CARMELITE STUDIES

EDITH STEIN SYMPOSIUM
TERESIAN CULTURE

John Sullivan, OCD
Editor

ICS Publications
Washington, DC
1987

ICS Publications
2131 Lincoln Road, NE
Washington, DC 20002

Typeset by the Carmelites of Indianapolis

Library of Congress Cataloging in Publication Data

Edith Stein symposium.
(Carmelite studies; 4)
Includes bibliographies.
1. Stein, Edith, 1891-1942.   2. Teresa, of Avila,
Saint, 1515-1582.   I.Sullivan, John, 1942-
II. Series.
BX4705.S814E35   1987   271'.971   87-26199
ISBN 0-935216-09-X

TABLE OF CONTENTS

ACKNOWLEDGEMENTS

We want to express appreciation for permission to print the following texts:

"Edith Stein the Woman," authorized by the author. © Freda Mary Oben 1984.

"The Economic Concerns of Madre Teresa" originally section four of the article "Ambiente Historico" in the volume *Introduccion a la lectura de Santa Teresa* (1978), pp. 88-103, authorized by Editorial de Espiritualidad, Madrid.

"The Doctorate of Experience," originally a chapter of the volume *Experiencia y realismo en Santa Teresa y San Juan de la Cruz* (1974), pp. 163-84, authorized by Editorial de Espiritualidad, Madrid.

"Remarks of the Pope about Edith Stein," found in the English edition of *Osservatore Romano* (nos. 18, 21 and 22, 1987), authorized by the Editor, Vatican City.

ABBREVIATIONS

For citation of the major works of either St John of the Cross or St Teresa of Jesus we will continue to use the following abbreviations adopted in Vol. I of *Carmelite Studies*:

ST JOHN OF THE CROSS

A = The Ascent of Mount Carmel   In A and N the first number
N = The Dark Night   indicates the book
C = The Spiritual Canticle
F = The Living Flame of Love

ST TERESA OF JESUS

L = The Book of Her Life
W = The Way of Perfection
C = The Interior Castle   In C the first number indicates the Dwelling
F = The Book of the Foundations

INTRODUCTION

This fourth volume of CARMELITE STUDIES has been a while in coming. More than ever the series continues to be what bibliographers call an "irregular series." Our original intention would have led to a biennial cycle of publication designed to allow adequate time for production, dissemination and assimilation between volumes before calls for others would arise from our public. The public has been active in requesting new commentaries on the Carmelite heritage since the appearance of the third volume on St Teresa's centenary in 1982; still, spreading knowledge of this heritage has involved a growing number of tasks for I.C.S. and many of the latter have kept the Chairman (and Editor of this series) from compiling the present set of studies. I feel safe in presuming our readers' indulgence, while I extend deep thanks to the authors and translators (in some cases) of the following articles for their generous patience. Another source of the delay was an embarrassment of interesting personal activities, such as a sabbatical leave and commencement of duties as general editor of I.C.S.'s new Collected Works of Edith Stein. Regardless, since there's no time like the present, I'd now call the reader's attention to a brief description of what is contained in the parts of this volume.

Late in September of 1984 I.C.S. was privileged to co-sponsor a symposium about "The Life and Thought of Edith Stein" along with the Friends of the Library of the Catholic University of America and the School of Philosophy of that same institution of higher learning. Personal biographies listing the accomplishments of the authors of the papers of that symposium stand at the beginning of their texts: they are all devoted interpreters of Edith Stein and are continuing their efforts to make her better known to the English-speaking public, especially after her beatification on 1 May 1987 in Cologne. In particular, Dr Freda Mary Oben has recently completed a fine translation of Stein's *Essays on Woman* which will take its place alongside *Life in a Jewish Family*, the first volume in our series of the Collected Works of Edith Stein and also recipient of the award for Best

Spirituality Book of 1986 from the Catholic Press Association. Dr Oben has graciously agreed to publication of her paper on "Edith Stein the Woman" here, before it appears in a volume of other studies by her about the new Carmelite Blessed.

In the Spring following the Catholic University Symposium the Teresian/Discalced Carmelites celebrated their sexennial General Chapter in Frascati, near Rome. An important theme which emerged for long-term consideration by the Order's membership was cultural adaptation. During the papacy of John Paul II a fair amount of reflection about culture and cultural adaptation has gone on (see the 1987 publication of the Department of Education of the United States Catholic Conference, *Faith and Culture: A Multicultural Catechetical Resource*): publishing the working papers presented in this second part will show how some leading interpreters of the thought of Teresa and John view the topic against the background of the experience of those two Doctors of the Church. It is to be understood that the texts presented here were originally designed for discussion at the General Chapter of 1985 and were not drafted with the critical apparatus of either footnotes or bibliography. All the same, the expertise of their authors in the Teresian heritage vouches for their worth as so many urgent invitations to serious reflection/ action regarding cultural adaptation now and in the future. The authors have shown great kindness in allowing publication of their own reflections with the current format and in the sometimes quaint English rendition of some valiant official(s) at OCD headquarters in Rome.

The third part harkens backward a little, in the direction of the 1982 centenary of St Teresa. All the studies concern Teresa of Jesus, and they examine her rich personality from several promising approaches. It is gratifying to complete publication of the landmark article of Teofanes Egido about the "Historical Setting of St Teresa's Life" that appeared in part in Volume One of CARMELITE STUDIES. This section of the article speaks about Teresa's financial concerns and its appearance can serve as a reminder for the expression of belated thanks to the Spanish Embassy's Cultural Affairs Office in Washington, DC for a generous grant to publish the handsome Teresian symposium poster (which itself was included in part as a frontispiece for the last volume of CARMELITE STUDIES).

Concerning the fourth part of this volume, it seems the delay in publishing has opened the door to the inclusion of some very timely texts about the recent beatification of Edith Stein/Sr Teresa Benedicta of the Cross. While plain documentation is not one of the assigned goals of CARMELITE STUDIES, I feel this set of texts emanating from authors in Rome will be useful to our readership and shed light on the ramifications of the Pope's gesture of proclaiming Edith Stein one of the blessed in heaven. A fair amount of controversy surfaced in the press at the time of the beatification: perhaps reflections like the ones made available here, and in the first part of this book, will contribute to a fuller, more-balanced image of this great woman of our century.

This volume of CARMELITE STUDIES will begin a practice of omitting initials after the authors' names which would indicate either academic accomplishments and/or affiliation with religious orders. One ought not interpret this editorial option as a bow in the direction of creeping (or galloping) secularization, but simply a move toward simplicity. Furthermore, the usual "bio" preceding the text of an author identifies her or him adequately for the reader.

John Sullivan
Editor

PASSING OF AN I.C.S. MEMBER/TRANSLATOR

Since publication of the last volume of CARMELITE STUDIES one of our members and most willing collaborators moved on to the eternal dwelling places. Fr John Clarke, whom so many of our readers know through his fine translations of the works of St Thérèse, died on 15 February 1987. Many will remember that one of the articles in the inaugural volume of this series, entitled "St Thérèse of the Child Jesus and Spiritual Direction," was translated by Fr John.

His devotion for St Thérèse was unflagging: even in the last days of his struggle with cancer he kept busy proofing his version of the second volume of the *Letters of St Thérèse* or *General Correspondence* which we plan to publish next year and dedicate as a posthumous tribute to him. Many of us Carmelites will continue to remember him as a kind confrere, educator and superior from north of the border (he was born in Montreal) who frequently outdid most of us in tackling heavy manual labor chores. John was a well-rounded individual, and we know he will be sorely missed. Happily for him, he will be at home with Thérèse, there where she said we find "no indifferent glances," and where he certainly will deepen his attachment for her in the embrace of God's merciful love.

J.S.

EDITH STEIN SYMPOSIUM

"The Life and Thought of Edith Stein"

EDITH STEIN THE WOMAN

Freda Mary Oben

Freda Mary Oben has devoted many years as a Jewish Catholic to studying the life and writings of Edith Stein. She has shared her knowledge of Stein in many ways: through a recent translation of Stein's Essays on Woman (*ICS Publications, 1987*), *many articles, a doctoral dissertation, participation in TV and radio dialogues, and public addresses. This text will appear soon in a book about Edith Stein which Alba House will publish under the title* Edith Stein: Scholar, Feminist, Saint. *We are both pleased and grateful to Dr Oben for her authorization to publish this excerpted text in* CARMELITE STUDIES.*

The pretty village of Birkenau in Germany received its name in token of the lovely birch trees growing everywhere in such profusion. This pretty little village, emptied of its inhabitants, became the extension of the Auschwitz Concentration Camp. In the transport of 559 people which arrived there from Holland on August 9th, 1942, there were two sisters, Edith and Rosa Stein.

Because of the horrible travelling conditions, many had already died in transit. Many survivors were suffering from psychological breakdown. Edith was still wearing her Carmelite habit, and so conspicuous was she by her appearance and manner that one of the guards later testified that he turned to another guard and said "That one is sane, anyway."[1]

3

The people were ordered to form lines of five. The SS doctor selected 295 persons he considered fit for work. The others, 264 including Edith and Rosa, were driven in lorries to huts in the nearby woods where they were told to undress for showers and delousing.

During this summer of 1942, two farm cottages were being used for the gassing—a red and a white one. It is believed that Edith was led to the latter. A former guard of Auschwitz writes "Nobody would have thought it credible that in those insignificant little houses as many people had perished as would have filled a city."[2]

These victims came to their death completely duped. They were disarmed by the lovely pastoral scene and the matter-of-fact small talk of the "Sonderkommandos" and SS men. Those who did show panic were shoved inside quickly. If any became hysterical, they were quickly forced to the back of the cottage and shot.

The cottages were windowless. As soon as the strong, air-tight doors were bolted down by screws, Cyclone B acid was discharged through vents in the ceilings. In about fifteen to twenty minutes it was over for all.

In the autobiography of the camp commander, Rudolf Hess, we find the following passage:

> During the summer of 1942, the bodies were still being placed in mass graves. Towards the end of the summer, however, we started to burn them, at first on wood pyres bearing some 2,000 corpses, and later in pits together with bodies previously buried. . . . Bodies were burnt in pits day and night, continuously . . . By the end of November all the mass graves had been emptied.[3]

Last March, I stood by the remains of the white cottage which is flanked by a large birch tree. Several of the former mass graves are still discernible near the cottage. The pits are marked by large white crosses. My guide told me that the ashes of the cremations had been used as fertilizer for the surrounding fields or else simply dumped into the nearby pond or Vistula River.

We walked to the edge of this pond. The calcium remains along its edges can be seen clearly. He retrieved a fistful of small bits of white bone from the mud and placed it in my hand. Time stopped for me.

I had come to the camp, now called the Auschwitz Museum, to do research on Edith Stein, the famous German philosopher, educator and feminist. After a two-hour interview with the camp director, I was shown about the camp by a young man from the camp Archives and then given material and photographs from the Archives. I am indebted to them for this new and authentic description of her death. Yet there are no formal records of Edith because the prisoners designated for death right from the train were never registered.

I then went to find the beginnings of Edith's life in Wroclaw, Poland. Formerly known as Breslau in Silesia, this lovely medieval city of religion and culture was ceded back to Poland at the end of World War II. Edith was born the eleventh child, the seventh surviving, to Siegfried and Augusta Stein on October 12, 1891 in a small house on Kohlenstrasse. The parents had come from Lublinitz just a half year before her birth to seek a better living.

In that year, this date fell on the Jewish Day of Atonement, "Yom Kippur", and Edith explains in her autobiography that this correlation of events was so important to her mother that it was the paramount reason why her mother held her so dear. She describes another tender association. On a very hot day in July, Mrs Stein was holding a mere twenty-one month old Edith as Mr Stein made his farewells: he was going on a long trek to a distant forest for his lumber business. Edith called after her father from her mother's arms, and this moment was the last memory Mrs Stein retained of her husband, for he was to die of sunstroke that very day.

Edith confesses that she was a headstrong child. At times merry and saucy, she was at other times most naughty and willful; in fact, she became infuriated when she could not have her own way. Her mother now took charge of the lumber business, and the elder sisters took turns caring for Edith and her sister

Erna who was also quite small. At times her sister Else resorted to locking a naughty Edith in a dark place. Edith writes that, when lying in her tantrum on the floor she saw this coming, she would deliberately make herself rigid, and once locked in, did not submit to her fate but lay screaming and kicking the door until she was liberated, usually by her mother.

Although she worked, Mrs Stein remained the center of the home and was for Edith always an image of the proverbial woman of faith, courage, and industry. Her mother went to synagogue with the elder brothers and sisters on the Jewish high holy days; yet, the business remained open on Saturdays, and prayers in the home were recited in German and not Hebrew.

She was a precocious child who, according to her sister Erna, was indoctrinated into the field of literature when she was only four years old! She writes:

> One of my earliest memories is of my eldest brother Paul carrying Edith around the room in his arms and singing student songs to her, or showing her pictures in a History of Literature and lecturing her on Schiller, Goethe, etc. She had a tremendous memory and forgot nothing of all this.[4]

Edith writes of herself as a seven year old experiencing a secret, inner life which she was unable to express. She envisioned a radiant life of happiness and glory. [This inner life which she keeps quietly hidden within her is, of course, what she develops so beautifully in her vocation as a contemplative. She could not readily talk about this interiority even when she was older; she was known to be reserved.] Reason had taken hold and her disposition changed. Temper tantrums were no longer possible for she felt shame in seeing others lose their tempers. At a very early age she attained a self-mastery and the quality of trustful submission.[5] We shall see this beautiful bent of her soul later in her complete surrender to the will of God.

But at the age of fifteen, a dual blight hit her soul. The child who had wheedled her way into school on her sixth birthday — even though it was the middle of the semester — announced suddenly to her mother that she did not want to continue school!

And she writes, moreover, "I dropped prayer consciously and by my own free decision."[6] She went to help her sister Else in Hamburg with the children and house. But six months later, she informed her mother that she intended to return to school and then go on to college. Edith was to be among the first group of women entering a university. She had evidently discovered at her sister's that domesticity was not exactly her cup of tea!

When she was seventeen, she started to attend the Girls' High School in Breslau. I would like to place her now from time to time in the historical scene because it will help us to understand better her spirituality. This same year, in 1908, another high schooler, the nineteen-year-old Adolf Hitler, had already failed the entrance exam to the academy of arts and was reading anti-semitic newspapers in Linz.

During her last years in high school, the Stein family moved into the spacious house at 38 Michaelisstrasse, now called Nowowiejska. The architectural beauty of this house is evident. The large two-storey brick building is now covered with grey plaster. It is divided equally in two parts. I counted nineteen windows in the front alone!

The spacious street adjoins a park where children play by the lake. Nearby, the tower of St Michael's Church looms high, the church to which she was to steal away quietly in future years for the 6 A.M. mass. I am sure she heard the chimes tolling even in her young years, but then she was deep in the bosom of her family with loads of aunts, uncles, cousins, and joy. This strong love for her family and theirs for her was to form an integral part of her nature and help to determine her fate. At this time, an orphaned Hitler was hiding in Vienna and dodging conscription by the Austrian army.

She enrolled at the University of Breslau in 1911. An incident which occurred the next year reveals her deep concern for humanity and its disorders. She was twenty and had just read a novel painting in most frightening colors the link between student alcoholism and amorality. She reacted violently. Nauseated, she lost her trust in humanity and was submerged under a pain of cosmic weight. It is an early instance of her concept of co-responsibility which we find developed to perfection in her adulthood.

She was cured, she writes, by attending a concert of Bach (whom she calls her "Liebling") where Luther's hymn, "A Mighty Fortress Is Our God" was also sung, and she responded with rising joy to the third verse:

> Though hordes of devils fill the land
> All threatening to devour us
> We tremble not, unmoved we stand
> They cannot overpower us.

Her "cosmic pain" fell away. Certainly, the world was bad. But if she and her friends stuck together, they could get rid of all the devils![7] Let us note, she has said "friends": she has not used the word God whom we consider the protagonist against the devil in that song.

This was shortly before her 21st birthday and Edith has confessed that she was unable to believe in a personal God until she was 21. We ask, of course, what happened then? The answer is clear: she transferred from the University of Breslau to the University of Göttingen. At Breslau she had thought to write a thesis in the department of Experimental Psychology but was definitely disenchanted. The light awaiting her intellect and soul was elsewhere: it beckoned to her through her reading of Husserl's second volume of *Logical Investigations*.

So charming is her description of this old university town, of the school of philosophy and its Philosophical Circle that I invite you to read it for yourselves. She describes her arrival there in the summer of 1913: "Dear old Göttingen! I don't believe that anyone who did not study there between 1905 and 1914, during the short spring-time of the Göttingen phenomenology school, could ever imagine what that name conjures up for us."[8] And I invite you to retrace the landmarks of her life there as I first did ten years ago when, as a virtual pilgrim filled with a sense of beauty and excitement, I first came to Göttingen.

There is a plaque on the house where she roomed: Edith Stein,

Philosopher, 1913-1916. I walked past St Albani Church from which she had heard the Angelus ring three times daily, then on to the market place to admire the Goose Girl fountain which still stands. I stopped for coffee at the *Kron und Lanz* coffee shop of which she speaks. And then I walked through the very building which housed the philosophy seminars she attended.

She loved nature and took frequent hikes and picnics with her friends. I followed her route to Nikolausberg almost expecting to come upon the "three wind-stripped trees" which had reminded her of Golgotha, an image indicating that this Jewish girl had a few unnamed thoughts. I sat on the edge of a wheat field filled with pink and white flowers, and in that solitude and silence, I felt the deep love which Edith had for the German land.

Her love for art, music and literature drew her on longer journeys. She climbed the hill from Eisenach to Wartburg Castle where the Middle High German poets had written, where Martin Luther translated the Bible, and where Elizabeth of Hungary had lived; years later, she was to capture this saint beautifully in an essay. She went to Weimar to pay her respects to her childhood idols — Goethe and Schiller, and her compassionate heart was moved by the "miserable little room in which Schiller died." I, too, visited Eisenach and Weimar, which is now in East Germany, but I must confess I did not climb that huge hill to the Schloss as she did — I took a cab!

She makes a minute description of the Göttingen Philosophy Circle, many of whose names will be familiar to you: Adolf Reinach, Theodor Conrad and Hedwig Martius, Dietrich von Hildebrand, Alexander Koyré, Fritz Frankfurter and Fritz Kaufmann. "But" she writes, "the one who most deeply impressed me was Hans Lipps." He was two years older than she was. And he was such an ardent philosopher that at one time in a heated discussion, he emptied his cigar into the sugar bowl! This was the young man for whom Edith had a genuine attachment which was broken off. He died in World War II.

Now we come to a beautiful story of conversion, an ongoing conversion into sainthood. We keep in mind that Edith has said that her conversion was a mystery in God, but she has left clear clues in her words, writings and deeds.

Edith had changed universities in the pursuit of truth. She considered herself an atheist, yet she was to write later that whoever searches for truth is actually searching for God whether he acknowledges this or not. As a young girl of twenty, she had great confidence in her own intellect: no one could tell her anything! But she always took the prerogative of a critical view concerning other people, and her wit was apt to be caustic. Now, when she came to the University of Göttingen, she found that the great intellects there were investigating the essence and structure of supernatural truths which were just as real as other phenomena.

Edith's friend, the philosopher Peter Wust, explains ". . . from the very beginning, there seemed to be in the intention of the new philosophical perspective something hidden which was completely mysterious, a searching back for objectivity to the sacredness of being, to the purity and chasteness of things, 'of the thing in itself.'" Edith's friend and colleague, Hedwig Conrad-Martius, recognized an affinity between the Jewish radical spirit and the movement of conversion in this group. She describes the existing challenge in these words: "Can the scientist even take the responsibility not to come to terms with the problem of the existence of a thing which has suddenly appeared in a very impressionable sense as able to exist?" [9]

This was, of course, part of the Religious Revival affecting all disciplines, and Edith's atheism was confronted by the phenomenological ideal of objective clarity. Revelation became a viable object of scrutiny. She studied the Greek philosophers, but there was a return to medieval Scholasticism, for Husserl, who had converted in 1887, easily admitted his debt to St Thomas. And at some time in a linguistics course, she studied the Lord's Prayer in Old Gothic and was very affected by it.

Her teacher, Adolf Reinach, influenced her especially by what she calls his "natural goodness." And Edith writes also that many of the younger phenomenologists were influenced more by Max Scheler than they were by Husserl. In this period of a returning Catholic fervor, Scheler lectured on religious subjects such as humility and the essence of holiness. We shall see later how deep his impact was on this young girl so sensitive to the workings of another soul. In keeping with this trait, her doctoral thesis was to define empathy. This was to be her first attempt to treat the major theme of all her works, the structure of the human spirit.

While Edith was involved in this search for truth, which she describes as a prayer in itself, Hitler was finally found in Munich in 1914 and escorted to the Austrian Consulate; that fatal summer he willingly joined the "German Colors" for the war. He was to claim that "the First World War taught him more about the real 'problems of life' than thirty years at a university could have done."[10] Reinach also enlisted that summer, and Edith, after passing the state exams in history, philosophy and German, served for six months at the Weisskirchen Epidemic Hospital in Moravia; she nursed soldiers of the Austrian army infected with spotted fever, dysentery, and cholera.

We find here a striking instance of her independence as a 24-year old. She writes: "My mother opposed me vigorously . . . she declared energetically, 'You will never go with my consent!' and I answered with equal determination, 'Then I shall have to go without your consent.'"[11]

After this she taught for eight months at the high school in Breslau where she herself had studied and then, on August 3rd, made the trip to Husserl to receive her doctorate "summa cum laude." He had been given a chair in phenomenology at Freiburg University, and it is a recognition of her singular genius that of all his students, many of whom were to become famous, Husserl now invited Edith to come as his first assistant in October. On her way back to Breslau, she stopped to see Mrs Reinach. This anticipated visit in 1916 ends her autobiography, *Life in a Jewish Family.*

However, another visit to Anna Reinach was soon to change Edith's life. Adlof had died at the front in 1917 and Anna asked for Edith's help in the arrangement of his papers. The testimony of two priests bears witness of the importance of this visit in Edith's conversion. Fr John Nota writes that she described this incident to him some time before her arrest, and she still felt the dynamic impression made by Mrs Reinach who had been baptized as a Protestant just as her husband had been at the front. Anna was able to console Edith rather than be consoled because of her faith in a loving God.[12]

Also, Fr Johannes Hirschmann, in a letter of May 3, 1950 to the Mother Superior at the Cologne Carmel, writes the following: "Sister Theresia Benedicta herself distinguished between the cause of her conversion to Christianity from the cause of her entrance to the Catholic Church... The most decisive reason for her conversion to Christianity was, as she told me, the way and manner in which her friend Mrs Reinach made her offer in the power of the mystery of the cross after her husband died at the front during the First World War."[13]

We can see here again that Edith's great gift of relating to people allowed her to experience the essence of the Christian faith. But all this required a period of gestation: it was to be another five years before her decision.

Time does not permit me to describe the beauty of Freiburg where Edith served as Husserl's assitant for eighteen months: the city itself, the surrounding Black Forest, an enchanting world, where Edith tramped with friends and visitors, the Günterstal area where they lived and where Husserl now lies buried.

Edith taught Husserl's beginning students, referring to them laughingly as her "philosophical kindergarten," but she had been employed primarily to get Husserl's manuscripts in order for publication. She had the formidable task of transcribing his notes from Gabelsberger shorthand, elaborating, if necessary, and editing. Her colleague Roman Ingarden explains how difficult this really was since Husserl's creativity compelled him to write in bursts, in fragments, but never to reread or to revise his manuscripts. After trying unsuccessfully to encourage Husserl to study her elaboration of his *Ideen* (Ideas), she left this post in 1918. Ingarden writes that Husserl had failed Edith: he did not fulfill his end of their working arrangement.[14]

However, during this time, Edith had been writing articles herself: "Psychic Causality" and "The Individual and Community." While in high school, Edith had campaigned as a suffragette; now, in 1918, she canvassed for the German Democratic Party; and this led to an interest in the structure and function of the state and to her later study, *The State*. These three works were soon published in the *Jahrbuch für Philosophie und phänomenologische Forschung* and represent her purely phenomenological contributions as distinct from her Thomistic works.[15]

Attempts to get another university position failed even with a letter of unqualified recommendation from Husserl, probably because there were few women teaching then in the universities. Another letter was written about this time. In 1919, Hitler wrote to a military officer, presenting the views of the German Workers' Party concerning Jews. In this, his first political manifesto, he lists the "crimes" of the Jews and suggest not only a legal struggle to remove all Jewish privileges but also, as the final objective, the removal of all Jews from their midst.[16]

During the next three years, the dramatic trauma of her conversion developed. When she wrote the essay "Plant Soul, Animal Soul, Human Soul," it seemed to her friends that she had already accepted the Christian faith.[17] Indeed, from Fr Hirschmann's letter, we know that Edith wanted to become a Christian but she had hesitated as to which denomination to join. Many of her friends had become Protestants. But her basic reason for entering the Catholic Church was her reading of St Teresa of Avila's autobiography for which she had been prepared by the fervent Catholicism of Max Scheler.

This happened during a prolonged visit to the home of her good friend Hedwig Conrad-Martius in the summer of 1921. Many members of the Göttingen Philosophy Circle still came from time to time to help gather fruit and to talk philosophy. Hedwig describes the religious crisis they were undergoing during that visit: "it was as if we were both walking on a narrow mountain ridge, aware that God's call was immanent." She writes that Edith, always reserved, was at this time intensely quiet.[18]

After her friends went out one evening, Edith was left to entertain herself with a book. By chance, she picked up *Leben der*

Heiligen Teresia von Avila (*Life of St Teresa of Avila*) and did not close the book until dawn. She tells us herself that she said then, "This is the truth."[19] So convinced was she of the truth of St Teresa's experience that she had to acknowledge the source of that experience as Truth itself.

That very morning, she went directly to buy a Catholic catechism and a missal. On January 1st, 1922, she was baptized at St Martin's church in Bergzabern. This lovely Church nestling at the foot of hills is devoted to her memory. Cards of the church are issued bearing her name. A street by the church is called Edith Stein Strasse. The new youth building was constructed in her memory — the Edith Stein House. The new altar, made in the shape of an unsymmetrical T, is not only the symbol of the crucified Christ but is also a sign of the name Teresia Benedicta a Cruce, Teresa Benedicta of the Cross, Edith's name as a religious.

When the priest who baptized Edith died — Fr Breitling — both the Jewish and Christian communities attended his funeral mass. All this can be found in the *Festschrift* issued by that church. But I was lucky enough to stand one day before the font where she was baptized. On the wall by the font, there is a plaque dedicated to her. It depicts the scene from I Kings 19:17: a scone and water have been placed at the feet of a sleeping Elijah by the angel who bids him "Get up and eat or the journey will be too long for you." The words on the plaque are in German and read: "Steh auf und iss/ Sonst ist der Weg für dich zu weit." The *Festschrift* suggests that it is the heavenly bread awaiting Edith at the baptismal font, the Eucharist, which alone enabled her to ascend the Mt Horeb of her life through the gas chamber, where she died for her people and her faith.[20]

So strong was my sense of her presence there at the basin that it was really too much for me: in a sudden panic, I actually ran out of the church.

Edith was to write in *Finite and Eternal Being* that the resurrected Christ is the model and guide for all human formation. In 1921, Hitler had seized power and was proclaimed leader of the National German Workers' Party; when writing *Mein Kampf* after his unsuccessful putsch resulted in his imprisonment, he presents his concept of the Aryan as the highest image of God and humanity and of the Jew as the exact antithesis. He does not hesitate to use Scripture, believing that his actions are in accord with God's intentions.

Edith had wanted to become a religious immediately after her baptism. But this was not permitted by her spiritual director because she was prominent as a lay woman and, moreover, they could not inflict further cruelty upon her mother. Instead, she taught for eight years at the oldest Dominican convent in Germany — St Magdalena's in Speyer. Her students were high school girls, postulants, and nuns preparing to teach.

And now she realized that her intellectual work could indeed serve her faith. She had wanted to study the intellectual foundation of Catholicism and turned to St Thomas Aquinas. Through him she learned that her intellect was a means of giving herself to God. And we remember that Aquinas writes of "This light in which we human beings contemplate truth . . . the light of grace and the light of glory. . . ." Through the clear luminosity of her writings, Edith exemplifies that "This light is not only placed in each human learner directly by God Himself, it is also by its very nature a created participation in that supernal light which God Himself is."[21]

At the suggestion of her friend, the Jesuit philosopher-theologian Erich Przywara, she set to work as a translator: the letters and diaries of Cardinal Newman (J. H. Kardinal Newman, *Briefe und Tagebücher bis zum Übertritt zur Kirche, 1801– 1845*); *The Idea of a University* (J. H. Kardinal Newman, *The Idea of a University*);[22] Thomas Aquinas' *De Veritate* (*Des Hl. Thomas von Aquino Untersuchungen über die Wahrheit*).[23] There was as yet no adequate German edition of *Truth* from the Latin and her work was actually a brilliant commentary as well as a translation. This two-volume study made her famous for it was a decisive step in the relationship between phenomenology and Neo-Scholasticism.

During these years at Speyer, she was also working on *Potenz und Akt*, the embryo of her greatest philosophical work, *End-*

liches und Ewiges Sein (Finite and Eternal Being).[24] And on
Husserl's seventieth birthday, she contributed an important
seminal work, a comparative study of Husserl and Aquinas,
Husserls Phänomenologie und die Philosophie des Hl. Thomas.[25]

She had made great strides in scholarship; let us also note
here that during these years at Speyer, her personality was
undergoing a great transformation.

She had taken the three private vows (yet so intense was her
prayer life that she was apt to stay all night in the chapel strictly
against the wishes of her spiritual director!). She termed God
"The Master Educator" and she was a very good student. Her
critical, even caustic bent had been replaced by the spiritual
maternity she was to consider woman's greatest gift whether
married or single. Her colleagues and students describe her as
gentle, patient, modest, loving, humble, happy, lovable, serene,
balanced, charitable and holy. She taught that Christ is the perfect model and Gestalt of all personality, and on this she, too,
was formed.

In order to find the right perspective for the education of girls
and women, she had turned to an analysis of woman's nature
and vocation. At this time few were interested in gearing the
educational system, which was strictly masculine, to the feminine psyche. She challenged the system by her analysis of woman's unique nature and intrinsic value.

And she was the first to reveal the link between woman's nature and religious education. She shows the motivation for such
religious education as placed in the very nature of the student.
Borrowing an image from St Thomas, she describes the image
of God planted as a seed in the human soul: the seed comes to
development by the supernatural aid of grace and the natural
help of education, plus, of course, the student's own inner dedication. And this full development of personality implies a wholeness of the person because it is the whole person that is needed
for God's service. This requires a balanced development of all
physical and psychical powers.

In the lectures that comprise *Die Frau*, from which I am now
taking this material, Stein presents an ontology of woman — a

study of her being, nature and role proper to happiness. Basic to this ontology is her belief that the human species is a dual one and that woman is to be considered as a species apart from the man.

She finds that woman's vocation is threefold: human, individual and feminine; the fulfillment of one of these vocations depends on the fulfillment of the other two. She sees woman's unique strength, as I have noted, in a spiritual maternity which should be exercised through her professions and represents her femininity regardless of marital status. She upholds the Church's ideal of marriage; the family should always come first for the woman. Yet she claims that as long as children are properly cared for by loving people, the mother is free to exercise her profession—unless it does, indeed, make problems. She believes that woman's nature best qualifies her for certain professions but that, actually, there is no work performed by a man that a woman cannot do!

Yet the woman differs from the man in the relationship of body to soul and in the relationship of her faculties. She is emotion-centered and thus requires intellectual training to develop objectivity. The woman's view is personal—geared towards the person and relationships, and she is driven to develop herself and those about her to a total humanity. Objectivity is also needed to help her avoid a hyper-feminine personal attitude which is apt to make her a nuisance. The essence of the pedagogical goal is to teach her to relate properly to others and to understand the world so that she can better serve.

The justice of the cause of feminism is evidenced by the singular fact that a woman of such holiness as Edith Stein was a feminist. Indeed, she was the intellectual leader of Catholic feminism in Europe. She delivered lectures constantly, these lectures of *Die Frau*, for the League of Catholic Women and the Association of Catholic Women Teachers which actually formed the Catholic Women's Movement. She became their "voice," speaking at their annual conventions, acting as their advisor in plans of reform and in discussions with government officials.

She advocated that Catholic thought must meet the challenging questions of the time: sexual problems, teachings on marriage and motherhood, woman's vocation, etc.:

> The traditional Catholic handling of these questions or, indeed, the traditional disregard for them could and should be reformed if it is to meet the challenging questions of the time. The setup of a genuinely Catholic broad-minded approach to marriage and sexuality and the educational principles to be derived from this should therefore be considered as an urgent problem in contemporary education. This means the education of all youth, including young girls.[26]

She rallied the Catholic woman to get involved. The following lines are from Edith Stein's address to a group of Catholic university women in Switzerland:

> Let's get to the point . . . Do we grasp social problems, the burning problems of today? Do they concern us also? Or are we waiting until others find some solution or until we are submerged by the billows of chaos? Is such an attitude worthy of an academic woman? Must we not try to help in deed as well as in thought? . . . We must get in touch with the social ferment of the masses and understand their physical and spiritual needs . . . I have reached the core of a burning question . . . Are we familiar with the work of the adversary? In the mine fields of today's society, can we justify looking backwards continuously while our adversary wages war against our views?[27]

We must not forget that Edith was attempting to counteract the growing Nazi ideology which would reduce women to "church, kitchen and children." She urged, rather, that it is the mission of the twentieth-century woman in a very sick society to act as "healthy, energetic spores supplying healthy energy to the entire national body."[28] But she cannot help others to be whole unless she is a whole person herself. And in the growing Nazi ideology which subjected woman completely to men's dictates, she urged that women be trained in value judgments so that they can understand the world in which they must serve and relate properly to others.

But she was in too much demand as a speaker, and, in 1931, she left her teaching duties at Speyer. At Breslau, she continued to work on *Potenz und Akt*. Attempts to secure a teaching post at the University of Freiburg failed although her former fellow student and colleague Heidegger now held the chair there in phenomenology; in fact, she felt herself treated by him with considerable ill-will. Then, in 1932, she accepted an important post at the German Institute for Scientific Pedagogy in Münster.

On September 12th of that year, she participated in a conference held in Juvisy, France by the Thomistic Society. She was the only woman invited to attend. Although Daniel Feuling, OSB gave the paper, a reading of that day's proceedings reveals that Edith made a considerable impact. Professor Rosenmölh writes:

> The discussion was dominated entirely by Edith Stein. Certainly she had the best understanding of Husserl, having been for years his assistant in Freiburg, but she developed her thoughts with such clarity, in French when necessary, that she made an extraordinarily strong impression on this learned company of scholars.[29]

Among "this learned company" were Maritain, Koyré, Gilson and Berdiaev. A letter of the following November indicates that she apparently visited with the Maritains in Meudon at the time of the conference in Juvisy: she recalls the day with joy and thanks him for sending her a copy of his text *Degrees of Knowledge*.

Another letter of Edith written at this time to a religious in Speyer expresses Edith's growing difficulty of living in the secular world. Her interiority had developed so strongly that she feared she was projecting a quality troubling to the other women teachers. The innermost part of her being had become her world. She was to explain this is a line found in *Finite and Eternal Being*: ". . . those who live the interior life have always experienced being drawn into their innermost parts by that which draws more strongly than the total exterior world: the invasion of a new, forceful, higher life—the supernatural, divine life."[30]

Edith was suffering for she, indeed, had a vocation as a contemplative.

On January 30, 1933, Adolf Hitler became "Reichskanzler" of Germany. Edith's Jewish presence was now an embarrassment at the Institute, and although she stayed there throughout the summer, her last lecture was on February 25th. She writes of these last days in Münster, ". . . now on a sudden it was luminously clear to me that once again God's hand lay heavy on His people, and that the destiny of this people was my own."[31]

We have now come to the turning point of Edith Stein's life. Clearly, she foresaw the danger which awaited not the Jews alone but also the Christians. She tried to obtain a private audience with the Pope to urge that he write an encyclical on behalf of the Jews. When this failed, she wrote a letter to the Pope which was personally delivered by her spiritual advisor, the Abbot of Beuron.

She knew, then, full well the reality of the coming evil. Indeed, Edith's entreaty for action by the Pope as early as the spring of 1933 is so conspicuous in its singularity that historians have noted it as such. We ask: why did she not fly the country early as others did; Freud in 1932, then Einstein—they understood. In fact, just that past November she herself had been thinking of going to work in London. And in that month of crisis, April, she was given an opportunity to teach in South America where she would have been with her brother Arno. Instead, she chose the cross.

She has described this crisis in her essay "The Road to Carmel." She writes: "I spoke to our Savior and told him that I knew it was His Cross which was now being laid on the Jewish people. Most of them did not understand it; but those who did understand must accept it willingly in the name of all."[32]

She spent thirteen straight hours of prayer at the St Ludgeri Church in Münster. I have seen a beautiful plaque dedicated to her there on a wall by a large iron cross; it commemorates those hours of prayer because it was then that she made her great decision to enter Carmel. It was her belief that the Carmelite order excells in a free and joyous participation in Christ's redemptive action. And it was the intention of her innermost being to offer up her prayers and life in reparation for both Jew and Nazi, for the persecutor as well as the persecuted.

Now, this would come very hard to ordinary people like us, no doubt. But let us consider her own words: "Saints who are determined to confidently maintain a courageous love for their enemies have experienced that they have the freedom to so love . . . their behavior is led by supernatural love."[33] Her intention to pray for the Nazis was in keeping with St John of the Cross who writes "God sustains and is present substantially in every soul, even that of the worst sinner."[34]

Three weeks after her decision to enter Carmel, she wrote again to Maritain. Since her last letter to him seven months prior, her whole world had changed. Yet, she said nothing of her hopes for Carmel, telling him only of the termination of her post and asking him not to fear for her because God works all things to the good.

Edith writes to another friend that she believes this friend would want to take upon herself the excess of misery and pain being experienced by so many if only she understood their despair. As all saints have done through time, Edith had set herself on God's side to fight the sins and disorders which were causing this terrible misery, pain and despair. Her weapons were prayer and the face of love. And what sadness she must have felt over this misery, not only as a Jewess but as a Christian for, after all, it was the so-called "Christians" who were among the brutal oppressors. She believed that only the Passion of Christ could save the world, and she wanted a share in that. The Jewish girl born on the holy Jewish Day of Atonement understood well what redemption is.

Yet Edith's anguish was intensified by her family's lack of understanding. Her conversion had been most painful to them, but her entrance into Carmel in 1933, at the very onset of their persecution, was unbelievable. There was a touching incident at this time involving Edith and her niece "Susel," and they have both described it.

Susan was at that time twelve years of age and she had heard much talk. She saw her grandmother suffering over the certainty of never seeing Edith again. Her grandmother was eighty-four years of age and no longer travelled, and Edith was to be fully cloistered.

Edith writes of this meeting with Susan: "'Why are you doing this now?' she asked . . . I gave her my reasons as I would to an adult. She listened thoughtfully and understood."[35] Susan, however, describes it differently in a lovely little essay, "Erinnerungen an Meine Tante Edith Stein" (Reminiscences of my Aunt Edith Stein).

> It was characteristic of my aunt that she did not ridicule my words or answer me condescendingly. She was serious and attentive; she said she did not consider her step as a betrayal; she was leaving no one in the lurch. Her entrance into Carmel did not guarantee her any safety and would not eliminate the actual world outside. She would always be a part of her family and always remain part of the Jewish people even as a nun.

But Susan adds, "A cleft existed between her and her family which could not be reconciled although, on the other hand, we could not stop loving her."[36]

This was all part of Edith's personal, unique cross. Her redemptive role was unique in its duality: as a Jewess, she suffered for her people, and as a Christian, she underwent the passion of Christ her Lord, united to Him as He suffered for Jews and Gentiles.

On October 14th, 1933, two days after her forty-second birthday, she entered the Lindenthal Carmel in Cologne. This was the eve of the feastday of the Order's founder. St Teresa had led her home.

Her investiture took place the following April and was attended by many people of repute in the world of philosophy, religion, and academia. She adopted as her religious name Teresia Benedicta a Cruce, Teresa indeed blessed by the cross. But there is also a correlation to the Benedictine Abbey at Beuron and its Abbot, Raphael Walzer, who had been her spiritual director; she had a great love for the celebration of the liturgy at the Abbey and had spent both Christmas and Easter there for many years. Fr Hirschmann writes that Edith confessed to him that she had a great devotion to her name, a singular love, for it contains the mystery of her conversion.

Her friends who attended the investiture were all struck by her transformation. Hedwig writes that Edith had always been childlike and amiable, but now she was enchanting in her child-like laughter and happiness. During my visits to the Cologne Carmel, I have spoken with nuns who lived with her and they remember her so. They remember her laughter. She said once to them, "I have never laughed so much during my whole life as I have these two years as a novice."

Her stories and humor enchanted the nuns, but above all, they were struck by her humility, her modesty. She never referred to her importance in the outside world. And, over and over again, I have heard that Edith had a special gift for relating to people; she intuitively felt the state of mind of others and knew what they needed and how to encourage them. Her love and goodness were natural. She herself had a need to help other people.

I asked if she had shown signs of still being artistically inclined and received an enthusiastic "Yes!": she loved plastic sculpture and kept a silver Japanese vase in her cell by the Madonna; she had copies of paintings on cards (Rembrandt was her favorite); she had a great love for music, wrote poetry, and created little plays for the nuns' entertainment. The young lady who had so enjoyed dancing, hiking, boating, tennis, theater, concerts, and literature was now content behind the cloistered walls.

She continued to do her intellectual work which they believed was the fruit of her intense prayer life and devotion to truth. Her first endeavor was to write *Life in a Jewish Family* for she had started this during the painful months at home before she entered Carmel. She writes in the Preface that she had a dual motivation: she wanted to honor her mother on whose memories she relied, and she wanted to present the true nature of Jewish humanity to the young Nazis being taught to hate Jews by way of a false stereotype.

Edith had a strong power of concentration and creative energy which the nuns attributed to her deep powers of prayer and contemplation; this enabled her to finish *Endliches und Ewiges Sein* in nine months by giving up her free time and recreation. And I must mention that one of the high points of my visits to the Cologne Carmel was the discovery that Edith's translation of Psalm 61 is included in *Gotteslob*, the official prayer book used at all masses daily in Germany: hymn no. 302.

Both nuns I interviewed at Cologne felt that Edith, in a deep fidelity to her people, wanted to experience their actual suffering. The Nürnberg Statutes were declared shortly after she took her first vows in 1935. Among many severe injunctions, Jews were deprived of all legal rights and books were burned. The following spring, 1936, the Nazis marched into the Rhineland.

This was a very hard year for Edith. Her mother died of cancer on September 14. It was the feast day of the Exaltation of the Holy Cross and the day on which the nuns annually renewed their vows. Edith said afterwards, "As I was standing in my place in choir waiting to renew my vows my mother was beside me. I felt her presence quite distinctly."[37]

This is believable, given the special bond of love between them and Edith's intuitive power which was now developing into a mystical nature. Her sorrow was relieved by a special cause for rejoicing, for her sister Rosa came to her at Christmas and was baptized. She had been a believer for many years.

Because Edith as a born Jewess had lost her right to publish, *Endliches und Ewiges Sein* could not be published under her own name; it was proposed that the work be published under the name of a Nazi sympathizer but Edith refused. When the text finally did appear in 1950, it was acclaimed as invaluable toward a much needed rehabilitation of Catholic thought.[38] Aristotle, Plato, Duns Scotus, Thomas Aquinas and Husserl underlay the basis of her analysis, but her method was phenomenological. She herself explains in the opening of the text that she is attempting to contribute to a philosophical issue of much contemporary importance: the question of Being through an examination of the relationship between Thomistic and phenomenological thought.[39]

In March, 1938 Hitler invaded Austria and, in September, the Sudentenland. Edith's final vows were in April of that year. Her great trauma was now upon her. On Good Friday, she writes in a poem dedicated to the Virgin Mary — and Edith had an abiding, deep love for Our Lady — that those whom Mary chooses as companions must stand with her at the foot of the cross to purchase new life for souls. At the end of October, ten days before the fatal "Night of Crystal," she writes in a letter that, like the Jewish Queen Esther who was singled out from amongst the Jews to plead to the king for her people, she, also, will plead — to the heavenly king — for her own people.

We know the havoc of "Kristallnacht" on November 9th, when synagogues, Jewish homes and businesses were destroyed, and thirty to forty thousand Jews were sent to concentration camps which already existed as early as 1933. Edith and the nuns feared for each other's safety, and during the night of December 31st, she fled to the Carmel in Echt, Holland.

The Echt Carmel is a small, unpretentious row house in a quiet village. Last year, I saw her cell, I held her bible, I saw her formal chapel cape. I asked the present prioress if she knew whether Edith had been melancholy there. "No," she said: in seclusion, Edith's face indicated she was lost in thought, but in the company of the nuns she was most cheerful and friendly.

And amusing anecdotes about Edith are tenderly remembered. She was unhandy at housework. Holding the broom in front of her and pushing it, she would walk up and down the room — just pushing it! The nuns would burst out into laughter and that did not embarrass Edith in the least. Her sewing was so inadequate that when she finished working on something, like a little scapular, the Prioress would take it quickly to another nun and tell her quietly to fix it!

Edith was in charge of professions and taught the novices Latin. But she was also concerned with the intellectual and spiritual advancement of the nuns who did the manual work. In those days, the nuns who did the gardening, cooking and laundering did not have library privileges; Edith asked that they be allowed to read good books and attend lectures. She did not succeed.

However, her poetry and other writings of this time show that, inwardly, Edith suffered much travail. It was clear during the days of 1939 that the world was heading for war. On January 30, Hitler declared that should the Jews cause another world war, they would bring about their own extinction. On March 25th he stated, "Poland should be totally subjected." The next day Edith wrote the following note to the Prioress. It was Passion Sunday:

> Dear Mother, I beg your Reverence's permission to offer myself to the Heart of Jesus as a sacrificial expiation for the sake of true peace: that the Antichrist's sway may be broken, if possible without another world war, and that a new order may be established. I am asking this today because it is already the twelfth hour. I know that I am nothing, but Jesus wills it, and He will call many more to the same sacrifice in these days.[40]

In June she wrote her last will. She concluded with a joyful acceptance of her death foreordained by God, for the sake of God's glory, the Sacred Hearts of Jesus and Mary, the intention of Holy Church, the deliverance of Germany and world peace, and for her family living and dead.

The Germans broke into Poland on September 1st. It was the beginning of World War II. A few weeks later on the feast day of the Exaltation of the Holy Cross, Edith wrote an impassioned essay, "Hail Cross, Our Only Hope." This former nurse of World War I reveals here a personal anguish in her inability to personally attend the wounded and dying and to console others in their misery. But she ecstatically affirms that there is an actual power of healing and consoling available even to the cloistered religious, for compassionate love and prayer is at one with Christ as He "soothes, heals and redeems."

The following lines from one of her poems reveals an agony alike to Christ's in the Garden of Gethsemane: "Bless, O Lord, the sinking mood of those who suffer/ The heavy loneliness of troubled souls/ The restlessness of human beings in mortal pain/ Which none would trust to tell a sister."[41]

In 1940, Edith's sister Rosa came to Echt and acted as portress for the nuns. She wanted to become a religious but, instead, became a third order Carmelite, for Hitler invaded Holland in May of that year. Starting on September 1st of the following year, both sisters were forced to wear the Yellow Star of David on which was inscribed the word "Jew."

They had to report periodically to the Gestapo. On one such visit, Edith greeted the officer with the habitual greeting of Catholic Germany: "Praised be Jesus Christ!" The officer stared at her but said nothing. She later explained that she had been compelled to do this, foolhardy as it could have been, because of her clear recognition of the eternal struggle between Christ and Lucifer.[42]

In an attempt to get Edith out of the country, the Prioress applied to the Le Pâquier Carmel in Switzerland. However, they could take only Edith and she refused to go without her sister. This caused further delay. In time, arrangements were made for Rosa at a house for third order Carmelites near Le Pâquier. Now, all that was needed was authorization from the Dutch authorities.

Meanwhile, Edith was writing works of a mystic bent: *Wege der Gotteserkenntnis-Dionysius der Areopagit* (*Ways to Know God-Dionysius the Areopagite*)[43]; *Kreuzeswissenschaft* (*Science of the Cross*)[44], a study of the life, theology, and poetry of St John of the Cross. The spirituality described in a passage here was now hers: "Thus, the bridal union of the soul with God for which it is created is purchased through the cross, perfected with the cross, and sealed for all eternity with the cross."[45]

In her essays on Heidegger, Edith writes that metaphysics alone cannot explain the innermost life of the soul—only mystics like St Teresa of Avila can do this. It is clear that Edith herself was a mystic as well as a scientist.

And she was objective to the end as well. She was certainly not set on death although she was prepared for it: she writes that she is carrying on her person the line Matthew 10:23 which reads, "When they persecute you in one town, flee to the next."[46]

On July 1st, 1942 the education of Jewish Catholic children was forbidden in Holland by the Nazis: this meant the children could not attend Catholic schools, their only means of learning.

The Dutch bishops protested this action as well as the deportation of the Jews in a pastoral letter on July 26th. In retaliation on August 2nd, the Nazi authorities ordered the arrest of all Dutch Catholics of Jewish extraction. Edith and Rosa were among those picked up that evening. People, aghast, gathered at the door of the convent. The last words heard as the two sisters left the convent were Edith's as she said to Rosa, "Come, let us go for our people."[47]

They were taken to three camps during the next week: first, to two Dutch camps—Amersfoort and Westerbork; finally, to Auschwitz. Witnesses who survived the camps have testified to the holy love manifested by Edith.

Many of the mothers were in despair and had even given up caring for their own children.

> The most distressing thing was the condition of the women. It was in this that Edith Stein showed her worth. Sr Benedicta took care of the little children, washed them and combed them, looked after their feeding and their other needs. During the whole of her stay there, she washed and cleaned for people, following one act of charity with another until everyone wondered at her goodness.

She is described by a Dutch guard of Westerbork:

> When I met her in the camp Westerbork I knew this was truly a great woman. She was in the hell of Westerbork only a few days, walked among the prisoners, talking and praying like a saint. Yes, that's what she was. That was the impression which this elderly woman gave, though, on the other hand, see seemed quite young. She spoke in such a clear and humble way that anybody who listened to her was seized. A talk with her was like a visit to another world.[48]

Edith was finally effecting Christ's ministerial action as He "calms, soothes and redeems." Months before, she had written the following:

> I am quite content in any case. One can only learn a "Science of the Cross" if one feels the cross in one's own person. I was con-

vinced of this from the very first and have said with all my heart "Hail Cross, our only hope."[49]

The Dutch Red Cross reported that the two sisters were in the transport which left Westerbork on August 7th and arrived in Auschwitz the early hours of the 9th. We know the rest.

Edith had written, "I have an ever deeper and firmer belief that nothing is merely an accident when seen in the light of God, that my whole life down to its smallest details has been marked out for me in the plan of divine Providence and has a completely coherent meaning in God's all-seeing eye."[50]

Without trying to speak for God, what can we understand as the meaning of her life? First I see her as a symbol of the inherent unity between Judaism and Christianity and as a hopeful sign of their ensuing reconciliation. Indeed, St Paul tells us that Christ has already reconciled Jew and Gentile by the cross, creating from both a new humanity in His peace.

And I believe that God is working through her to affirm this reconciliation. I believe that through *her* passion, He is creating a resurrection of the human spirit and of brotherhood. St Augustine tells us that Christ's Resurrection was God's supreme and wholly marvellous work. To rise, He had to die and so it is with Edith. I see her martyrdom as making wonderful things happen.

The Holocaust was a death of the human race. Edith stands for the ten million people who died in the flames of the crematoria: six million Jews and four million Christians. We must pray that this fire of purgation will cleanse both faiths and put an end to their hostilities, effecting a redemption of total humanity.

And Edith believes that Christ's redemptive action is for all men: that all humanity is included in the Mystical Body of Christ.[51] Each person is a unique revelation of God and is to be honored so. Hence, forty years before Vatican Council II, she declared that she cannot believe that salvation depends on the exterior limits of any church. She becomes a symbol, then of universal dimension because she points to that universal realm of brotherhood above all barriers of nation, race, and religion.

Edith wanted a share in Christ's redemptive action and she teaches us to assume a similar role. Each person, she writes, is co-responsible through prayer for the salvation and redemption of the many who comprise the human community.[52] She incarnates the essence of holiness itself.

And because she is a model of holiness, she becomes a model of human spirituality. Edith was a true Jewish heroine as well as a saintly Christian. She pitted herself against the forces of evil like the great Hebrew women we find in scripture: Deborah, Ruth, Esther, Judith, and Mary. Of course, she is specifically a model of Christian spirituality and holiness. For us Christians she reveals the truths of our faith as truths: they are not mere abstractions but experiential, passionately lived truths which teach and heal us by their very organic power.

Edith is one with Christ because she went His way of the cross. She gave herself totally to His ministry of love and reparation on earth. She believed that love conquers hate and evil, and it is the cross which is the sign of that victorious love because hate cannot triumph over the love inherent in self-sacrifice. The cross is triumphant because it wins the redemption of the world.

This salvific power is desperately needed by society as a whole, and, surely, God grants us saints just when we need them! Edith Stein shows us the way out of our contemporary materialism, secularization, and even paganism through the power of love and prayer. In this day when technical science has become a God and is throttling the human spirit, she demonstrates that the search for truth is guided by the spirit of truth and that, indeed, the love of God surpasses all knowledge. She presents a viable balance of reason and faith. That is why Peter Wust wrote of her, "A bride was led to the altar whose life might be taken as a symbol of the intellectual movement of the last decade."[53]

Finally, she has a mission to strengthen women, to help them find their full humanity as persons and as women. I have spent the greater part of my adulthood preparing to bring Edith Stein to the public because I know she is the model from whom we can all learn.

There is a difference between the giving of self for love of God and the unbalanced, abject surrender of some modern women enslaved by their passions. Rare among women, she was a philosopher, a highly successful professional as well as a holy woman. She must in some way help us to find the true way towards our mission as God's special instruments of love to fight evil.

Edith reveals the beauty of God as Creator of humanity because of her own beauty. His beauty is in her. His intention of woman as a vehicle of divine love is fulfilled in her. She *is* the image of God. She manifests his qualities of self-giving, goodness, forgiveness, purity, holiness. She is another Christ.

She shows us the person of full humanity. Over a hundred years ago, a French Abbé, Abbé Constant, wrote that when women unite themselves to intelligence and love, they will give birth to a divine race.[54] Edith Stein was such a woman — God's lovely instrument: love and intelligence in her, in all her writings, in all her deeds to uplift the human race. Please God, we will be worthy of her sacrifice.

NOTES

1. See Teresia Renata de Spiritu Sancto (Posselt), *Edith Stein*, trans. Cecily Hastings and Donald Nicholl (New York: Sheed and Ward, 1952), 236.
2. *KL Auschwitz Seen by the SS*, ed. Kazimierz Smolen (Auschwitz: Panstwowe Museum, 1978), 175-76.
3. Ibid., 73.
4. Posselt, *Edith Stein*, 12.
5. *Aus dem Leben einer jüdischen Familie*, vol. 7 of *Edith Steins Werke*, ed. L. Gelber and R. Leuven (Louvain: Nauwelaerts, 1965; 2nd unabr. ed. Druten: "De Maas & Waler," 1985). The incidents described here are to be found in this autobiography of Stein's childhood and youth (with references to the 1st edition).
6. Ibid., 90.
7. Ibid., 145-46.
8. Stein's own description of her student days at Göttingen can be found in chap. 7 of her autobiography *Aus dem Leben* and in chap. 3 of Posselt, *Edith Stein*.
9. Hedwig Conrad-Martius, "Edith Stein," *Hochland*, 51 (Oct. 1958,1):40.
10. Adolf Hitler, *Letters and Notes*, ed. Werner Maser (New York: Bantam Books, 1974), 40.

11. Stein, *Aus dem Leben*, 231-32.
12. Hilda Graef, *Leben unter dem Kreuz* (Frankfurt a. Main: Verlag Josef Knecht, 1954), 37. Subsequent citations to Graef's *Leben* will be to her own translation of this work, *The Scholar and the Cross*.
13. This writer was granted the courtesy of examining the letter of Fr J. Hirschmann at the Edith Stein Archives in the Carmel of Cologne.
14. See Roman Ingarden, "Edith Stein on her Activity as Assistant of Edmund Husserl," trans. Janina Makota, *Philosophy and Phenomenological Research*, 23 (Dec. 1962,2):155-61.
15. Edith Stein, *Jahrbuch für Philosophie und phänomenologische Forschung* vols. 5 (1922) and 7 (1925).
16. Hitler, *Letters and Notes*, 211.
17. Posselt, *Edith Stein*, 64.
18. Conrad-Martius, *Edith Stein*:38, 42.
19. See chap. 11, "The Road to Carmel," in Posselt, *Edith Stein*, 116-32.
20. *Festschrift Sankt Martin 1879-1979* (Bad Bergzabern: Katholische Pfarrgemeinde Bad Bergzabern, 1979).
21. Msgr Eugene Kevane, "St Thomas Aquinas and Education," *The Catholic University of America Bulletin*, (April 1961,4):2,6. See Thomas Aquinas' *Quaes. Disp. de Magistro*, art. 1 and Summa Theol., I, q. 12, art. 5.
22. See J.H. Kardinal Newman, *Gesammelte Werke*, vols. 1 and 2, ed. Daniel Feuling, OSB, Erich Przywara, SJ and Paul Simon, trans. Edith Stein (München: Theatiner-Verlag, 1928-1933).
23. *Edith Steins Werke*, vols. 3 and 4. Stein's *Werke* will be designated below as *Werke*. Erich Przywara acknowledged his own debt to Stein and to Husserl in his Preface to *Ringen der Gegenwart*. He attributed much importance to Stein's contribution to the relationship of Neo-Scholasticism and Phenomenology. See particularly his "Neo-Scholasticism in Germany," *The Modern Schoolman*, 10 (1933):91-92.
24. *Werke*, vol. 2.
25. *Festschrift Edmund Husserl (zum 70 Geburtstag gewidmet), Supplementband Jahrbuch für Philosophie und Phänomenologische Forschung* (Halle: Niemeyer, 1929).
26. *Werke*, 5, 96-97.
27. Ibid., 224-25.
28. Ibid., 212.
29. See "La phénoménologie," *Journée d'études de la Société Thomiste* (12 septembre 1932), vol. 1 (Juvisy: Eds. du Cerf, 1932).
30. *Werke*, 2, 407.
31. Posselt, *Edith Stein*, 117.
32. Ibid., 118.
33. *Werke*, 2, 410.
34. Karol Wojtyla, *Faith According to St John of the Cross*, tran. Jordan Aumann (San Francisco: Ignatius Press, 1981), 49.
35. Posselt, *Edith Stein*, 128-29.

36. *Edith Stein*, ed. Waltraut Herbstrith (Freiburg im Breisgau: Herder, 1983), 71.
37. Posselt, *Edith Stein*, 168.
38. See Rudolph Allers, "Endliches und Ewiges Sein," *The New Scholasticism*, 26 (1952):480–85.
39. *Werke*, 2, Intro., ix.
40. Posselt, *Edith Stein*, 212.
41. Waltraut Herbstrith, *Das wahre Gesicht Edith Steins* (Bergen-Enkheim bei Frankfurt/Main: Verlag Gerhard Kaffke, 1971), p. 169.
42. Posselt, *Edith Stein*, 198.
43. Edith Stein, *Wege der Gotteserkenntnis-Dionysius der Areopagit* (München: Verl. Gerhard Kaffke, 1979).
44. *Werke*, vol. 1.
45. Edith Stein, *The Science of the Cross: A Study of St John of the Cross*, ed. L. Gelber and R. Leuven, trans. Hilda Graef (Chicago: Henry Regnery Co., 1960), 241.
46. Graef, *Scholar and the Cross*, 225.
47. Edith Stein, *Briefauslese 1917–1942* (Freiburg im Breisgau: Herder, 1967), 136.
48. See Posselt, *Edith Stein*, chap. 7, "The Way of the Cross," for a coverage of Stein's arrest, imprisonment and death.
49. Stein, *Briefauslese*, 127.
50. Herbstrith, *Das wahre Gesicht*, 147.
51. *Werke*, 2, 482.
52. *Werke*, 6, *Welt und Person*, "The Ontological Structure of the Person and Its Epistemological Problem," 161–62.
53. Posselt, *Edith Stein*, 147.
54. l'Abbé Constant, *l'Assomption de la femme* (Paris: Aug. le Gallois, 1841), 4.

EDITH STEIN'S PHILOSOPHY
OF PERSON

Mary Catherine Baseheart

Mary Catherine Baseheart is a Sister of Charity of Nazareth who is Professor of Philosophy at Spalding University in Louisville, KY. She has published various studies on Edith Stein in the past and is currently preparing a book on Stein's philosophy with the projected title of Light and Darkness: An Introduction to the Philosophy of Edith Stein.

If we are really to know Edith Stein, we must know her not only as a holy and heroic Jewish woman, a saintly Carmelite nun who was a victim of the Holocaust, but we must know her also as a philosopher, for her philosophizing is central to her total being. To think of Edith Stein without philosophy would be like thinking of Keats without poetry, Shakespeare without drama, or Knute Rockne without football. From her earliest college years at Breslau and at Göttingen, then at Freiburg as a doctoral student of Edmund Husserl and later as his assistant, she was a scholar and teacher whose life was filled with study of the history of philosophy and with research and discussion of contemporary thought with her peers and professors, especially with Husserl and his circle, including among others Martin Heidegger and Max Scheler. After turning from atheism to Catholicism in 1922, she continued to meet and collaborate with leading European philosophers while she was teaching at Speyer and at Münster. She translated the *De Veritate* of Thomas Aquinas into German, in addition to editing Husserl's manuscripts and writing numerous original works of her own, some of which were published in Husserl's *Jahrbuch*. She delivered lectures of a philosophical nature in many cities of Germany. At the meeting of the Société Thomiste at Juvisy in 1931, devoted to the consideration of phenomenology and Thomism, she was, so to speak a "star witness."[1] After her profession as a nun in Carmel in 1935, she was directed to resume her philosophical research and writing, and she produced some of her major works in the Carmels of Köln and Echt, until her death at Auschwitz in 1942.

A 1982 study of Stein[2] lists some forty works of hers, a large percentage of which are philosophical in nature. Because of the Nazi ban on books by non-Aryan writers, many of her works could not be published at the time they were completed, but many have been published posthumously. Especially to be noted are the volumes of the series entitled *Edith Steins Werke*, edited by Lucy Gelber and Fr Romaeus Leuven, OCD, and published by Nauwelaerts. One of the first of these to be translated into English is, the autobiographical *Life in a Jewish Family* published by the Institute of Carmelite Studies. Another work of hers in English which should be mentioned is her grandniece Waltraut Stein's translation of *Zum Problem der Einfühlung, On the Problem of Empathy*, published by Nijhoff in 1970. American scholars have been slow to investigate Stein's philosophy, but several significant studies have appeared in Europe.

If we follow the development of Edith Stein's thought from its beginnings to its final stages, we find one center of interest on which her philosophy focuses, one central theme that is like a thread running throughout her work: It is that of the human person.[3] Her philosophy of person takes its point of departure from her early studies in psychology, proceeds through questions related to the philosophy of man, discovering the inevitable link of the essence of person with the question of an ontology of spirit, and culminates in her metaphysics of God as Person.

As a young college student, Edith Stein specialized in psychology at the University of Breslau, her native city, where she studied from 1911 to 1913 under Professors Hönigswald and

William Stern. It was in Stern's seminar in 1912–1913, devoted to problems in the psychology of thought with reference to the works of the Würzburg School, that she came upon quotations from Edmund Husserl's *Logische Untersuchungen.* The reading of the second volume attracted her to phenomenology and convinced her that here was the work of a great philosopher. Her own words explain her decision to go to the University of Göttingen to study under Husserl:

> All my psychological studies had led me to the view that this science had not got beyond its infancy, that it still lacked essential, clear, basic concepts, and that it was in no condition to work out these concepts for itself. And what I had so far learned about phenomenology had captivated me precisely because it set itself this task of clarification and was fashioning the very conceptual tools one needed.[4]

She was quick to realize that psychology was still a science in search of itself, in spite of the brilliant scholars who were contributing to its development. In her turning to the task of clarification, her psychological studies stood her in good stead. Her in-depth knowledge of theories of Wundt, of Dilthey, of Theodor Lipps and William Stern, among others, served her well, both positively and negatively, in developing her philosophy of person.

She and the other young students who flocked to study under Husserl at Göttingen were attracted, she tells us, by his *Logical Investigations* because they seemed to find in this work an apparent "radical turning away from critical idealism of the Kantian or the Neo-Kantian variety." They regarded the work as a "new scholasticism," because it did not begin from the subject and then proceed to things: "Knowing was once more a process of reception whose laws were received from things and not—as in critical idealism—the imposition of laws upon things."[5] But in 1913, history was being made in Husserl's theory. *Ideen I*[6] had just appeared in the *Jahrbuch,* and many of Husserl's pupils were quick to realize and resist the impact of his emerging transcendental idealism.

It should be noted at the beginning of this study of Stein's philosophy that she was in many ways a true disciple of Edmund Husserl. She worked within the framework of his phenomenological terminology and method — but only up to a point. She used to advantage the method of descriptive analysis of the phenomena of consciousness — the turning to the "intentional object," of which the subject, the *I*, is conscious in its stream of lived experience. She also affirms in theory and in practice Husserl's "eidetic reduction," that is, the process which leads from the psychological phenomena to the essence, from fact to essential universality, the process which focuses on the "things" of experience, the *cogitationes* and their *cogitata*, and probes them by way of descriptive analysis. But for Stein these " things" of experience presuppose things of the fact world, the existence of which Husserl "brackets." She never gives assent to Husserl's phenomenological reduction, the epoché (ἐποχή); that is, the suspension of judgment in regard to the transcendent existence of the objective correlates of the *cogitata*.[7]

Stein recognized implicitly the impossibility of Husserl's ideal of a totally presuppositionless philosophy. Nevertheless, she agrees with him that philosophy should be carried on as "rigorous science."[8] She finds a parallelism between phenomenology and Thomism: (1) in regard to the end pursued: a system having objective validity and laying claim to the title of science (the "weasel word" here is *objective*); and (2) in regard to the intelligibility of being, the affirmation of an essential, intelligible structure, or *logos*, in all that is, and the power of reason to attain this intelligibility.[9] These were principles which she held firmly in her philosophizing.

In exploring the subject of her philosophy of person, this paper will depend on Stein's own texts and will attempt a developmental approach, beginning with her first work, entitled *On the Problem of Empathy*, which has been referred to above.[10] In it she initiates efforts to attain an ontological foundation of psychology and human sciences (the *Geisteswissenschaften*) within the framework of Husserl's phenomenology. It was written as a doctoral dissertation under Husserl for the Ph.D. awarded her by the University of Freiburg in 1916. Although the work shows affinity with Husserl's phenomenology, Stein exhibits, young as she is, a marked independence in appropriating his ideas in her own way and for her own purposes. Thus in a foreword to the English translation of the work, Edwin W. Straus remarks on Stein's existential approach as contrasted with the predominantly epistemological interests of Husserl.[11]

The scope of this first published work of hers is broader than the subject of empathy, and its primary significance for this paper lies in its revealing analyses directed toward the uncovering of what it means to be a person. The result of her intricate, descriptive analyses of the conscious experiences of the *I* is the arriving at the knowledge of the person as an integral totality, a being who belongs to the world of nature and to the world of spirit (*Geist*). As nature, the psycho-physical individual is subject to the laws of causality; as spirit, the person is subject to the laws of meaning. She explores *meaning* in the context of motivation, which brings her to concrete analyses of attitudes, feelings, values, and cognition, and their interaction.

She begins with the awareness of one's own being that is concomitant with the acts of consciousness. This is the awareness of the *I*, the self, which is simply given as the subject of experience, brought into relief in contrast with the otherness of the other when another is given. Using the Husserlian term, she calls it the *pure I*, the *I* in the I perceive, I think, I am glad, I wish, and so on. Yet the *pure I* is empty in itself; it depends for its content on experience of an outer world and of an inner world, and so, upon reflection, the *I* is revealed as the subject of actual qualitative experiences, with experiential content, lived in the present and carried over from the past, experiences which form the unity of the stream of consciousness. Further, she maintains that as we examine inner perception, we find one basic experience, which, together with its persistent attributes, becomes apparent as the identical "conveyor" of them all, their substrate. She calls this substrate the soul (*Seele*). But, she continues, this consciousness is body-bound consciousness. The body given in consciousness is sensed as "living body" (*Leib*) in acts of inner perception and in acts of outer perception. It is outwardly perceived as physical body (*Körper*) of the outer world; but this double givenness is experienced as the same body. The result of her analyses thus far is the disclosure of the psycho-physical individual.[12]

Even at this stage, Stein observes, there have been intimations of the self as *Geist*, spirit, in feelings and perceptions which appear linked with knowledge and felt value and which thus go beyond the psycho-physical. The manner in which she proceeds to "constitute" the knowledge of the person as spirit (she calls it the *geistige Person*) is strikingly original in that she arrives at rationality by way of analyses of feelings. She does not begin with what she terms "theoretical acts" such as perception, imagination, ideation, and inference, she says, because in these one may be so absorbed in the object that the *I* is not aware of itself. Instead she concentrates on feeling (for example, the feeling of joy), since here the *I* is always present to consciousness. But feeling always requires theoretical acts, and involves values, and both of these lead to the constitution of the rational.

Sentiments of love and hate, gratitude, vengeance, animosity —that is, feeling with other people for their object—are acts revealing spirit, *Geist*, which is characteristic of personal levels. In the act of loving, one experiences a grasping or intending of the value of a person. One loves a person "for his or her own sake." In a feeling of value one becomes aware of the self as subject and as object, and every feeling has a certain mood component that causes feeling to be spread throughout the *I* and can fill it completely. Feelings have different depth and reach, different intensity and duration, and these are subject to rational laws. The *I* passes from one act to another in the form of motivation—the meaning context that is completely attributable to *spirit*. Thus the person as spirit is the value-experiencing subject whose experiences interlock into an intelligible, meaningful whole.

Analysis of strivings, volitional decision, and willing follow. Every willing is based on the feeling of "being able"—"I can." Every act of feeling as well as every act of willing is based on a theoretical act. The act of reflection in which knowledge comes to givenness can always become a basis for a valuing. Cognitive striving and cognitive willing involve feeling the value of the cognition and joy in the realized act. Personality is thus a unity based in experience and distinguished by rational laws. Person and value-world are found to be completely correlated.

Personal attributes such as goodness, readiness to make sacrifices, the energy which I experience in my activities are conceivable as attributes of a spiritual subject and continue to retain their own nature in the context of the psycho-physical organization. They reveal their special position by standing outside the order of natural causality. Action is experienced as proceeding meaningfully from the total structure of the person.[13]

Much of this first work, it is obvious, is pheonomenological psychology, but it definitely goes beyond empirical psychology in its coming to knowledge of spirit as the specific characteristic of person and in its attempt to grasp the essence of spirit. This concept is necessary to Stein's concept of empathy, since only the person as spirit can go beyond the self and relate cognitively and affectively to others in the full sense of these relations.

You may ask why this early work has been considered somewhat in detail, perhaps with some tedium and certainly with oversimplification. There are two reasons: (1) because it shows Stein's method; and (2) because this work sketches in outline the framework of the structure of the person, which she fills in in her subsequent investigations.

Edith Stein's next work, *Contributions to the Philosophical Foundation of Psychology and the Human Sciences*, published five years later, in 1922, continues her search for a deeper knowledge of the self as person. In it appear several sentences which may express her own state of mind at the time she wrote it; they treat of the struggle that ensues when a convinced atheist realizes the existence of God in a religious experience, cannot avoid belief, but does not assent to it because unqualified faith might upset his/her scientific view of the world.[14] Edith Stein did assent, for she was baptized on New Year's Day, 1922.

The work contains lengthy, painstaking descriptions of the phenomena referred to in her first work, which add further evi-

dence of the person as capable of theoretical acts that go beyond
the sensuous and of affective acts that demand spirit. Motivation
is analyzed more comprehensively in all its manifestations: instincts, strivings, attitudes, moods, feelings, willing and acting.
Especially effective is her descriptive analysis of the freedom of
the person in acts of will. She recognizes the complexity of the
influence of the outer and inner situation on the decision, reso-
lution, and execution of the will act, but she holds firmly to the
freedom of the person within proper limits. She meets and finds
untenable the arguments regarding determination by the strongest motive and also determinism on the basis of the principle of
association.[15]

Stein devotes many pages in this work to the attempt to distinguish between psyche and spirit in the human being. The psychic
life, she holds, has to do with the soul, with its constant and vari-
able dispositions; this life refers to a subjective consciousness,
monadic and closed. Spirit, on the other hand, has to do with
objectifiable contents of intentional acts: thoughts, ends, values,
creative acts. This is why their bearer is never a simple subject of
acts, but an individual person with a qualitative point of view,
incarnating a unique spiritual value. A true science of spirit, she
states, should recognize the autonomy and individuality of the
person, while recognizing at the same time that every person is
subject to general laws of nature and of psychic life. Although the
latter are less precise than the former, knowledge of these laws
can afford the basis of a limited prevision, the eidetic possibilities, of what *can* take place, not what *must* or *will* take place.[16]

In spite of all her efforts, Stein never quite distinguishes between soul and spirit in this work, possibly because she was holding too strictly to Husserlian notions and also, perhaps, because
her concern in this context was to distinguish between psychology
and the *Geisteswissenschaften*. Stein herself admits that the
boundaries between soul and spirit cannot be strictly drawn.
Later, in *Endliches und Ewiges Sein*, she will reach her final
position on the question. More important at this point is her vision of the person as totality of qualitative particularity formed
from one central core (*Kern*), from a single root of formation

which is unfolded in soul, body and spirit.[17] In some respects her views seem close to the personalism of her former psychology professor William Stern, for whom the person in an individual totality whose defining property is purposive activity and who is at one and the same time turned back on the self and open to the world.

The third work to be considered in this paper, *Finite and Eternal Being (Endliches und Ewiges Sein)*,[18] represents the maturation of Edith Stein's thought. Completed in Carmel at Köln in 1936, it is the product of a mind nurtured not only by Husserl's phenomenology but also by her intensive study of Aristotle and Aquinas, Bonaventure, Scotus, and Augustine, but especially of Aquinas. It is a metaphysical work, subtitled *Attempt at an Ascent to the Meaning of Being*. Stein sees the problem of the meaning of being to be inextricably linked to the recognition of a First Being. Early in the work, she enters upon the ascent to the infinite and eternal being by way of an analysis of the experience of the finitude of the *I*.[19] Toward the end of the work, after many chapters treating the structure of concrete being in terms of potency and act, essence and existence, substance and accident, matter and form, she returns to the question of: What is *Menschsein*?[20] What is human being?

Stein acknowledges the mystery of man, since the entire conscious life, upon which she has relied for knowing what it means to be human, is "not synonymous with my being." It is only the lighted surface over a dark abyss, which she must seek to fathom.[21]

Without going into the entire fathoming process with her, which would be repetitive in part, our attention will be focused on advances over her previous works and on the summation of her philosophy of person. In this work her concept of the soul is explained further and more clearly. Soul is herein defined in the Aristotelian-Thomistic sense as the substantial form of a living body.[22] Thus there is a plant soul, an animal soul, and the human soul, each differing essentially from the other. As form, the soul is the principle of life and movement and gives essence-determination to the being. Man is neither animal nor angel—he is both in one.²³ The awake and conscious *Ichleben* gives access to the soul just as sensuous life gives access to the body. When the *I* goes beyond originary experience and makes the self an object, the soul appears to it as thing-like or substantial, having enduring characteristics, having powers or faculties which are capable of and in need of development, and having changing attitudes and activities.²⁴

Mention should be made here of Stein's theory of individual form. Each human being has not only universal essence by also individual essence. These are not two separate essences but are a unity in which the essential attributes join together in a determinate structure. The following quotation explains her position:

> To the essence of *this man* it belongs that he easily flies into a rage, is easily appeased, that he loves music and likes to have people around him. It does not belong to his essence that he just now went into the street and was surprised by rain... To the essence of *man* it belongs that he has a body and a soul, is endowed with reason, is free. It does not belong to his essence that he has white skin, blue eyes, was born in a big city or took part in a war or died of a contagious disease.²⁵

Thus, humanity is part of the individual essence of Socrates.²⁶ His individual essence makes the whole essence and every essential trait something unique, so that the friendliness or goodness of Socrates is other than that of other men.²⁷ Individual essence is not static, she holds; it can change, and she avoids Leibnizian strictures on freedom by emphasizing that not all that is grounded in essence follows necessarily.²⁸ This theory of individual essence, it is obvious, contributes to her emphasis on the uniqueness of each person.

In this work Stein still holds to her original distinction between soul and spirit, which has been noted in her earlier works; but here the distinction appears to have become a matter of the *I*'s progressive awareness of *spirit*. She writes:

> As form of the body the soul takes the middle position between spirit and matter ... As spirit it has its being in itself (*in sich*)

and can rise above itself in personal freedom and take up a higher life in itself. It does not radiate its essence unconsciously or involuntarily but goes out of itself in personal freedom into its spirit-activity. . . . Spirit and soul are not to be spoken of as existing side by side. It is the one spiritual soul which has a manifold unfolding of being. . . . The soul is spirit according to its most inner essence, which underlies the development of all its powers.[29]

The person, the *I*, then, is a three-fold oneness: body-soul-spirit. As spirit the human person is the bearer of his/her life — holds it in hand, so to speak. The person's knowing, loving, and serving and the joy in knowing, loving, and serving are the life of spirit, the proper sphere of freedom. And again she affirms that under spirit we understand the conscious and free *I*; free acts are the privileged realm of person. The *I* to which body and soul are proper, the same *I* which encompasses the spirit *I* is the living-spirit-person, the conscious, free *I*.[30]

For Stein the threefold unity of man — body-soul-spirit — is the image of the Triune God. From here *Finite and Eternal Being* proceeds into theology, where we will not venture just now. Certainly Stein agrees with Scheler that the being of the person is perfected in the person's relation to God. In a later work also, *World and Person* (*Welt und Person*),[31] Stein takes the person from the realm of natural reason to the realm of grace, showing that all human powers are enhanced in the higher realm, without loss of individuality. Thus Stein sees the person with the eyes of faith and of reason.

Stein's philosophy of person comes through in many of her other works, not considered in this paper, and particularly in her life. In the compilation of her lectures on woman, delivered in German cities around 1930, entitled *Die Frau*,[32] we find Stein the psychologist, Stein the teacher and educational theorist, and Stein, the intensely religious convert whose lay apostolate was to culminate in the contemplative life of Carmel; we also find Stein the philosopher, whose philosophy of education is directly related to her philosophy of person. Education, she states, is the formation of human personality. In each human being there is a unique inner form which all education from outside must respect and aid in its movement toward the mature, fully-developed personality. The humanness is the basis of fundamental commonalities. All persons show forth the image of God, and so education must help all of them to develop their powers of *knowing, enjoying,* and of *creative making* in order to image God's *wisdom, goodness,* and *power.* "Intellect is the key to the kingdom of the spirit... The intellect must be pressed into activity. But ... the training of the intellect should not be extended at the expense of the schooling of the heart. The mean is the target."[33] The disciplines should be taught not in a purely abstract way but should be related to the concrete and personal as far as possible.

Her philosophy of woman likewise grows out of her philosophy of person. She presents the being of woman under three aspects: her humanity, her specific femininity, and her individuality. Her treatment of woman as a member of the human species is quite traditional, but she adds that within the human species there is a "double species" of man and woman; here the term *species* is definitely used in a non-traditional sense. She does hold that differences in gender, rooted as they are in bodily structure, are the basis of personality differences, but the differences in personality apply only in general; for some women have characteristics which are considered typically "manly," and some men have characteristics that are "womanly." There is no profession that cannot be carried on by women, she maintains, and some women have special aptitude for some professions that have been considered as belonging principally to men, such as that of doctor.

Edith Stein's life gives eminent expression to her philosophy of person, for she lived her personhood in the fullest sense of the word. Certainly her philosophy originated in the fullness of her own experience, of her shared experiences with other human persons, and ultimately in her experience of God. Her belief in the dignity and uniqueness of every person and her capacity for love as well as for knowledge are seen in her relations with members of her natural family and those of her religious community as well as in her personal and professional relationships with her colleagues, particularly Edmund Husserl. In spite of her divergence from some of his fundamental theory, her friendship for him and his for her endured until the end. He was always very proud of her. She seems to me to be a role model for philosophers in the manner in which she entered into dialogue, without rancor over disagreement and with proper respect for and openness to others' ideas.

In the attempt to give a comprehensive overview of Edith Stein's philosophy of person, in theory and practice, it is obvious that I have sacrificed depth to breadth. It is an effort to explore virgin territory; there are few landmarks, and I have indicated some of the difficulties in finding one's way. I want to study the German texts more thoroughly, to finish some of the translation that is under way, and I hope for the publication of translations by others who are studying Stein's works. There is also need for comparative studies; for example, the comparison of Stein's treatment of *Leib*, living body, with that of Merleau-Ponty's *corps vécu*; of Stein's *Lebenskraft*, life force, with Bergson's *élan vital*; of Stein's theory of individual form with that of Duns Scotus and that of her contemporary Jean Hering; and of course, further exploration of Stein's adaptation of Husserlian themes and methodology to large philosophical questions.

Some general conclusions, however, can be drawn at this point regarding the value of Edith Stein's philosophy of person. One may cite the strong case which she makes for the unity of the person while facing its immense complexities in what she terms the body-soul-spirit human being; the existential character of her investigation in the turning to the *things themselves* in the outer world, while at the same time describing and analyzing the intentional objects of consciousness; the enriching of the classic Boethian definition of person as "an individual substance of a rational nature" through extensive disclosures of motivation proper to the person and through the exposition of the essential connections of feelings and attitudes with reason, even in their initial stages. Finally, her stand with Max Scheler in regard to the dignity and worth of the human person, the highest of all earthly values, which she grasped and justified even in the purely philosophical context of her life before she turned to religion, and even more in her Christian philosophizing in faith.

Edith Stein's philosophy, it seems to me, holds a depth of meaning and speaks to many, in fact, to all classes of persons. It speaks to philosophers and scholars in general of the openness, good feeling, and honesty which should characterize their dialogue in search for truth. It speaks to women of a balanced feminism that promotes the full flowering of women's gifts. It speaks to teachers and students in emphasizing the respect for the individual in the context of a vigorous curriculum (I mean that in the original meaning of the term: "race course") of humanistic, scientific, and professional studies. In the manner in which she blended her identity as Jewish and Christian, she shows the way to break down the barriers that divide people of different race and/or religion. Her grand niece, Waltraut Stein, in an article in *Spiritual Life* (1967) sees in her aunt a symbolic realization of the relation between the Jew and the Christian — of the love that can bind them together in peace.[34] For all people of God who are seeking God she is an example of the harmony that may be achieved in the union of the intellectual life and the spiritual life.

Finally, Edith Stein's life and philosophy call us to live below the surface, to what she calls "self presence," that is, to live in the innermost part of our being. If the personal *I* lives there, she says, it will be closest to the meaning of all happenings and open to the demands that are made on it; it will be best prepared to gauge their importance and bearing. The person who lives recollectedly in depth, will see small things in their wider relationships, can estimate their importance and is on the way to final forming and perfecting of his/her being. It is from the interior, too, that one's own being radiates outward and casts its spell on others.[35] Edith Stein's life in philosophy has the power to cast a spell on us today, inspiring us to live less on the surface and more in the depths of our being to encounter ultimately the Eternal Being, the Person *par excellence*.

NOTES

1. "La phénomenologie," *Journée d'études de la Société Thomiste* (12 september 1932, Juvisy), vol. 1 (Juvisy: Eds. du Cerf, 1932). Hereafter cited as *Journée.*

2. Matthieu Barukinamwo, *Edith Stein. Pour une ontologie dynamique, ouverte à la transcendance totale,* vol. 169 in series 23 of European University Studies (Frankfurt a. Main: Peter Lang, 1982), 45–47.

3. Reuben Guilead also remarks on this. See his *De la phénomenologie à la science de la croix, l'itinéraire d'Edith Stein* (Louvain: Nauwelaerts, 1974), 12.

4. Quoted in Sr Teresia Renata de Spiritu Sancto (Posselt), *Edith Stein,* trans. Cecily Hastings and Donald Nicholl (New York: Sheed and Ward, 1952), 22.

5. Ibid., 34.

6. Edmund Husserl, *Ideen zu einer reinen Phänomenologie und phänomenologischen Philosophie,* vol. 1, ed. W. Biemel (The Hague: Nijhoff, 1950). First published in the *Jahrbuch für Philosophie und phänomenologische Forschung,* vol. 1, (1913); English translation, *Ideas: General Introduction to Pure Phenomenology,* trans. Boyce Gibson (New York: Macmillan, 1931). Hereafter cited as *Ideen 1.*

7. Edith Stein, "Husserls Phänomenologie und die Philosophie des hl. Thomas v. Aquinas," *Festschrift Edmund Husserl (zum 70 Geburtstag gewidmet), Supplementband Jahrbuch für Philosophie und Phänomenologische Forschung* (Halle: Niemeyer, 1929). Hereafter cited as *Festschrift.* Also *Journée,* 75, 88.

8. Edmund Husserl, "Philosophie als strenge Wissenschaft," *Logos,* 1 (1910–11): 289–341; English translation, "Philosophy as Strict Science," trans. Quentin Lauer, *Cross Currents,* 6 (1956): 227–46; 325–44.

9. *Festschrift,* 316–17.

10. Edith Stein, *On the Problem of Empathy,* trans. from the German *Zur Problem der Einfühlung* by Waltraut Stein (The Hague: Nijhoff, 1970).

11. Ibid., v–vi.

12. Ibid., 35–47.

13. Ibid., 87–102. See Karol Wojtyla, *The Acting Person* (Boston: D. Reidel, 1979).

14. Edith Stein, *Beiträge zur philosophischen Begründung der Psychologie und der Geisteswissenschaften,* repr. (Tübingen: Max Niemeyer, 1970), pp. 43–44. First published in the *Jahrbuch für Philosophie und phänomenologische Forschung,* 5 (1922).

15. Ibid., 79ff.
16. Ibid., 86ff.
17. Ibid., 204-15.
18. *Endliches und Ewiges Sein*, vol. 2 of *Edith Steins Werke*, ed. L. Gelber and R. Leuven (Louvain: Nauwelaerts, 1950). Hereafter cited as *EES*.
19. Ibid., 53-59.
20. Ibid., 336ff.
21. Ibid., 337.
22. Ibid., 340.
23. Ibid., 343.
24. Ibid., 346-47.
25. Ibid., 70.
26. Ibid., 144.
27. Ibid., 151.
28. Ibid., 71.
29. Ibid., 423.
30. Ibid., 347.
31. *Welt und Person*, vol. 6 of *Edith Steins Werke*, ed. L. Gelber and R. Leuven (Louvain: Nauwelaerts, 1962).
32. *Die Frau*, vol. 5 of *Edith Steins Werke*, ed. L. Gelber and R. Leuven (Louvain: Nauwelaerts, 1959).
33. Ibid., 80-83.
34. Waltraut Stein, "Edith Stein, Twenty-five Years Later," *Spiritual Life*, 13 (1967): 244-51.
35. *EES*, 404ff.

EDITH STEIN AND
MARTIN HEIDEGGER

John Nota

*John Nota is a priest of the Society of Jesus, born in the Nether-
lands and now residing most of the year in North America where
he teaches philosophy. He knew Edith Stein personally in Echt,
Holland. At the recent beatification ceremonies in Cologne he
was one of the official "witnesses" who gave personal descriptions of their contacts with Bl. Teresa Benedicta of the Cross
before her tragic death.*

In 1933, the year that Adolf Hitler became Chancellor of the
Third Reich, Martin Heidegger accepted reluctantly his
appointment as Rector of the University of Freiburg and gave
his inaugural lecture, his famous "Antrittsrede" as rector. Heidegger used to be the assistant, later the successor of Edmund
Husserl in Freiburg.

In this same year, Edith Stein, Husserl's first assistant in Freiburg, well acquainted with Martin Heidegger, had to resign
from her teaching post because of her non-Aryan blood. She
was Jewish.

This paper intends to give an exposition of Edith Stein's philosophy, mainly in its relation to Heidegger's thought, from
about 1929: how she developed her philosophy in unity with her
life, how she responded to the challenge of the Hitler regime.
She remained faithful to the phenomenological approach in her

philosophy, also in dealing with Heidegger's important works as *Being and Time*. She did not live in anxiety, but in hope, even when she had to die in the gas chambers of Auschwitz on August 9, 1942.

LIFE

The persecution of Jews and Christians which started in 1933 did not come as a surprise to Edith Stein. Her former colleague at the Magdalena College of Speyer, Baroness Uta von Bodman, told me during a commemorative meeting at the Edith Stein Carmel in Tübingen (August 1982), how one night in 1930, the French occupation forces left the city and the German army took over. Teachers and students went to celebrate the event that took place at midnight. Everybody was excited about the regained freedom, symbolized in the parade of the German soldiers to the light of the torches' flames. Edith Stein, however, was very quiet. Uta von Bodman asked her why she did not share the enthusiasm of the crowd, of all the spectators. Edith answered: "They are going to persecute first the Jews, then afterwards the Catholic Church." Her friend could not believe it. "Wait, and you will remember my words," Edith said.

She did not remain passive, but visited several professors for her "Habilitation," one of them Martin Heidegger. The result of her efforts was negative, as about ten years previously. The handicaps of former years had only increased. She was still a woman and Jewish, but had also become a well-known Catholic. Another event proved her intuition of Speyer true. It happened in 1933, in Münster, where she was teaching at the Pedagogical Institute, the *Marianum*. One night, she told later, she was not able to enter her own house, either because she had forgotten her key, or because somebody else had a key left in the lock from the inside. A friendly passerby, a Catholic teacher, noticed her predicament and said: "My wife invites you to stay overnight at our house." Edith accepted the friendly invitation and, enjoying some fruit from her hosts, she heard him talking about the political situation. American papers, he said, wrote about cruelties to the German Jews:

> There was no confirmation of these facts. I do not want to re-
> peat them. The important issue here is the impression I received
> that evening. I had already heard more often about severe mea-
> sures against the Jews. But now I all of a sudden realized that
> God had again laid his hand heavily on his people and that the
> destiny of this people was also mine. I did not show my host what
> was happening in my soul. Apparently, he did not know about
> my descent. In such cases I used to give the right information,
> but I did not do it now. I thought it would have been a kind of
> violation of the right of hospitality to disturb his night's rest by
> such a revelation.[1]

But she made up her mind that she had to do something in
the Jewish question. In her personal prayer she told God that
she was willing to suffer with her people and for her people, if he
wanted her to. She also decided to go to Rome to ask the Pope to
write an encyclical against the persecution of the Jews. When
she discovered that there would be no chance of a private audience, but only an audience in a small group because of the Holy
Year 1933, she wrote a letter to the Pope. She heard that her
sealed letter was handed to the Pope, and she received later his
blessing. She did not know, however, as we know now from the
archives, that in 1938 Pope Pius XI decided to ask Father John
La Farge, SJ to make a draft for an encyclical against racism
and antisemitism. But then the war broke out in 1939, the Pope
had died and his successor wrote an encyclical about peace:
"Summi Pontificatus." He used parts of the draft for a more urgent purpose: world peace, as a condition for an end to racism
and antisemitism.[2]

Edith Stein was not allowed to teach anymore and she decided
that the time had arrived to do what she had wanted to do a long
time previously: she applied to enter the convent, the Carmel of
Cologne.

After a while her superiors allowed her to continue her work
as a philosopher and she wrote her impressive synthesis of phenomenology and scholasticism in her *Finite and Eternal Being*.
She finished the book in September 1936 and received the galleyproofs, but the law against Jews in Germany made publication

impossible. In 1941, when she was in Holland, she asked me to see if publication in Holland or in Belgium would be possible, but the Nazi occupation caused the same problem. Edith Stein was resigned to it and said to me that it would become a posthumous work. As a matter of fact the book was published in 1950, eight years after her death.[3]

It is impossible to deal with the content of this volume of 485 pages in one talk, but I will limit myself here to the relation between the philosophy of Edith Stein and the philosophy of Martin Heidegger. In her original text Edith Stein deals with Heidegger several times and in a very explicit way in an extensive addition to the book ("Anhang") which is entitled "Martin Heidegger's Existential Philosophy." Here she gives an exposition of *Being and Time*, of *Kant and the Problem of Metaphysics, The Essence of Ground* and *What is Metaphysics?*, followed by a profound critical evaluation of Heidegger's thought. The editor in 1950 left out this section completely, with the excuse that Edith Stein did not take into account the later Heidegger after 1936. In 1962 the addition finally got published in Vol. VI of the *Edith Stein Werke*. It consists of 66 pages.[4]

FINITE AND ETERNAL BEING

To understand Edith Stein's philosophy one has to take into account the development of her philosophy. Elsewhere I wrote about her first years, how she turned away from the positivistic psychology of her day to Edmund Husserl because philosophy to her meant a search for truth: truth about herself and a meaning to her life, truth about man, her fellow men and women, about the human person and society. The phenomenological method helped her a great deal, but she did not agree with Husserl's idealism. Already in 1917 she decided that only a realistic philosophy could be the answer to her phenomenological experience.[5]

Her conversion to the Catholic Church did not decrease her philosophical interest, but on the contrary increased it. She became acquainted with Thomas Aquinas, John Henry Newman, by means of her translations and by her studies. Erich Przywara, SJ was a particularly important inspiration. In 1929 she wrote an article in the Husserl-festschrift: a confrontation of Husserl and Thomas Aquinas. It is an interesting program for her future philosophical activity. In our present context I would like to mention that E. Przywara wrote later in an article that actually Edith Stein composed "an also artistically important dialogue between E. Husserl and Thomas Aquinas . . . which, unfortunately, according to a wish of Martin Heidegger she had to change into a so-called neutral article."[6] Heidegger contributed to the same Festschrift his *The Essence of Ground.* In her great ontology, prepared by an unpublished study on "act and potency," she ranges herself under "the born phenomenologists"[7] and she is going to be helped by the "philosophia perennis — the perennial philosophy." She also mentions that Heidegger's *Being and Time* is at the background of her thinking. This appears again and again in her book. Already the title is significant: "Finite and Eternal Being, an Attempt at an Ascent to the Sense of Being." She is aware of Heidegger's complaint about the oblivion of Being and the concern for beings. She makes the distinction, but then she analyzes the authors, especially, Thomas and Aristotle, together with her phenomenological experience and discovers the important distinction between finite beings and eternal Being.

A first step to this discovery she expresses in the phrase Augusta Spiegelman Gooch in her dissertation rightly considered as characteristic: "All Being is Being of a being."[8] Edith Stein agrees with Thomas Aquinas there is a distinction between τὸ ὄν — be-ing and ἡ οὐσία — essence in finite beings, whereas in the First Being one may speak about a real one-ness. Moreover there is a real distinction between all kinds of beings around us, but there is also being within us and so she takes as a starting point of her search for the sense of Being her own being: "The fact of the own being." (p.35)[9] In her own being she discovers the temporality of being, but at the same time the idea of a pure Being reveals itself to us. This Being does not contain anything of non-being, it does not present a "no-more" nor a "not-yet," it is not temporal, but *eternal.* (p. 36f.)

To quote her words: "Thus the conscious life of the ego is dependent in its content on a double transcendence, on an outer and inner world... Can one say that the ego might have its being from itself? That apparently would not be in agreement with the remarkable qualities of this being we discovered. We are confronted with the puzzling uncertainty of its whence and its whither... It experiences itself as alive, as being present, and at the same time coming from a past and living into a future. The ego and its being are necessarily just there, it is a thrown into *Dasein*! That is the extreme opposite to the absolute autonomy and self-transparency of a being by itself." (p. 51f.) We just do not have that experience, but the mixed experience of being independent *and* dependent.

This double-aspect Edith Stein discovers in her own being confronts her with the phenomenon of anxiety, an anxiety finally for "nothingness." But she disagrees with Heidegger that the phenomenon of anxiety would be the dominating vital feeling. Of course, a superficial way of life may hide the basic uncertainty which is part of our being when we do not go beyond our being. But that does not point to a "freedom to death" attitude as the only rational attitude in life. "Because of the undeniable fact that my being is a passing being that goes from moment to moment and is exposed to the possibility of non-being — because this is accompanied by another fact, just as undeniable as the former, that *I am* notwithstanding this passing by, that I am *kept in being*, from moment to moment, and that I contain a permanency within my passing being, I know that Somebody supports me and this gives me rest and certainty. It is not the self-conscious certainty of a man who stands on his two feet by his own power, but the sweet and blessed certainty of a child that is being carried by a strong arm. This certainty is after all not less a rational certainty. Or would one call a child 'sensible,' when it would live continuously in anxiety, because mother might drop it? So I am confronted in my own being with another Being which is not mine, but the support and cause of my being that does not have this support or cause by itself." (pp. 56-57) "In other words my temporal being reveals to me the presence within me of an eternal Being." (p. 57)

Edith Stein shows herself a real phenomenologist in her description of temporality, finitude, infinity, eternity:

Temporal being is a movement of existence; an always new shining (*Aufleuchten*) of actuality. The being that is temporal does not possess its being, but is being given its being again and again. In this way we are confronted with the possibility of a beginning and ending in time. Here we find a description of one sense of finitude: that which does not possess its being, but needs time to arrive at being, would be accordingly the finite. Even in case it would be kept without end in being, it would not yet be *infinite* in the full sense of the word. Authentically infinite is that which *cannot* end, because it does not receive being, but it *possesses being*, is *Lord of being*, is *Being itself.* We call it the *eternal Being.* This being does not need time, but is also Lord of time. Temporal being is finite, eternal Being is infinite. But finitude means more than temporality, and eternity means more than impossibility of ending in time. That which is finite needs time to become *that what* it is (*das-was*). And that is a *thing-like limitation.* That which is put into being, is being put into being as *something.* As something which is *not nothing,* but also not *everything.* And that is the other sense of finitude: *to be something and not everything.* Accordingly *eternity,* as full possession of Being means: *there is nothing one is not,* i.e. *to be all.* (p. 60)

In a finite being in general Edith Stein discovers the distinction especially between being and being this particular being, the distinction between my ego and Being itself. But she wants also to go deeper into the distinction between the being of the ego and its experience. This lived experience can only be an experience because of its content. There is a difference between the joy you may have at the success of your work and the work itself. Even when Thomas and other philosophers or psychologists tell me in a definition what joy is all about, there is first of all the phenomenological experience of joy and that is the only way to its essence. Two things become clear: Edith Stein remains a phenomenologist, notwithstanding Herbert Spiegelberg's statement,[10] and her examples, as expressions of her own phenomenological experience, are again and again about joy. This is not because everything was so great in 1934 and later, but because, notwithstanding her anxiety and her concern for her relatives, she is still in her deepest self full of joy and trust. The analyses help her to acquire a deeper understanding of the essence, the whatness of joy, so of essence and essential being in general.

In a second section of her book she tries another approach, i.e., the study of Thomas Aquinas (especially *De ente et essentia*), Aristotle and others, as an historical complement to her phenomenological attitude. This helps her to come to a better insight into the meaning of τὸ ὄν — be-ing, οὐσία — essence or being in an excellent way, τὸ ὄν ἧ ὄν being as such. In her historical and philological research she remains the phenomenologist and supports, e.g., her view about life, about plants, with her personal analyses and with the analyses of her friend Hedwig Conrad-Martius. Her conclusion is again that the questioning of Being receives a multiple answer. She discovers eternal and finite being, and in all finite being it is necessary to distinguish between Being-*Sein* and being-*ens*. The Augustinian and Aristotelian approach, the starting point from the ego and the starting point from the world, led to a similar result: the separation between possible and real Being and being, and the foundation of the real and possible in an essential Being and being that lies beyond the separation. As Aristotle considers the question about being ὄν and οὐσία as similar, and as οὐσία means finally "being in an excellent way," and moreover several beings show several excellences of being, she wonders if it would not be possible to discover the meaning of Being and being as such in οὐσία. She disagrees with Heidegger's identification of οὐσία and sense of Being.(p. 257f.) Her interpretation is that οὐσία is a being in an excellent way, where we see the fulfillment of the sense of being, or being as such τὸ ὄν ἧ ὄν. And so the question of Being as such leads us to the question of the sense of Being. She sees the doctrine of the transcendentals as an effort to define being as such(p. 263). Her surprising conclusion is that the transcendentals only hold for being and not for Being. She considers the transcendentals as a development of a special something that finds its fulfillment in Being as its Essence (*wesenhaft*). Human imagination cannot make a sense; we do discover, however, in all finite beings the development of a sense. The plurality of beings finally finds its unity and its sense in the pure first Being.(pp. 307-11)

The first Being is pure Being, because here is nothing of non-being, as in a finite temporal being that once was and once will not be, or as in the factual limited being that is something and not all. Here is no transition from possibility to actuality, from potency to act, and so we may call pure Being also pure Act. All this is pointing to the difficulty to define (*bestimmen*) pure Being, where Being (*Sein*) and *being* (*Seiendes*) cannot be separated anymore. So we also call pure Being the first Being (*Seiendes*), but then Being (*Seiendes*) in a sense that transcends all transcendentals and may only be called Being according to the *analogia entis*. This eternal Being, origin of all finite being, goes beyond all determination. Being and Essence coincide, and Edith Stein is close to this other famous Jewish philosopher, Moses Maimonides, in his negative theology. She would on the other hand disagree with Heidegger who says in his "*Letter about Humanism*" that Being surpasses even God.[11] According to her the pure Being can only be a Person. Her metaphysics of being culminates in a philosophy of Person. The cause of finite beings must be intelligent and loving and cannot be anything else than personal. But then human language has to be silent. The only word we can say is: "God is—God."(p. 317) But when God himself reveals himself to us, then we have to listen. And here she tries to come to a synthesis of her philosophy and her Christian faith, rooted in Judaism, by quoting the words of Exodus 3:14: "I am who I am." She elaborates this by starting again from the human ego where we experience a limited unity of ego and being. In God, the fullness of Being, there is no limitation. God who says "I am," says at the same "time": "I live," "I know," "I will," "I love."(p. 319) He is Being in Person. Now person, according to Edith Stein, is always *Mitsein*—being with, and so it is in agreement with her philosophy when she continues beyond her philosophical approach and says that a God who is love cannot be just a lonely person. Love, as a "yes" to a good, is quite possible as the self-love of an ego. But love is more than an affirmation like this, than an "estimation of values." Love is the surrender of the self to a "Thou" and a higher unity in a mutual surrender. As God is love itself, then divine Being must be a Oneness of a plurality of Persons, and his name "I am" must be identical to a: "I give myself completely to a Thou," "I am one with a Thou," and so also a: "We are." The sense of finite beings consists in the unity of all finite beings in the Logos.(p. 321ff. and also p. 460)

Returning from God to his creation Edith Stein develops how all creation is an image of God. Human beings are God's image in a special way. In this context she develops her philosophy of man, of the ego, soul, person. Here she meditates on the word of Genesis, how God, who is the triune God according to her Catholic faith, created humankind according to his image: male and female he created them. Edith Stein makes clear that this includes a sexual difference and elaborates on the specific aspects of man and woman. God created man and woman according to his image as spiritual-personal beings.(p. 470f.) One wonders, if this was the reason that it was "no good" that one would be alone, because the deepest sense of spiritual-personal being is mutual love and oneness of a plurality of persons in love. The Lord gave Adam a help as his counterpart (*wie ihm gegenüber* is according to Edith Stein the best translation from the Hebrew), a companion, corresponding to him as one hand to another. She was almost exactly like him and still a little bit different, and so she was capable of a proper and complementary action, according to her bodily and psychic being. We are allowed, Edith Stein thinks, to interpret the 'to be in one flesh' not only as an essential unity of the bodily nature (*Wesensgemeinsamkeit der leiblichen Natur*), but at the same time as a crossing of life-happenings which let grow from both a unity of being. In that case a still deeper unity will be possible for the souls, because on the level of the spirit there is a communion that does not have its equal on the level of the body; the created image of the love between the eternal Father and the divine Son. All creatures have their own nature, not one nature together as the divine Persons. But the human souls are able, because of their free spirituality, to open themselves to each other and to receive the other into oneself in loving surrender. "And when the greater power of surrender corresponds to the nature of woman, then in the loving union the woman will not only give more, but also receive more than the man."(p. 470) The importance of being a woman becomes even clearer in the union of man and woman in marriage. Human beings are superior to other creatures insofar as they represent God as a spiritual being and so their bodily union is to be considered as an expression and result of their spiritual union. "The child is as the fruit of this mutual surrender, or rather the embodied 'gift' itself. The gift is a third person, an autonomous creature and as 'creature' in the full sense of the word a gift from God."(p. 471) The question may be asked what this creature owes to God, what it owes to the parents. But the important issue for Edith Stein is that the new creature receives from the first moment of its *Dasein* in the mother's womb a bodily-psychic nature of its own, familiar to the parents and still something very special. The thing that is of interest to her is that this new human being is carrying its own being — although not yet in a free conscious way — and starting its development. It receives food, grows and forms itself. This is not only for the body, but also for the soul, as the experiential wisdom of people considers the emotional condition of the mother, in the time between conception and birth, of normative significance for the future of the child. Edith Stein may confuse contemporary feminists when she says that the motherhood of Mary is the archetype of all motherhood, not just for the time of pregnancy, but beyond it. She sees the surpassing meaning of motherhood in regard to human fatherhood in the fact that Jesus is born from a human mother, but did not have a human father. When his food was to do the will of his heavenly Father, then the mother whose nature would be his first food, should be dedicated to this Father's will with all power of her soul: "let it be unto me according to thy word." Mary's Son is the final form where all human being receives its sense. His person is the marriage of heaven and earth where all finitude finds its fulfillment in eternity.(p. 473f.)

Excuse me for quoting this theological thought from Edith Stein. I could not resist the temptation to show that there are more ways in feminist theology that what some feminist theologians would make us believe. They would say that Edith Stein is a philosopher. And rightly so. But this woman-philosopher knew more about theology than many professional theologians of her and our time and, moreover, she wrote from experience and lived it. Her philosophy cannot be separated from her religion. But let us go back to her explicit philosophy.

ANHANG — ADDITION ON HEIDEGGER

After the summary of her own metaphysics I would like to summarize also the "Anhang" of her book on Heidegger's philosophy. As I mentioned before, she had this addition printed in the galleyproofs, as part of her *Finite and Eternal Being,* but the present editor published it in Vol. VI of her *Werke,* as a chapter of the book *Welt und Person* (World and Person). At the beginning of the "Anhang" Edith Stein writes: "It is impossible to sum up in a few pages the richness and power of the often truly enlightening explorations that are contained in Heidegger's great torso *Being and Time.* Perhaps no other book of the last decade had influenced philosophical thought today so much as this one . . . "[12] In her critical evaluation Edith Stein is going to deal with three issues:

(1) What is *Dasein?*
(2) Is the analysis of *Dasein* faithful to the experience of *Dasein?*
(3) Will this analysis do to ask the question of the sense of Being is a right way? (p. 90)

Dasein

With Edith we may be brief about the first question: What is *Dasein?* When *Dasein* means human being or man, and man's essence would be his existence, then she wonders how essence and being may coincide in man. Of course, *Dasein* is not just Being, but a special mode of Being, and the only being from which one may expect an answer about the sense of Being. The positive reason to use the term *Dasein* is that it is essential to its being to be *there,* i.e., open to oneself and within a world wherein one is always directed to a there. The negative reason is that Heidegger rejects the traditional (?) definition of man as consisting of two substances: body and soul. Heidegger does not deny that man has a body, he just does not talk about it. As for the soul, he thinks that the term is not clear, and without denying the importance of the spirit, he prefers another clearer approach and talks about *Dasein.*

Analysis and Experience of Dasein

In her critique of Heidegger's analysis of *Dasein* Edith Stein expresses her admiration for this analysis and for the distinction between authentic and inauthentic being, but she wonders why he does not continue to give more clarity and even why he stops where the phenomenological experience tells him to go on. When I experience myself as thrown into the world, then nobody can tell me that I am not supposed to ask any questions about somebody who did the throwing. There is no objection to the fact that human life means first and foremost a living together with others and according to the tradition, before the proper authentic being comes to the fore. After all, Max Scheler emphasized this much earlier. But a philosopher has to ask about the foundation of the factuality, and then the distinction between the "one-self" and the proper self, and the term existential and form of existence may need some more clarification. (p. 94)

Edith Stein gives her own phenomenological analysis of "one." She disagrees with Heidgegger's denial to talk about ego and person and points to the very different meanings of the expression "one." "Being with others" (*Mitsein*) is a part of man's being and cannot be called inauthentic. Actually, person is called to be part of a community *and* individual person, and to live both aspects of being human in the right way, many must leave the "being with" on the lower level, to be with and for others in a better way. Edith Stein's analysis points to a development in man from a less perfect stage to a more perfect stage, and she wonders how Heidegger starting from fallenness without a Fall, can ever switch to a better stage just by himself. A state of degeneration can hardly explain the origin of an authentic self, especially because the authentic self has to make the call of conscience to the self. (p. 100)

Edith Stein gives another re-experiencing critical analysis of Heidegger's qualification of *Dasein* as "Being-unto-death." First of all she asks the question: "What is death?" Heidegger's answer is: "The end of *Dasein*." And Heidegger immediately adds that he does not want to make a decision by this statement about the possibility of life after death. Only when we will know the ontological nature of death, we may ask meaningfully about life after death. Edith Stein is puzzled by this attitude. When the final sense of *Dasein* is "being-unto-death," then the sense of *Dasein* should become clearer by the sense of death. But how is this possible when you can only say about death that it is the end of *Dasein*? Is this not a completely vicious (*ergebnislos*) circle? (p. 101) As a matter of fact Heidegger is not so much concerned about death, but much more about the way we experience death. His opinion is that death or dying (he does not make here a strict distinction) are not experienced with others, but as "existential," belonging to our own *Dasein*. Edith Stein is going to deal here again with three issues:

(1) Is there an experience of our own death? (Heidegger says: Yes.)

(2) Is there an experience of the death of others? (Heidegger says: No).

(3) What is the relation between 1 and 2?

By dying Heidegger means not the transition from life to being dead, but something that belongs to *Dasein* as such. Edith Stein notes here an ambiguity: Death and dying as the end toward which *Dasein* is directed, and at the same time this directing itself. According to the first meaning death would be something to come, according to the second meaning *Dasein* itself would be a continuous dying. Both meanings are justifiable, but we should be clear which one we are dealing with. (p. 102)

In case we would take the first meaning we may ask the question: Do we have an experience of death?

Yes, we do, Edith Stein answers. In the literal sense we will have this experience only when we really die, but somehow we have an anticipation of death in our own body. Heidegger talks about it in his "being-unto-death," although, according to Edith Stein, Heidegger stresses the future too much at the expense of the present and neglects completely the fulfillment which is actually essential to all experience. In Heidegger's interpretation we have to distinguish between anxiety as the ontological disposition which reveals us our being-unto-death and the determination which accepts this disposition. Here we understand anxiety. Heidegger interprets anxiety as being afraid of the own being and afraid for the own being. Edith Stein wonders, if it is the same aspect of Being you are afraid of and afraid for. One is *afraid of* the nothingness of our being. But that one is *afraid for* is Being as a fullness, which one would like to keep and not let it go — something which Heidegger does not mention in his analysis of *Dasein* and which would give it its ground and foundation. When *Dasein* would not be in some way a participation in the fullness of Being, there would not be any anxiety *of* the possibility of non-being and *for* the possibility to be. But when it is a participation of this fullness, then dying would be a loss of the fullness as far as a complete emptying, and death emptiness or non-being itself. But anxiety alone would not do to give us the certainty of the inevitability of death. The natural and healthy vital feeling would be strong enough to counter it. However, there are other situations that give us an experience of dying: a serious illness, the threat of a violent death. Being preoccupied with other people or other things is completely over in the serious illness, you are only concerned for your own body. But with most people even that will come to an end and then the question is: to be or not to be. The question of being is not "being in the world," but "what next?" is the real question of death which is being experienced in dying.

But people who have been confronted with death and then returned to life are the exception. Most people know more about death by the dying of others, even when Heidegger affirms that we do not experience the death of others. Of course, we do not have the same experience of my death and the death of the other, but we do have an experience, especially when we care for the other, when we love them (remember, her mother was dying in those days). Edith Stein describes the experience of death with children and makes it clear that this experience will do to shake the indifference of the "one dies." Whoever witnessed a real agony of death knows better. It is a violent break of a natural unity and when the struggle is finally over then the man or woman is not anymore. What is left is not him or herself. Where is this self? Where is that which made him into a living human being? Heidegger, who excludes any consideration of soul and body, does not deal with these questions, but the lack of an answer here makes it impossible to know the full meaning of death. Faith knows an answer; but even in our experience there is some confirmation of a life that goes beyond this world. Heidegger is right in saying that nobody can take away somebody else's death. Each individual person has his/her death, as he has his/her *Dasein*. So dying is different with different people: not only for the fact that some people die hard and some just drop asleep, but also that often the dead person lies after the agony as a victor — in majestic rest and deep peace. Sorrow about the loss of the beloved one sometimes gives place to the experience of the greatness of the event. Edith Stein wonders, if the mere ceasing of life, the transition from being to non-being could be able to produce such an impression. And is it sensible to think that the spirit which put this mark on the corpse does not exist anymore?

Edith Stein knows about dying from her experience as a nurse during the war and later in the convent and she describes how sometimes, even before the moment of death, all vestiges of struggle and suffering disappear, how the dying person becomes transfigured by a new life, so that all who are present can see it. His or her eyes look into a light that is inaccessible to us, and its shine remains present on the lifeless body. This experience makes clear that *Dasein* as being-unto-death is not being unto an end, but to a new kind of Being. The meaning of death is the transition from this life to another life, even when it has to be through the bitterness of the violent break of natural *Dasein*.

The meditation on death should give us a better insight into authentic Being to which we are called from inauthentic *Dasein*. We may discover within *Dasein* itself three modes or stages of Being: natural life, life of grace, life of glory. Of course, this is a consideration inspired by faith. When one replaces the life of glory by non-being, then one would put instead of life of grace the being-unto-the-end.

Fortunately there are also in Heidegger some clues to a fuller and not to an emptier being, expressions from which one may conclude that there is more to Being than being-unto-death. We read about determination (*Entschlossenheit*), which includes the understanding of the situation of the moment (*jeweilig*) one cannot predict and of what is required from us to cope with it. *Authentic* life means to realize your very own possibilities and to respond to the requirements of the moment. (p. 107)

But once you admit this, you must be consistent and admit also that this realization includes an essence or a special nature with which we are thrown into *Dasein* and which needs our free cooperation for its development. The understanding of the *moment* and the *situation* points to an implicit affirmation of an order or a plan which man did not design himself, but of which he is part and in which he has to play his role. That again means that *Dasein* is related to a Being which is not his, but his ground and purpose.

Heidegger's philosophy of the importance of the moment that offers a fullness that should be exhausted makes clear that "moment" here is more than a point of time. This is difficult to combine with his rejection of eternity and his identification of being and time. When we are supposed to exhaust the moment, we cannot run from moment to moment, but we must open and surrender ourselves to the moment. We stay, we linger, till a new call tells us to go on. That means that our temporal being includes a timeless dimension and is not just temporal.

Heidegger agrees that we cannot exhaust all our possibilities, and he calls the decision to do one thing and forget about others an unavoidable guilt which is part of the fact that we accept our *Dasein* with *determination*. He does not distinguish between this kind of guilt and the guilt in an avoidable and therefore sinful failing to do what is required. Edith Stein thinks that Heidegger should be more down to earth in his description of persons of determination who never *lose time* and always *have time* to do what the moment requires them to do. For saints will often be sorry that they do not have enough time to do everything that they are asked to do and to have always clarity about the best choice. They just trust in God who will help those of good will and they know too well that they are not infallible and that only God is the disclosed one without any limitations (*der unumschränkt Erschlossene*).

The failure of our temporal being to arrive at a complete development of our nature makes clear that the authentic being we are able to achieve in time is not our final being. Edith Stein reminds her reader of Nietzsche's: "All lust yearns for deep, deep eternity." And "lust" does not mean here, she interprets Nietsche, lust in the narrow sense of the word, but deep satisfaction in the experience of the fulfillment of a desire. It is typical to her that Heidegger talks about *care* as the quality of human being, that man is concerned in his being about Being. He does not mention that which gives fullness to human being: joy, happiness, love, and so one wonders why man should be so concerned about a being that runs from nothingness to nothingness. Edith Stein opens her heart to express her joy about human existence:

> This being is not only a temporal extending, always *ahead of itself*: man *desires* to receive the always new gift of Being, to be able to exhaust whatever the moment at the same time will give and take. Whatever gives him fullness, that he does not want to leave, and he would love to *be* without end, and without limits, to possess it completely and without end. Joy without end, happiness without shade, love without limits, a maximum of life without slacking, the most powerful action that is at the same time perfect rest and freedom from all tensions — that is *eternal bliss*. That is *the Being for which man is concerned* in his *Dasein*. He reaches out for the faith that promises it to him, because it opens to him the sense of his being. Man will be *in the full sense*, when he will be *in the full possession of his nature*. Part of it is *openness* in the double sense: as transition from all possibilities into actuality (the perfection of Being) and — with Heidegger — as unlimited understanding of one's own being and understanding of the totality of Being as far as the limits of one's own finite being allow it . . . (p. 110)

Here we need the moment of Kierkegaard and Heidegger where the distinction between moment and permanency has been sublated, where the finite arrives at the highest possible participation of the Eternal, a medium between time and eternity, which Christian philosophy describes as *aion* (*aevum*).(p. 110)

After her own description of the beauty and the bliss of the fullness of Being, Edith Stein shows her sincere disappointment about Heidegger's concept of eternity that misses the point completely. Heidegger says: "When God's eternity would permit a philosophical *construction*, then it could only be understood as a more original temporality *without end*." She answers: A being that has arrived at the fullness of its being is not anymore *concerned* about its being. In the surrendering itself to the Eternal Being its temporal being becomes filled by eternal Being. Care and temporality are not the final sense of human being, but — also according to Heidegger — something that has to be overcome to arrive at the fulfillment of its sense of being.(p. 111)

Heidegger's doctrine about time, as he wrote it down in *Being and Time,* and even after his deepened analysis of time in *Kant and the Problem of Metaphysics*, does need a change of direction. The dimension of the eternal should be made explicit. Temporality and its three ecstasies should be experienced as the way in which the finite participates in the eternal. Heidegger loves to stress the importance of the future. That is all right, but it should be done in a double sense. First, with Heidegger one should consider the future from the *care* for the conservation of one's own being, born out of the understanding of its transitoriness and nothingness, but second, as a fulfillment to come, a transition from the dispersion of temporal being to the recollection of the proper simple Being that is filled with eternity. The *present* should be done justice as a mode of being of fulfillment that opens to us the understanding for the fullness of Being, and the past should be seen as the mode of Being which, amidst the transitoriness of our being gives us the mark of permanency.(p. 111).

As a conclusion to this section: "Is the analysis of *Dasein* faithful?" Edith Stein summarizes: In a certain sense one may give an affirmative answer insofar as Heidegger describes with great insight a mode of human being. He goes into its deepest levels. But there is no better way to describe this mode of being which Heidegger calls *Dasein* and human being as such than to call it "*unredeemed being*." It is unredeemed as for the inauthentic fallen being of everyday-ness, but also as for the authentic being. The former is the flight from the authentic being, the escape from the question: to be or not to be. The latter is the decision in favor of non-being, against being, the rejection of the true real being. Heidegger's interpretation is not only insufficient and imperfect — because he limits himself to one mode of being — but also a falsification of this mode of being, because it is being taken out of context and so it cannot give its true sense. The being of everyday-ness is ambiguous, because it may cause at least the misunderstanding, as if communal life would be identical to fall-enness, and authentic being identical to being lonely. Actually both being alone and communal life have an authentic and in-authentic form.

Sense of Being and Analysis of Dasein

Edith Stein's third question in regard to *Being and Time* is whether the analysis of *Dasein* will do as a foundation for asking the question of Being in the right way. She agrees with her friend Hedwig Conrad-Martius that Heidegger did a fantastic job to open a door that had been closed for a long time and that he had the key in his hands to a doctrine of Being by his starting point in the ego. But then he closes the door, locks it and does not use the key anymore. It is an excellent idea to start from the question about the sense of Being to whose sense belongs the understanding of Being. But this important starting point is not the only starting point, because the subhuman world also has a sense and we may discover this sense in our confrontation with its appearance. Heidegger would deny this, because sense and understanding of being are one, and thus the world of mere entity and instrumentality (*Vorhanden-zuhandensein*) remains in the dark with him.

Actually he has to wrestle with one great prejudice, i.e., the temporality of Being and he is trying hard to justify this preju-dice. Because of this he closes his eyes to eternity, he does not admit a distinction between *Dasein* and *Wesen*, there is no sense outside of understanding sense, no eternal truths, independent from human thought. He closes himself even to the possibility of a discovery and does not take seriously other thinkers, who show that openness for more than finite being. (p. 113f.) Edith Stein has the impression that Heidegger tries hard to prove that human being is the ground of all being and that everything may be reduced to it, but that at the end of *Being and Time* this remains doubtful. She wonders why the reviews of *Being and Time* stress so much the influence of contemporary thought and seem to forget about Kant and the Greeks. She is going to say something more about Kant in dealing with the Kant book.

Edith Stein deals with this book mainly to find more clarity about the sense of Being. She quotes Heidegger's challenge to his critics that they have to prove "that the transcendence of *Dasein* and so its understanding of Being is *not* the most inner finitude in man; that the foundation of metaphysics does not have this most inner relationship to the finitude of *Dasein*, and finally that the basic question of the foundation of metaphysics is not included in the problem of the inner possibility of understanding of Being."(p. 120f.)

To make his standpoint clearer Heidegger says: "And even when the impossible would be possible, i.e., to prove rationally that man is a created being, then the qualification of man as *ens creatum* would only prove again the fact of his finitude, but not the essence of this finitude nor would this essence be defined as the fundamental situation of being of man."(p. 221) With some irony Edith Stein says, "With the tradition we are convinced that the impossible is possible," i.e., that human reason is able to prove the fact of being created. Of course, this does not mean the special mode of creation . . . but the necessity not to be *per se and a se, by oneself and from oneself*, but *ab alio, from another*, which follows from the fact that man is *something*, but *not all*. Is this not the real sense of finitude? Heidegger touches this issue, when on the last page of the Kant book he asks the question: "Can the finitude of *Dasein* even be developed as problem without an affirmation of infinity?"[13] Edith Stein gives the answer: *"Finitude can only be understood in opposition to infinity, i.e., to the fullness of Being. The understanding of Be-*

ing by a finite spirit is as such always already a breakthrough from the finite to the Eternal."(p. 122) Here we find at the same time an answer to Heidegger's three challenges and she is disappointed that the Kant book does not go beyond the solution of *Being and Time.*

According to her opinion the other publications she was able to deal with, viz., *The Essence of Ground* and *What is Metaphysics?*, do not show any essential change. The statement that openness to a divine Being is not being denied and the rhetorical question, if freedom should be affirmed as finite according to its essence, are not very helpful to her. She considers it more like a denial of the God of monotheism.(p. 129)

The Freiburg inaugural lecture *What is Metaphysics?* does not want to teach, but intends to inspire and foregoes a strict scientific approach. The language is to Edith Stein more mythological and deals with "Nothingness" almost as with a person. She still makes her objection to Heidegger's interpretation of the Greeks and Christian theology about making and creating. To give some inkling of her own position, let me quote the following:

> Is it right, when Heidegger says that Christian dogmatics does not ask either about Being or about Nothingness? It is right, insofar as dogmatics does not *ask*, but *teaches*. [and in a note — "To state this more precisely: dogmatics can ask whether something belongs to the doctrine of faith or not; but what has been established as dogma is for dogmatics not questionable anymore."] But that does not mean that dogmatics does not care about Being and Nothingness. Dogmatics talks about Being by talking about God. And dogmatics talks about Nothingness in many contexts, e.g., by talking about creation or mentioning about a created being that it includes a non-being...
> And so, the question "*Why then beings at all, and not rather Nothingness?*" (which is) the question by which man's being expresses itself, is transformed into the question about *the eternal Ground of finite being.*(pp. 134 and 135)

But this is not yet the final word. She wants to be completely fair to Heidegger and gives him all the benefit of the doubt she may be able to give. So she adds a final note to her text, quoting from a conversation Heidegger had with Daniel Feuling, OSB. Heidegger defends himself against an interpretation that all Being and all beings would be finite. "The concept of Being is finite, but this doctrine does not say anything about the finite or infinite character of being and Being itself." Then her comment is: "Here we find the sharp separation between Being and understanding of Being which we missed in the writings, and so the possibility of an eternal Being remains open." (note, p. 134f.)

Perhaps she would have been more satisfied, if she would have been able to be acquainted with the later Heidegger. She died in 1942, as a victim of the Hitler persecution of Catholic Jews, but her critique of Heidegger was finally published in 1962, and one wonders if Heidegger ever took the time to read it and what might have been his reaction.

After Edith Stein finished her metaphysics she wrote on Pseudo-Dionysius and his symbolic theology, and her final book is on St John of the Cross. She was still writing it on August 2, 1942, the day that the SS officers came to the Carmel convent in Echt and told her that she had to leave immediately. On August 9 she died in the gas chambers of Auschwitz. I am sure from my meetings with her, the last one three weeks before her death, and from all her writings from 1922 on, that the end meant to her the beginning, the overcoming of time, finitude and cross, in the eternity of the living, loving triune God.

NOTES

1. See J. H. Nota, "Edith Stein und der Entwurf für eine Enzyklika gegen Rassismus und Antisemitismus," *Communio*, 5 (1976): 154ff.
2. Ibid.: 157ff.
3. *Endliches und Ewiges Sein*, vol. 2 of *Edith Steins Werke*, ed. L. Gelber and R. Leuven (Louvain: Nauwelaerts, 1950).
4. *Welt und Person*, vol. 6 of *Edith Steins Werke*, ed. L. Gelber and R. Leuven (Louvain: Nauwelaerts, 1962), 69-135.
5. See J. H. Nota, "Some Aspects of Edith Stein's Philosophy" (article in preparation); and, in general about Edith Stein's philosophy, Reuben

Guilead, *De la phénomenologie à la science de la croix, l'itinéraire d'Edith Stein* (Louvain: Nauwelaerts, 1974).

6. E. Przywara, "Edith Stein," in *In und Gegen* (Nürnberg: Glock und Lutz, 1955), 63. Edith Stein's article in *Festschrift Edmund Husserl (zum 70 Geburtstag gewidmet), Supplementband Jahrbuch für Philosophie und Phänomenologische Forschung* (Halle: Niemeyer, 1929): 315–38.

7. Stein, *Endliches*, xi.

8. Augusta Spiegelman-Gooch, "Metaphysical Ordination: Reflections on Edith Stein's *Endliches und Ewiges Sein*," MS International Academy of Philosophy, Liechtenstein. Quotations from *Endliches*, 177.

9. All page indications found in the text are from *Endliches und Ewiges Sein*, until indicated otherwise.

10. H. Spiegelberg, *The Phenomenological Movement*, 3rd ed. (The Hague: Nijhoff, 1902), 238.

11. M. Heidegger, "Brief über den Humanismus," *Wegmarken, Gesamtausgabe* vol. 9 (Frankfurt a. Main: Vittorio Klostermann, 1976), 331.

12. Edith Stein, "Martin Heidegger's Existentialphilosophie," *Welt und Person*, 69. The page indications in my text from here forward will come from this book.

13. M. Heidegger, *Kant und das Problem der Metaphysik*, 2nd ed. (Frankfurt a. Main: Vittorio Klostermann, 1951), 222.

EDITH STEIN AND THOMISM

Ralph McInerny

Ralph McInerny is director of the Jacques Maritain Center of Notre Dame University at South Bend. He is a well known writer in the field of philosophy and a popular novelist as well. This paper was delivered as a post-luncheon talk and it elicited many spirited reactions.

INTRODUCTION

"**W**e may expect that critical studies on her philosophy will multiply rapidly with the issuance of her collected works and the recognition of her high philosophical genius."[1] James Collins wrote those words 32 years ago and it is safe to say that his expectation has not been realized. Nonetheless, at the time he expressed it, it seemed eminently reasonable. What happened? What went wrong? Did close study of the works of Edith Stein fail to disclose high philosophical genius? Hardly. The sad truth is that for some decades her writings have been all but ignored. A glance at the bibliography in Carla Bettinelli's *Il Pensiero di Edith Stein*[2] suggests the beginning of an answer. Most of the titles listed appeared before or during the Second Vatican Council.

In this paper, I shall suggest that the neglect of Edith Stein is due to the very thing which guarantees that her influence will be great in the future. The temporary eclipse of interest in her writings is part of the recent relative neglect of the thought of

Thomas Aquinas among Catholics. Nonetheless, Edith Stein provides us with an important model of how we can respond to the Church's wish as to the role St Thomas Aquinas should play in our intellectual and spiritual lives.

EDITH STEIN AND ST THOMAS

As is well known, Edith Stein turned to the study of St Thomas Aquinas after she had been fully trained as a philosopher in the phenomenological school of Edmund Husserl. The role of St Teresa of Avila's autobiography in Edith Stein's conversion is equally well known and Carmelite spirituality was to define the convert's life. "This is the truth." It might be said that training in any philosophical tradition would put truth before one as a principal ideal and that, consequently, there is nothing of particular significance in Stein's way of expressing her appreciation of St Teresa. Nonetheless, training in phenomenology, particularly the kind of phenomenology to be found in Husserl's *Logical Investigations*, entailed a desire for truth, a thirst for objectivity, which, in a passage Hedwig Conrad-Martius quotes from Peter Wust in her tribute to her late friend, contained a built-in orientation to Catholicism:

> From the beginning there was a great secret hidden in the intention of this new philosophical orientation, a nostalgia for a return to the objective, to the holiness of being, to the purity and chastity of things, the things themselves (*zu der Sachen selbst*). For, even though the modern curse of subjectivism was not completely overcome even by the father of this new orientation of thought (Husserl), the opening to the object peculiar to the original intention of this school pushed many of his disciples along the way toward things, toward real contents, toward being itself, indeed even to the Catholic demeanor to which nothing is more natural than always to allow things to be the measure of the knowing spirit.[3]

Conrad-Martius (in whose home Edith Stein read the autobiography of St Teresa) goes on to suggest that in this sense of the term all phenomenologists could be called Catholics. That Edith Stein pressed on from phenomenology into Catholic thought is clear not only from her study of St Thomas, but from the translating into German of works of Cardinal Newman, including *The Idea of a University.*

The influence of Erich Przywara, SJ on Edith Stein during the early years of her Catholic life must never be forgotten. The new convert wished to steep herself in the intellectual foundations of her new faith. As she put it in the Preface to *Finite and Eternal Being*:

> This book is written by a beginner for beginners. At an age where others can claim the title of master, the author found it necessary to start anew. Formed in the school of Edmund Husserl, she wrote a number of works employing the phenomenological method. These treatises appeared in the *Jahrbuch* of Husserl. It was thus that her name became known at a time when she had ceased philosophical work and no longer thought of a public career. She had found the way of Christ and his Church and was occupied with drawing the practical conclusions from this discovery. During her teaching career at the Dominican Normal School at Speyer, she had a chance to familiarize herself with the true Catholic milieu and quite soon there woke in her the desire to learn and understand intelligible principles of this world. It was almost natural to begin with the works of St Thomas Aquinas.[4]

It was by undertaking the formidable task of rendering the *Quaestiones disputatae de veritate* into German that she began again her philosophical studies. How better, one might ask, could one become better immersed in the Catholic outlook than by translating Newman and Aquinas? Anyone who has done translating will know how intimately one becomes involved in the text, adopting its rhythms and its cadence, turning over its thoughts until appropriate expression in the target language is found. It is a species of collaboration with the author. In the cause of the translation of the *De Veritate* Edith Stein is said to have found not only a German expression for St Thomas, but a phenomenological one.

In her contributon to the festschrift put together on the occasion of the 70th birthday of Edmund Husserl, Edith Stein made an explicit comparison of the thought of Husserl and St Thomas.[5] Having recalled Husserl's conception of philosophy as a strict science, Edith Stein takes up the following topics: Natural and supernatural knowledge; faith and reason; critical and dogmatic philosophy; theocentric and egocentric philosophy; ontology and metaphysics; the question of intuition: phenomenological and scholastic methods. The emphasis, in this comparison, is on knowledge. She speculates that, given the influence of the Catholic philosopher Brentano on Husserl, there is reason to expect an affinity between phenomenology and Thomism. But, it is the differences which stand out. For Thomas, the measure of knowledge is the divine knowledge in which ours is merely a participation.[6] The greatest difference between transcendental phenomenology and Catholic philosophy is that the former is egocentric, the latter theocentric. Indeed, as Elisabeth de Miribel has noted, Edith Stein presents the thought of Thomas in such a way that his philosophy and theology make one indivisible unit.[7] Stein even suggests that just as one speaks of natural and supernatural theology, so too one could speak of natural and supernatural philosophy.[8] Moreover, she rejects the notion that Thomas has produced a system; what we seek and find in him is a philosophy of life, one that answers the big questions, but in a sober rather than a heightened style.[9]

So impressed is Edith Stein by what she calls the theocentrism of Thomas that she attributes to him the doctrine that God is the first axiom of thought.[10] And there are other surprising aspects of her interpretation of her new master. But what stands out is her grasp of a central truth of Thomism and that is the orientation of the mind toward objective reality, truth. Human understanding is measured by what is, and is a participation in an understanding that is infinite. Grace elevates and perfects natural understanding and the human vocation is seen as ultimate union with God in the beatific vision. However defective her account may be with respect to the formal difference between philosophy and theology, she has grasped the unity and continuity of the intellectual life and its submersion in the spiritual life.

This effort to confront Husserl with Thomas was the beginning and not the end of her effort. Before she entered Carmel, she had written a long work on act and potency. This was in 1931. She entered Carmel in 1933 and, after her novitiate year, was asked by her superiors to continue her intellectual work. She turned once more to the earlier work on act and potency. The result was *Finite and Eternal Being*, which was written in 1935 and 1936, was set up in type and about to be published when the Nazi prohibition against the publication of books by "non-Aryans" stopped it. She retained some of the earlier work in the new one, beginning with a study of act and potency, but the work was now centered on the problem of being. In the preface, she expresses a good deal of diffidence about her ability to do well what she has set out to do. And, when the book appeared, there were criticisms.[11] Collins notes, as did others, the departures from the teaching of Thomas that Edith Stein explicitly makes: she locates the principle of individuation in form rather than matter; she speaks of spiritual matter in angels, who are pure spirits but not pure forms; the image of God is to be found in all creatures and not merely in humans; and she accords universals a special reality of their own. Scotus rather than Thomas is her guide on these matters. Collins's suggestion as to the reason for these departures is worth quoting in full:

> *Why* these somewhat peripheral criticisms of Aquinas are made and recourse had to Scotus is explained by a fundamental disagreement that is not announced and perhaps not fully recognized as such. Finite being is ultimately defined in terms of the unfolding of meanings. This is consistent with the contention that the pure forms or meaningful essences arrived at through phenomenological analysis of empirical data are ontologically more basic than either the act of real existing or the conceptions of our mind.[12]

This same suggestion, that Stein is insufficiently aware of the role of *esse* in the thought of Thomas is made by Geiger.

The time that Collins foretold 32 years ago is not here yet, I think, and I do not want to use this occasion to go into the niceties of the Thomisticity of Edith Stein's interpretations. Rather, I want to emphasize the way she picked up on the discussion of Christian Philosophy was being engaged in by Thomists at the very time she was writing on act and potency. Her references to Maritain in discussing Christian Philosophy, the whole drive of *Finite and Eternal Being* which may be said to culminate in *The Science of the Cross*, remind one of the argument of *Les Degrés du Savoir*. This leads me to suggest that she went into eclipse at about the same time that Maritain did (along with Thomism generally) and that she will now along with Maritain and Thomas Aquinas move into the light and, with them, play a significant role in the future intellectual and spiritual lives of many.

Among the stranger claims that have been made about Vatican II is that it deliberately downgraded the role of St Thomas as theological and philosophical mentor of Catholics, opening a free market of ideas and masters. Nothing could be further from the truth. Thomas is mentioned twice by name in conciliar documents, and this is unprecedented. But, like *Aeterni Patris*, the Council sees Thomas not as an isolated figure, but as in the forefront of a vast army of Catholic doctors and teachers. Since the Council, the popes have continued the long tradition of especially commending the thought of St Thomas. It is not the recommendation that has been wanting, it is the response to it. For a host of reasons, some more understandable than others, Catholics have turned away from Thomas. Where once he was the guide and mentor of philosophy and theology programs in Catholic colleges and universities, he is now all but forgotten. This is appalling. Consider by way of contrast the behavior of Edith Stein.

When she enters the Church she is already, as she tells us, a philosopher of no mean accomplishments. Her style of philosophizing is the phenomenological method as engaged in by Husserl in his first period, prior to the idealistic turn of the *Ideen*. Her attachment to phenomenology is not simply a disciple's allegiance. She herself has put it to good use in a series of studies which were published in the journal Husserl edited. After she becomes a Catholic, she ceases her philosophical work—her phenomenological analyses—because she is deriving the practical consequences of her conversion. Chiefly, this means that she is devoting herself to prayer, to the liturgy, to meditation. But it soon comes to mean the study of the intelligible supports of the faith. And she begins to study St Thomas. Why?

Why of all the great doctors of the Church does she turn first to St Thomas Aquinas? There seems little doubt that she does so because the Church has put him forth as the preeminent master of Catholic intellectuals. Her response is one of docility. And her response, let us not forget, is made despite the fact that she has been a phenomenologist for the better part of ten years. She has a formed mind, a trained mind. Still, like a beginner, she turns to Thomas and starts anew her studies. She cannot, of course, erase from her mind what she has already learned. It is inevitable that she will compare the new and the old, Thomas and Husserl. What we might expect is that she would submit Thomas to the test of Husserlian phenomenology. She does the reverse. It is Husserl who is judged by Thomism. How explain this?

One explanation must be definitively excluded. It is not open to us to think that Edith Stein regarded phenomenology and Thomism simply as different "languages," as ways of talking or thinking that one chose among by whim or accident or whatever. As if, before she became a Catholic, her friends were phenomenologists and so was she; and, after her conversion, she took on the outlook of her new Catholic friends. For one thing, many phenomenologists were Catholics who showed no interest in Thomas Aquinas. If all Catholics studied Thomas she would have been introduced to him by Scheler or Peter Wust. Having joined the Church, Edith Stein attended docilely to the ordinary magisterium, she became aware of the long tradition of singling Thomas Aquinas out as guide and mentor and she accepted him as her guide and mentor. But guide to what? Not to a new way of talking, to the patois of her new friends. No. She undertook the study of Thomas as a way to the truth.

The point is so obvious it is easily forgotten. Thomas is given us as our chief guide in philosophy and theology *in order that we may more surely arrive at the truth.* At the outset, one can only trust that this study will have that result. But it is the Church, the ordinary magisterium, that is being trusted. For one lively in supernatural faith, this is a sure and reliable guide. But the point of following the advice, again, is to arrive at the truth. We may be sure that if Edith Stein had not found Thomas to be a way to the truth, she would not have gone on studying him. She would not have measured Husserl by Thomistic standards and found him wanting by any other measure than the truth. It would be easy to show that Husserl was not a Thomist, but this is only interesting if not being a Thomist with respect to certain philosophical matters of moment is a defect.

In the wake of the Council, the kind of docility to the magisterium that Edith Stein showed has been in short supply. There has been no change in the way the Church sees the role of Thomas Aquinas in our intellectual and spiritual lives. The change has been in the ignoring of the advice, in a lack of docility. All this despite *Lumen Gentium*, 25. In such as atmosphere, the example of Edith Stein was not followed and this had to have the effect of making the contents of her writings of less interest.

It is difficult to see how that interest can easily take root in minds that do not, like hers, respond eagerly to the promptings of the magisterium.

The above suggests that one should see one's philosophical or theological work as integral to one's Christian vocation. But nothing is easier than to do philosophy in a way that makes it clear that we have become forgetful of the essential reason for doing it at all. In its classical beginnings, philosophy was the pursuit of wisdom, and wisdom in turn was defined as such knowledge as men can attain of the divine. The study of philosophy was not a cultural adornment, the fifty drachma course that assured success in Athens. *Lebensphilosophie* and philosophy were the same thing. Consider two of the most moving accounts of the philosophical life, that of Plato in the *Republic* and of Aristotle at the outset of his *Metaphysics*. I have in mind the parable of the cave, on the one hand, and, on the other, the gloss on the extraordinary claim that "All men by nature desire to know" which takes us from external sensation through memory and imagination to experience, art and play and onward and upward to knowledge of the first causes of all things. The cave is far more dramatic. Men are regarded as prisoners who must be unchained and led by stages out of a cave and into the light which will enable them to see things as they really are. The study of philosophy becomes synonymous with the pursuit of the good, the moral and intellectual tasks become mutually dependent: the overall aim is not merely to know, but to be — to be wise, that is, to be like God.

No wonder the Fathers found in pagan philosophy, particularly Plato, a *praeparatio evangelica*. It was the quest of human perfection that necessarily lifted the mind's eye beyond the evanescent things of this world. This vision is subsumed into the Christian vision. Man's new supernatural vocation and the grace that makes response to it possible can be seen as the culmination, the point, of philosophy.

Now what is certain in the case of Edith Stein — and indeed in all phenomenologists, if Conrad-Martius and Peter Wust are correct — is that she studied philosophy, not to win the plaudits of Husserl, not to gain a reputation, to publish, to dazzle, to have a successful career. She wanted the truth and a truth she could live and die for. When this truth was presented to her in the form of a person, as Christ, her whole life had to be reoriented. Now she knew that the point of life is to become holy, to allow Christ to live in her, to live his life. Her philosophical training provided a prelude to the life of prayer. Theologians like Thomas were to be read, not to become learned, not as a kind of intellectual game, but as providing reflections on the truths of faith. God did not become man in order that men might become theologians, but theology is one response to the truth that has been revealed.

Chapter VII of *Finite and Eternal Being*, which discusses the image of the Trinity in creation, provides a good illustration of the way Edith Stein combines philosophical, theological and mystical themes into a single fabric. She begins with a discussion of person and hypostasis, goes on to speak of person and spirit and then, discussing what it is to be a human person, speaks of body, soul and spirit and introduces St Teresa's *Interior Castle*. Trinity, angels, the image of God in creatures other than humans, but then interiority, the interior life. It seems to me churlish to say that she is mixing up diverse things, that this is an eclectic potpourri. After all, her first guide in Thomas was the *Quaestiones disputatae de veritate*.

I want to suggest that the importance of Edith Stein for Catholic philosophy consists chiefly in two things, one more substantive, the other more methodological. Earlier I quoted Peter Wust's remark about Husserl and subjectivism. The problem of the constitution of the object of thought leads the founder of phenomenology in the direction of idealism whereas Wust speaks of the naturally Catholic orientation of the original slogan, "To the things themselves." It is here that the Thomist will think of Thomas's insistence on the difference between what is true of *things as they are* and what is true of things *as we know them*. Edith Stein, in her festschrift comparison of Husserl and Aquinas hit upon this in her distinction between the egocentric orientation of phenomenology and the theocentric character of Thomism.[13] The world, for the phenomenologist, is always the "world for the subject." For Thomas, the human mind is measured by the reality created by God. One of the most perceptive comparisons in this early essay is reminiscent of what Thomas says of Platonism in the proemium to his commentary on the *De divinis nominibus* of Pseudo-Dionysius. I do not mean just Thomas's understanding of Platonism, namely, the philosophy which identifies the way things are and the way we know them, though that must occur to us. Rather, I think of the way Thomas, in the text cited, says that the Platonic Ideas are simply a mistake if meant as an account of human knowing, but *considered as ways of understanding God* they are of great value. So too, Edith Stein observes that Husserl's way of describing human knowledge, as unlimited, is simply wrong, but is nonetheless reminiscent of Thomas's way of describing the divine knowledge.

The only thing that can answer to the Transcendental Ego is God.

The methodological importance, so to say, of Edith Stein can be summed up in the phrase of John of St Thomas so much beloved of Jacques Maritain: *philosophandum in fide*. In the 1929 essay, Stein sees faith as an *axiom*, a starting point of philosophy. An initial reaction to this is that she has not yet understood the formal distinction Thomas draws between philosophy and theology. Perhaps a more fruitful response is to connect this with her interest in the soon to be much discussed topic of Christian Philosophy. If nothing else this discussion, major contributions to which were made by Maritain and Gilson, induces a wariness concerning the notion of "pure philosophy."

It is one thing to say that it is possible to define what a philosophical argument as opposed to a theological argument is. The latter will always contain at least one premise whose truth is accepted on the basis of faith rather than understanding. The external critic of the philosophizing of the Christian demands that the philosophical arguments be freed from all context and ambience suggestive of faith. Underlying this demand is the usually unstated assumption that the appropriate philosophical attitude is one of methodic doubt if not outright skepticism. With regard to religious beliefs, the appropriate philosophical attitude is agnosticism and doubt. But the controversy went on among believers as well and is perhaps best exemplified by the dispute between Etienne Gilson and Fernand Van Steenberghen. The latter held that the historian of philosophy should approach the writings of St Bonaventure, say, with the intent of separating out from the theological context all the purely philosophical arguments. These arguments, when appropriately arranged, give us the philosophy, as opposed to the theology, of St Bonaventure, and it does not matter that Bonaventure himself was not interested in producing a philosophy. Gilson counters by saying that the theological context is essential to whatever arguments, philosophical or theological, Bonaventure fashions. There is no other context that can appropriately contain the philosophical ones. This conviction of Gilson's, which grew with the years, lead to the retitling of his books so that the phrase "The Christian Philosophy of . . ." became almost de rigueur.

This is a large subject and I mention it only to suggest that Edith Stein, far from failing to get Thomas right, finds herself in some rather impressive Thomistic company in her disinclination to proceed otherwise than Thomas himself did, viz., doing such philosophy as he did in the course of doing theology.

CONCLUSION

Edith Stein and Thomism. I can hope here only to suggest some correlations, much as she herself had to confine herself to a few suggestions in her first comparison of Husserl and Thomas. I stress the truly edifying docility to the magisterium which led her, a philosopher of standing, to become a student again and sit at the feet of Aquinas. This leads very quickly to seeing Thomas as a means to seeing what is best in contemporary philosophy as well as to seeing where things go wrong. Reflection on this confidence points the way to seeing how important an ally Edith Stein is in the current flight against fideism.

The great danger for the believer is to be persuaded that he can hold his beliefs only on penalty of subjectivizing them, relinquishing any suggestion that he is giving his assent to objective truth. But the object of faith is the First Truth, He Who is, the measure of the created mind. Faith is a habit of intellect, not an eccentric quirk to be tolerated as such. Edith Stein reminds us of a better time when the believing intellectual, far from being apologetic about the faith and accepting the suggestion that it is intellectually suspect, glories in Revelation as a positive boon for the human mind. Seen from the vantage point of faith — *philosophandum in fide* — the efforts of philosophy are but a stage in those degrees of wisdom of which Maritain spoke, philosophical wisdom leading on to theological wisdom which in turn gives way to the wisdom which is a gift of the Holy Spirit. This progression is not of course deductive, but it draws attention to the primacy of the spiritual life as the real context within which all

human activities, including philosophizing achieve an importance which is eternal.

NOTES

1. James Collins, Review of *Endliches und Ewiges Sein* in *The Modern School-man*, 29 (1952): 145.
2. Carla Bertinelli, *Il Pensiero di Edith Stein* (Milano: Vita e Pensiero, 1976). A list of studies of Edith Stein is found on pp. 216–222.
   See now, prompted by the introduction of Edith Stein's cause for can-onization, *Gli Scritti della Serva di Dio Edith Stein—Teresa Benedetta della Croce—Carmelitana Scalza (1891–1942): Studio Ufficiale dei Due Teologi Censori della S. Congregazione per la Cause dei Santi* (Roma: Postulazione Generale, O.C.D., 1977).
3. I translate from the French translation of Hedwig Conrad-Martius's "Edith Stein" in *Archives de Philosophie*, 22 (1959, cahier 2): 164:
   Dès le début il a du y avoir un grand secret caché dans l'intention de cette nouvelle orientation philosophique, une nostalgie de re-venir à l'objectif, à la sainteté de l'être, à la pureté et à la chasteté des choses, des choses elles-mêmes (*zu der Sachen selbst*). Car, bien que même chez le père de cette nouvelle orientation de pen-sée (Husserl) la malédiction moderne du subjectivisme ne fut pas complètement surmontée, l'ouverture vers l'objet, propre à l'in-tention originelle de cette école, poussait beaucoup de ses discip-les dans la voie vers les choses, vers les contenus réels, vers l'être même, et même vers le comportement du chatholique auquel rien n'est plus conforme que de laisser toujours les choses mesurer l'esprit connaissant.
4. Edith Stein, "Avant-propos," *L'Etre Fini et l'Etre Eternel*, (Paris-Louvain: Nauwelarts, 1972), 1:
   Ce livre est écrit par une débutante pour des débutants. L'auteur, à un age où d'autres peuvent prétendre au titre de maître, s'est trouvé contraint de refaire son chemin. Formée à l'école d'Ed-mond Husserl, elle écrivit une série de travaux selon le méthode phénoménologique. Ces traités parurent dans les Archives Hus-serl. Ainsi son nom fut connu à une epoque où elle avait cessé ses travaux philosophiques et où elle ne songeait plus à une activité publique. Elle avait trouvé le chemin du Christ et de son Eglise et elle était occupée à en tirer les conclusions pratiques. Durant son professorat à l'Ecole Normale des Dominicaines à Speyer, elle eut

la possibilité de se familiariser avec le véritable milieu catholique. Ainsi, le désir d'apprendre à connaître les principes intelligibles de ce monde devait s'éveiller très tôt en elle. Il était presque naturel de commencer d'abord par les oeuvres de saint Thomas d'Aquin.

5. Edith Stein, "Husserls Phänomenologie und die Philosophie des hl. Thomas v. Aquinas," *Festschrift Edmund Husserl* (*zum 70 Geburtstag gewidmet*), *Supplementband Jahrbuch für Philosophie und Phänomenologische Forschung* (Halle: Niemeyer, 1929): 315-38.

6. Ibid., 318:

    Die volle Wahrheit ist, es gibt eine Erkenntnis, die sie ganz umfasst, die nicht unendlicher Prozess, sondern unendliche ruhende Fülle ist; das ist die göttliche Erkenntnis. Sie kann aus ihrer Fülle den andern Geistern mitteilen und teilt ihnen tatsächlich mit, je nach dem Mass ihrers Fassungsvermogens. Die mitteilung kann auf verschiedene Weise geschehen. Die natürliche Erkenntniss ist nur ein Weg.

7. Cf. E. de Miribel, *Edith Stein* (Paris: Eds. du Seuil, 1954), 68.

8. Stein, *Husserls Phänomenologie*, 320.

9. Ibid., 324:

    Die Menschen sind haltlos und suchen nach einem Halt. Sie wollen greifbare, inhaltliche Wahrheit, die sich im Leben bewarht, sie wollen eine "Legensphilosophie." Das finden sie bei Thomas. Von dem freilich, was heute unter diesem Namen bekannt ist, ist seine Philosophie himmelweit entfernt. Dithyrambischen Schwung wird man bei ihm vergeblich suchen.

10. Cf. Ibid., 325. Bertinelli, *Il pensiero*, p. 101, takes this to be Stein's understanding of the sentence she translated in *De veritate*, q. 1, a. 1: "Illud autem quod primo intellectus concipit quasi notissimum et in quo omnes conceptiones resolvit, est ens."

11. The review by Collins, mentioned above, is one of the most important, but mention can also be made of that by L. B. Geiger, OP in the "Bulletin de Philosophie" in *Revue des sciences philosophiques et théologiques*, 38 (1954): 275-77; Alois Dempf in *Philosophisches Jahrbuch*, 62 (1953): 201-4 and, on the occasion of the French translation, G. Cristaldi in *L'Osservatore Romano*, July 22, 1972.

12. Collins, *Review*: 143.

13. Stein, *Husserls Phänomenologie*, 325-27.

14. When I say this is a large subject, I do not mean to speak merely rhetorically. What I have just said about Thomas seems to me false. The Gilsonian position entails that the student systematically discount the importance of the commentaries St Thomas wrote on the works of Aristotle. But these commentaries constitute a significant fraction of the literary output of the saint. Moreover, they were not the natural products of his task as a teacher of theology: he produced them in his cell as a product of supererogation.

CARMEL
AND
CULTURE
General Chapter 1985

RESPONSE OF THE TERESIAN CARMEL TO THE SPIRITUAL SITUATION OF THE CHURCH AND THE WORLD TODAY

Augusto Guerra

Augusto Guerra is a former Provincial of the Castile Province of Discalced Carmelites. His preferred field of interest is contemporary spirituality, and he has written extensively about it. He is in frequent demand for courses on prayer. Since he gave this paper he delivered the inaugural lecture and a course at the newly established spirituality institute of the Discalced Carmelites in Ponce, Puerto Rico.

T he word "spirituality" continues to be a poorly defined or understood word. Often it is written in quotation marks in order to let the reader know that its sense is to be gathered from the context in which it is used and not merely from its definition.

This lack of a clear definition for "spirituality" necessarily affects any exposition regarding the "spiritual" situation, such as the present one. For this reason, I want to explain briefly what we mean here by "spirituality."

In our use, "spirituality" indicates "a style of living the Gospel in a given situation." More fully, but along the same lines, it can mean "the reformulation and reordering of the major axes of Christian life in function of the concrete present-day realities which we must live as well as the concrete services which we are called to render." It is a concept which I consider to be especially valid whenever we must describe the various progressive stages that ordinarily appear in the development of the spiritual life.

In keeping with this notion, I will outline the spiritual situation of our day as I see it. To do this, I will analyze a *few* facts and take note of the spiritual problematic that they raise. Afterward I will try to indicate those things which in my judgment could be a *part* of the response which the Teresian Carmel can make to this situation.

I will follow the inductive method which seems to conform better to historical truth and life. In that way I will try to avoid imaginary problems in order to concentrate on real ones.

SIGNS OF OUR TIMES

When we speak of the signs of our times we are referring to observable "facts" which bear an interior evangelical message within the facts themselves. We use this term in a broad sense: events, attitudes, ideologies, states of mind...

In approaching these signs of our times we will soon find ourselves running into *opposing*, even contrary signs, and find ourselves tempted to turn this into a logical discussion, impeccable in its deductive rigor. That would be a dangerous temptation since it would lead us to manipulate facts. We would demonstrate our lack of historical and critical discipline by suppressing or overlooking series of facts. Although it may seem that the facts we gather must follow a logical causal sequence and derive directly or indirectly one from another, and not merely follow temporally, a careful analysis of things would show us that the situation is not always so simple, and the appearance of a fact or its ascendancy is to be explained by other criteria.

In my listing of signs, I have chosen to limit myself to the period since the Second Vatican Council. It is our time of salvation.

True, we are all in debt to a much wider history, but this historical debt was "renegotiated" in a Council that was the final stage of many things and the starting point for many others. In contemporary spirituality, the Council is a watershed which should not be forgotten.

Therefore, I am listing *some* of the signs of our times, the ones that seem to be of particular importance in shaping spirituality.

The Second Vatican Council

The Council, which rediscovered and updated the concept of "signs of our time" was itself an unmistakable and important sign of our times.

For spirituality, Vatican II left a clear universal call to sanctity in the Church, expressed in a dynamic, down-to-earth concept of sanctity. Casuistry and the sometimes funny disquisitions it led to have been left behind. At the same time an important victory has been won over spiritual and ascetic moralism which wreaked havoc with traditional spirituality.

On the other hand, the Council took up traditional values. It taught the need to incarnate them in concrete realities to avoid our caricaturing Christianity. At the same time it *renewed* and *enriched* all the traditional values: it emphasized liturgical life; it turned eagerly to God's Word; it clearly and emphatically upgraded the communitarian aspect of the way we live and celebrate the faith; and it reminded us that our spiritual outlook and practices must be *updated* differently according to the needs of time and place.

Last of all, the vivid awareness of the fact that God's Spirit is present in every movement of history (GS 26) caused the Council to open spirituality to history, with all its problems, limitations and possibilities. As the first *official* sketch of Christian anthropology, *Gaudium et Spes* (GS) takes up in general the challenge of modern culture which places humankind at the center of its preoccupations. The rapid and profound changes of modern history make *updating* a task that cannot be avoided. The Council turned *pressing needs* into *preferential choices* for the Church.

And the final reply to the questions of humanity, are found in Jesus. However, we must observe that Jesus does not appear at the beginning of the reflections of GS, but only at the end of them. Jesus, then is not so much the one who asks questions as the one who answers them. The questions are posed by life itself.

Interconfessionality

Perhaps this sign for our times is somewhat surprising. Yet we would keep it very much in view, because it reflects a deep change in the attitude and practices of Christians. In its broader sense, we wish to emphasize here, interconfessionality means the relationships with other confessions within arm's reach today of the most restless Christians. It is undeniable that this situation has changed since the Council. Before it, one could not come into contact with *foreign* writings and ideologies. Various "defense mechanisms" "shielded" the Christian from these perils.

The change affected the educated most of all. Books which were unobtainable previously became familiar. Harvey Cox would admit: "I suspect that among the readers of my books, there are as many Catholics as the rest put together." And Paul VI would confess with concern that "the teachers of Catholic thought were often Protestant authors."

We cannot forget the impact which other forms of contacts with the various Christian confessions would produce among the *people*, especially ordinary people. *Emigration* and *tourism* opened doors through which people always observant of and curious about things which in one way or another are surprising, came to know values and attitudes and customs which raised questions for their own lives. Cooperation with our separated brethren was another important step; and *oversimplified treatments* in periodicals, at a time when some high-ranking prelates treated journalists like the theologians of the moment, gave many readers heretofore unimaginable ecumenical visions.

It would be a serious oversight to ignore the impact of interconfessionality on the spiritual situation of our time. It gave

Christians different new visions of aspects and values which Catholics had perhaps forgotten, erased from memory, or barely noticed. Pluralism seemed to be a normal possibility. The Christian could not help but begin to see as relative many things which had been presented to him as absolutes. The Council had spoken plainly of *treasures* and *riches* in reference to other Christian confessions. Now Christians came into contact with those treasures and riches which previously had been forbidden because of Catholic self-sufficiency.

Interconfessionality brought with it a previously unknown sense of freedom regarding the relationship between law and Spirit, something important for a time when society makes freedom its standard. This would involve a very novel or different way of conceiving, evaluating and respecting Tradition as well those interventions which might sound or look like obstacles against (or a sequestering of) one's own initiative or that of the invisible action of the Holy Spirit. A scarcely suspect Catholic writer could state that "the Protestant mentality tends to look to concrete, present realities and is sensitive to the intervention of the Spirit of God in history—that is beyond question." But we are only just beginning to see the problems and possibilities raised by interconfessionality and the conflicts it can generate.

Last of all, it would not be objective to ignore the fact that interconfessionality has created a sense of religious indifference on the part of many Catholics, or the fact that it has possibly strongly contributed to the acutely-felt problem of Christian and Catholic identity today. Consequently, if we extend confessionality to non-Christian religions—and as we said at the start we are taking this word in its widest sense—we are then faced with the huge problem of East-West dialogue which we will have more to say about presently. This problem will lead some to say, for example, that the Buddhist is an anonymous Christian; and it will lead others to say that the Christian is an anonymous Buddhist.

Interconfessionality is seen as one of the signs of these modern times and possesses a very important spiritual facet.

Appearance on the Scene of the World of Latin America

Up to a few years after the Second Vatican Council, Europe dominated the ideological world and imposed its thought on other peoples without meeting questions or resistance. Europe was the seat of truth. Medellin 1968 was a landmark in the history of universal Christianity, not just in the life of the local Christian church, because Latin America is not a ghetto. The multiple interests causing a stir there, its strong ties to various Christian countries of the Old World, the fact that in Latin America nearly everyone is a Christian, the expectation that in these lands a good part of the future of Christianity is at stake, the respect gained by Latin American thought since then, and the polemics it has raised, have all made of those lands a privileged place for observation. Latin America is, and has been for some years, one of the true signs of our times.

We must add, in order to come to our own specific area, that spirituality is not an exotic plant in Latin America. "From the first moments of the theology of liberation, the question of spirituality . . . has been a source of profound concern." These words are not glib affirmations after the fact, and they are not made in order to evade the difficulties we sometimes see liberation theology undergo when faced with accusations of horizontalism. It is certain that from the time the first pages of liberation theology were being written, spirituality has occupied an interesting place in it.

What problems does this sign of our times present to spirituality? Fundamentally, the one of finding a way to sing a song of the Lord in a foreign land.(Psalm 137) It asks us how we can live in a Christian manner in a dark night of injustice, a dark night that can spread to all parts of the world where any of those "diabolical labyrinths of death" or "our fringes of death" hold sway: poverty and exploitation, violence and oppression, racial and cultural alienation, industrial destruction of the natural environment, meaninglessness and abandonment by God. It would be difficult to find a place on earth where one or another of these labyrinths, and often several or almost all of them, are not present and not dominant and — this is important — are not responsible for violence in other regions.

Latin America speaks for the need to consider these pre-human problems as true problems of Christian life. It asks how is it possible to feel for a God who is so frequently associated with injustice and oppression. It asks how we can live in Paschal joy in a world of insufferable martyrdom. It demands to know how to speak and live in solidarity in a world which brings all peoples together, and then leaves them in solitude and in the most absolute abandonment.

All of this problematic, which is objectively very serious no matter how we may look at it here, conflicts with many real aspects of traditional spirituality when it admits humbly and realistically that even it does not have a sufficiently convincing answer for this situation. An *emerging spirituality* is a spirituality which is beginning to take shape, but not one that has taken shape.

Agnostic Environment

This is a sign that is not clearly defined and yet which strikes anyone who views it from the viewpoint of God's Spirit.

The influential cultural media, chiefly in the West, are dominated by a conviction that religion is a precritical magic residue, something primitive, that will disappear in a culturally developed world. Humankind, ought to be ethical, but not religious, still less, Christian (many believe it almost ridiculous to take Catholicism seriously). Perhaps it is the philosophers and intellectuals who insist on seeing things this way, but there is no doubting the lure of culture and development contains a fishhook that has caught many, especially among young people.

It would be difficult to deny this fact, however poorly defined it may be. The modern experience of *collective* and *mass* atheism, formerly unthinkable, echoes it and was recognized by the Council as one of the most disturbing facts of our world. No matter how often it is described as a "phenomenon of fatigue and old age," it continues to appear as an effect of progress and must be recognized as a fact. Calling it *anonymous Christianity* is another outdated approach used by many to give some sort of religious "control" over those who confessed their lack of belief.

Another echo of this agnosticism is the avidity with which many fanatic groups—the nightmare and embarrassment of humble and sincere Christianity—turn to a morbid sacralism and to supposed supernatural manifestations lacking in even the least inner logic and unable to stand up to even the smallest argument from common sense. By way of reaction, many think that a Christianity in which this *beatería* or fanaticism grows, and which seems to favor it rather than weed it out, is objectively despicable.

It is not easy to believe those who think that in the last few years there has been a strong rebirth of religious belief; nor can we believe those who think that our situation has been the normal one throughout history. Without making value judgments, we can say that the agnostic environment, flanked by atheism and magic pseudo-religion, appears as a sign of our times.

This sign also challenges us: it invites us to an intensive purification of our faith; to distinguish between religion and faith; to distinguish the religious instinct latent in the human personality from conscious or unconscious manipulation of religiosity; to distinguish temporary limitations of natural science from facile recourse to mystery; to attribute no factuality to supernatural causes when it is proven they are due to other socioeconomic motives (whether conscious or unconscious and which do not enter into individual culpability).

Agnosticism sets forth a serious problem of religious-cultural discernment, which needs more than a rudimentary approach today.

Fascination with the East

North America and Europe have watched with rapt interest an invasion from the East, both the Far East and the Near East. From the Far East have come Yoga, Zen, Transcendental Meditation and many other manifestations of religious subcultures in their wake. The Near East has given us Sufi Islam. They pose as centers around which the problems of our world may find solutions—our modern disenchantments that date back to the Enlightenment in the far-away eighteenth century which built the foundations of our modern society. And if, furthermore, we consider what these religious-cultural movements mean for the inhabitants of their places of origin (or at least major groups there), we may begin to suspect that the awareness of a religious East should be considered as a sign of the times.

The challenges posed by this sign are of many different kinds, but they are directed at spiritual persons and require an enlightening response from them. This awakening to the East in the West poses three *principal* problems.

1. Interior Experience

Mankind hungers and thirsts for interior experience and searches after an "essential identity" which seems covered or enclosed or even sequestered and manipulated by various "existential identities" which in the West (above all in the technical and intellectual West) are destroying people. Many are asking if a new humanity is rising up and to what point it is rising, or whether what is to rise up who would rather fly than eat (in the celebrated image of *Johnathan Livingston Seagull*).

2. Meditation as a Science

"Meditation" (within a widespread meditation movement) has stopped being something *exclusively* religious and has become a cultural and scientific reality with an undoubtedly religious base. Knowledge of "altered states of consciousness" are a challenge to spirituality, since the methods of meditation seem to have true affinity to Christian forms of meditation. Would it not be possible and convenient for everyone, in their different fields, to join cultural forces among scientists and spirituals in order to learn more about this deep and profound world of the conscious? On the other hand, this dialogue purely with science will be very difficult, since we already run into two interpretations of history which will not easily come to mutual understanding. However, it surely is an important challenge.

3. Religious Dialogue between East and West

Many important people think that the most interesting dialogue we can look forward to in the near future for Christianity is a religious dialogue between East and West regarding religious experience on the basis especially of mystical experience. Among the prophets and patrons of this exchange there is hardly anyone who does not explicitly recognize that mystics are called to be valid speakers in the dialogue. According to many, it seems obvious that such dialogue is possible and even easy (I have my doubts!) when it is based on religious experience, and that when it is based on ideas it becomes difficult and even impossible.

Confusion

In speaking of the signs of the times we mentioned *states of the soul* as possible signs of the times. And no one can deny that one of these is the *confusion* that besets many Christians.

While discussing the then current situation, Vatican II admitted:

> Caught up in such numerous complications, very many of our contemporaries are kept from accurately identifying permanent values and adjusting them properly to fresh discoveries. As a result, buffeted between hope and anxiety and pressing one another with questions about the present course of events, they are burdened down with uneasiness. (GS 4)

We experience this today. And it seems that this confusion, amidst anguish and hope, has actually increased, because the world has changed greatly in the twenty years since the Council and with a profundity and rapidity even greater than the changes noted by the Council. Some have even begun to call them *dislocations* instead of changes in order to indicate that they reflect a *disruption* rathen than an *evolution*.

This reference to confusion has nothing to do with pessimism. *Gaudium et Spes*, which noted this in the first place, was clearly an optimistic document. More important, however, is the Council's further observation: "The course of present history is a challenge to which mankind is obliged to respond." (GS 4)

This confusion raises the problem of finding ways to live spirituality in times of change and uncertainty. In the last few years it has become an object of study which grows more urgent with every important new development in life. How can we live a fidelity that is not pathological? Where can we find creative responses which take risks to the limit without being rash? These are fundamental elements of the response which Christians today are looking for.

THE RESPONSE OF THE TERESIAN CARMEL

The Council has asked us to respond to the problems raised by our history. What answers can the Teresian Carmel give to the questions raised by the signs of our times?

Before we answer these difficult, necessary and sometimes rash questions, we need to take a good dose of common sense which will keep us in the humility of spiritual infancy. The Teresian Carmel's response will not be magic, nor immediately forthcoming, nor evident. It does not have the kind of faith in God and individuals that works miracles, nor is it so valiant that it can pretend to solve all the world's problems. This dose of common sense is needed because it inspires and motivates us and opens the way to creative solutions. It has no use for fatalism, despair, or inertia. "Patience," tenacious step-by-step perseverance, "gains everything."

After making explicit mention we can approach the problem in two ways. The *first* is the path of the Teresian Carmel as promotor of spirituality. I believe that this response is worthwhile and necessary, even though it has less appeal and is less often followed than the second alternative. Although it may not appear substantial, it is no mirage in the desert air. Cultivating spirituality is a proper expression of our charism, our life, and our role in the Church. The *second* path is that of the Teresian Carmel as heir of a justly enviable spiritual heritage. This heritage represents for all a spirituality that we might not be able to define. All the same, we know it when we see it and have no trouble recognizing and testifying that Teresa of Jesus and John of the Cross were spiritual persons.

Vocational Call for the Sake of Spirituality

We believe in the existence of the charisms and gifts of God. We believe that all are brothers and sisters, that all of us have a basic commonality as Christians, and that all of us are People of God. But for that very reason we also believe that this People of God with its infallible instinct of faith has christened us "spirituals," knows us by that name, and in the same way acknowledges our activity fundamentally in the area of spirituality.

Our vocational call to spirituality means that we are called to attract and detect the Spirit of God in all times and places. We do not know whence he comes or where he goes, but we know that he fills the earth with the power of the Risen Lord and that he remains with us always. The Spirit does not take us out of the world: his is a mystery of ecclesial presence and presence to the world. Our task is to discover that presence and to second it.

In this sense our response must always be the open response of one who is attentive and watchful and seeks to face the Spirit's *problematic just as it appears in every time and place.* We must strive to discover, renew and make use of all the most appropriate *structures and interventions in every stage of history.*

Our contributions, from the viewpoint of professionals in the field of spirituality, could include:

1. Ideological Revision

Our first contribution could be an in-depth revision of programs of official spirituality. By that I mean, a revision of the programs of spirituality which are carried out wherever the Order officially sustains and supports it. This revision would mean not only that we would provide *guidelines*, but that we would *put those guidelines into practice*: In other words, create a new style for programs of spirituality. The Order as such should make itself responsible for this. It does not seem imprudent, much less objectively false, to say that we Discalced Carmelites sin in our programs with their emphasis on classics, on an elite, on intimacy. And they are elitist—the sense of the other terms needs no explanation—not only when they choose one class of persons to the detriment of others (usually a high class to the detriment of those of low condition), but also when they confer privilege on certain high stages, so to speak, or spiritual states or spiritual vocations in which only a few persons participate.

This ideological revision ought to follow along the lines of historic spirituality. That is not to say a spirituality which looks backward. On the contrary, it would be a spirituality focused on the present moment and firmly rooted in real life. I do *not* propose historic spirituality as an alternative to contemplative spirituality, but rather to give attention to the latter. If we postulate greater attention to the historical dimensions of spirituality, it is not in detriment to its contemplative dimension. If it were, we would be radically mistaken. Contemplation is not only not opposed to history, but must be situated in history in order to be real and rich. And history would no longer form the human person if it were to forget the contemplative dimension.

What is true in the conceptual order is paralleled in daily and professional life. One does not live historically by isolating prayer, ascesis or silence. One does not speak or write of commitment and then forget prayer, celebration, etc. Ironical attitudes toward this contemplative dimension have no place in an historical life. To the extent that we find them—and we do find them to the point that they are a "professional risk" for us—we can be sure that we are victims of the lingering wound of a serious dichotomy and a contradiction that we have been unable to resolve.

The proof of this is the fact that our contemporaries have only little faith in our programs. We do not make use of those specialized disciplines which form part of the environment in which they move and breathe. We often call them *auxiliary* in a pejorative sense. But spiritual persons need have no fear of the epithets of "naturalism" and "horizontalism" often hurled against those who make bold use of them and even those who use them with care and a certain "healthy respect." I am referring to psychology, sociology, literature, art . . . All of these are expressions of spirituality and, at the same time, they necessarily critically call "theology" into question. That is equally true of spirituality: either we accept an interdisciplinary approach or we lose the possibility of integrating spirituality.

Today this revision is not only more necessary than ever, but also easier. Both Vatican II and many postconciliar theologians write of "spirituality" and use this term frequently, with grace and to the envy of onlookers. Will we once again miss the train which would bring us to certain realism in spirituality!?

2. Set up Structures

Just as a faith which seeks to be practiced intelligently and not ingenuously cannot hold itself apart from any part of real life, in the same way the spirituality that we defend has need of adequate structures, if through it we are to fulfill our task in the world.

The General Chapter should make a central objective the establishment of a network of creditable spirituality centers with worthwhile tasks to accomplish. The Chapter should decide on an acceptable commitment to them and once the Order accepts it everyone should make every necessary sacrifice and provide all the real help needed to make them a success. We need to train persons who can respond to present-day needs; but we must also allow for the possibility that these persons may carry on their work in situations congenial to them. Even "intellectuals" will find activities that are complementary and mutually enriching and will not debase or distract them.

The same may and should be said of a network, however small (provided it is thought through and supported) of publications and other media. The commercialization of publications is of first importance *in today's market*, however saturated, as a means of getting the authors' work into the hands of the public. I believe that we need to make an intelligent start in setting up bookstores. The Order has scarcely distinguished itself in this field and we have been *too* dependent on others. (One must always depend on others, but that is not what I am referring to.)

Another structure that we must make use of is chairs of spirituality organized in other entities. We should take up this work in such a way that we can begin creating a Carmelite presence in them and hand it on to other members of the Order. This means that we have to open new trails for our spiritual presence in a public which in its turn will have a directive role in life.

In some way, also, we ought to take on diocesan responsibilities of a spiritual nature. This presupposes that we be part of joint pastoral programs within local churches where we may open new fields for spiritual ministry within the dioceses. The same may be said on the level of regional Conferences or national Conferences. These ways of being present imply, over and above what they require in themselves, a wide-open door through which we may step into other roles appropriate for us.

Finally, it will be very difficult to establish any of these or other structures and dedicate ourselves more to spirituality if we do not bravely attack the problem of setting priorities for our presence in the Church and the world. These are times when vocations are in short supply and in which many religious are working for a vocational reawakening. Yet, until we are willing to give a retreat or spirituality house preferential treatment over schools, we will not be able to accomplish anything worthwhile in this field which is truly our own.

3. Living

Three concrete aspects of life deserve our careful attention in this section:

(1) Our Community Life

We must live before we can do. We Carmelites live as community. We profess a markedly contemplative life as described for us in its essentials in our *Constitutions*. That description, however, does not derogate the unique character of individual communities or reject variations in lifestyle according to time and place. As we have said above, contemplation itself must be situated in history. Yet we may admit that we have fallen short in living an historical contemplative life and our poverty is notable in this regard.

Perhaps we have not been able to discover in contemplation something desirable and estimable. Maybe we need to catechize ourselves so as to realize once and for all that the contemplative aspect of our life is essential to it. Likewise, the time has come for us to face up to the fact that solitude, even apart from the importance given it by St Teresa, is fundamental to a healthy contemplative life. There is a pagan maxim which Catholic philosophers and theologians have made their own and which is especially relevant to us. It says, "One's worth can be measured by his capacity for silence." Our times are especially sensitive to this value, but we must know how to present it in a pedagogically sound way. We must make sure that we do not link it with attitudes or ideologies that have nothing to do with silence but only with ostracism.

(2) Living with the Poor

We should, and perhaps even must, be effectively present among the poor and the humble. We must avoid romantic illusions, but we must also be unafraid of being labeled "snobs." The Church's preference for the poor (Church of the poor) requires more than presence in parish ministry, in education, in health work . . . Once again it looks as if spirituality has nothing to do with real life. Perhaps few have felt it necessary to bring spirituality to these humble places. And yet, we would certainly fly in the face of the Gospel if we were to say that the spiritual life could not be lived except outside of the very social conditions in which God's own poor live.

Presence among the poor and life with the poor would awaken and challenge our provinces since it would break real ground for our spirituality, bring us down to earth, make us meditate a lot more in the difficult pastoral ministry of meditation, and would be an important cure for the angelism and artificiality which so frequently disfigure spirituality.

(3) Group Advancement

Since Vatican II Christian life has been characterized by the way it finds community expression. The experiences of small communities have helped shape this characteristic dimension. It challenges us, because life today is carried out and lived in groups.

There are all kinds of groups, and we ought not to close ourselves to any of them, but we should be especially open to prayer groups. They continue to grow beyond expectations. They offer an appropriate forum for our prayer ministry, a ministry abandoned in the Church and left to gurus and such like. Prayer, that Teresian and Christian subject, demands formation, conviction, practical application, and pedagogy. And perhaps more than anything else it demands discernment. It could be an escape, a refuge for persons who are not whole, or for the traditionalist seeking comfort in the idea that nothing can change in prayer. Certainly, not everyone interested in prayer will be maladjusted, but discernment is probably needed more here than in other places.

(4) Heirs of the Kingdom

Some words of E. Mounier come instinctively to mind: "It will not be by means of the derring-do of our grandfathers that we will respond to the anguish of our grandchildren." There is a tendency to look to the past as a golden moment to be treasured in reverent memory. We need to keep this in mind when we deal with our heritage, for without vigilance and great freedom of spirit our fidelity to the past runs the risk of becoming material repetition and an unhealthy attachment.

OUR HERITAGE

That said, we can turn to some considerations and proposals having to do with our heritage.

A Universal Patrimony

The judgment of history recognizes a dozen of our authors as classical in the best sense of that word. Chauvinism and uncritical attitudes toward them does not change that fact.

But these authors are not exclusively our own: they belong to

the Church and to humanity. To treat them like some embalmed
dead thing put away would be a sin against spirituality. Whether
we like it or not we are directly responsible for them in a way
that allows no subsitutes.

We must, therefore, make available to people of all conditions
the *writings* of these authors, together with the *tools* needed to
study them as well as *interpretations* and *up-dated applications*
of their doctrine. These are *four* essential tasks. None is new,
and none has been finished. We must thank all those who have
tenaciously worked and who continue to work on any of these
tasks, and we must constantly encourage those who seriously feel
called to this work. We must help others who might make a contribution to it discover and accept this vocation. And as a matter
of justice, and sometimes of simple courtesy, we must support
both psychologically and materially those who are carrying on
the most thankless, most misunderstood, and most overlooked
contributions to this field.

No money or support should ever be lacking in the Order for
this work. If, in the judgment of a Commission, there are works
that merit attention, they should be assured of publication.

Our Institute of Spirituality and the faculty of the Teresianum
in its seminary course, should not treat the students with such
"respect." Teresa of Jesus and John of the Cross should be represented by a chair there and courses on them should be an oblig-
atory part of the curriculum.

The Teresian Center at Avila might also be a good educational
resource for making known the doctrine of our Holy Parents.

In the tasks we have mentioned of *interpretation* and updated
application we need not, and perhaps should not, begin a course,
a book, or a study by referring directly to our authors, as if it
were always necessary to tack onto the end of whatever we have
to say "according to St Teresa" or "according to St John of the
Cross." What we need today, more than ever before, is to pick
out and analyze personal and community experiences with the
help of the truly valid contributions of our saints. We must know
how to *translate, incarnate,* and *relive* the great experiences,
the stages and formative values that shaped the spirituality of

our saints: that is the fundamental task for us today and at all times.

Concrete Subject Matter

If we were to try to propose here a series of concrete subjects to be addressed, we would have to list many and would stray from our purpose. I would simply like to say that our attitude here ought to be cool and dispassionate, but not fearful. One thing is certain: writers of our day from various backgrounds, who have made universal names for themselves, turn to our Holy Parents as teachers practically above question; and when some question is raised regarding their doctrine, it is usually because the various systematic studies approach these saints from a different viewpoint. Such criticisms are positive contributions. Such obviously different authors as Gustavo Gutiérrez and William Johnston, for example, come immediately to mind.

Our subject matter opens out to humankind's hopes for its future. May we learn how to implant that hope firmly in the culture of the world of today.

[ED's NOTE: the author indicated his desire to add—as a further "Sign of Our Times"—heightened interest in the role of *woman* in society, but he was unable to supply a text before we went to press.]

CHRISTIAN, HUMAN AND CULTURAL VALUES IN ST TERESA OF JESUS

Jesús Castellano

Jesús Castellano lives in Rome and, besides teaching at the Teresianum, is an advisor to several Vatican Congregations there. He shares in the training of Carmelites from around the world as a member of the Teresianum's formation personnel.

INTRODUCTION

St Teresa of Jesus constitutes a cultural phenomenon of widespread impact: (1) by reason of her person, her doctrine, and her literary style which have had and continue to have *wide impact in the Church and in society*; (2) because she was a woman who carried out a spiritual mission in the Church of her time and who left, unique among early writers and theologians, a theological and spiritual doctrine that grows out of her own Christian experience and bears the *seal of her Christian feminism*; and (3) for the openness to social and human values found in her writings and joined to her deep Christian, evangelical experience which embraces the summits of the *Christian mystical life*.

One spontaneously thinks of Teresa of Jesus as a person who shared fully in the vicissitudes of the cultural and spiritual currents of her times. She relived the experience of the gospel. With her books she gave to the gospel, and to the message of spirituality of the Christian life, the service of profound doctrine, of authentic witness and an exceptional literary expression. Her contribution takes its place deservedly among the great cultural expressions of all times. It has merited translations and studies in all languages. It has proven a spiritual phenomenon that has gained the attention of the highest sectors of human culture: the plastic arts, literary studies, philosophical and psychological analyses, theological writings, as well as journalism, fiction, cinema, television and legitimate theater.

John Paul II emphasized this special aspect of St Teresa in various remarks during his visit to Spain in November, 1982: together with St John of the Cross, she occupies a prominent place and she makes her presence felt in *universal culture* in a way that honors the Church and honors women.

Both the proclamation of the Doctorate of St Teresa by Paul VI in 1970 and the impact which her figure made during the Fourth Centenary of her death are indications that the saint is making her presence felt in the culture of today's Church and the world.

Our concern for presenting St Teresa in the context of a synthesis on the theme of *Culture* can be explained for various reasons.

First of all, it agrees with the Church's concern for giving to the gospel and to Christian life the weighty expression of a humanly rich experience which incorporates real values and stimulates interest in many areas of the cultural life of our society. St Teresa, like other saints, offers her witness to the cultural wealth of the gospel as it enters into human life and enlightens and elevates it.

Secondly, the values found in Teresian spirituality can be discovered in a coherent synthesis of humanism, sociability, spirituality and mysticism. The Church anxiously seeks such a synthesis today both because she is "specialist in humanity" and wishes to witness to and defend all human values, and because she is a herald of Christ the Redeemer who is the center of the cosmos and of history. St Teresa of Jesus offers exceptional, "expert" witness for this synthesis of values which looks to Christ, true God and true Man, as its archetypal point of reference, shaper of models, and index of values. Through the personal synthesis of her life and her written doctrine, Teresa points to a culture of *divinity/humanity*. Such a culture affirms that human values are open to the most genuine supernatural participation, as found in mystical experience, and that these values are open to an appraisal of all that is human since it was created by God and can be redeemed and elevated by Him in Christ Jesus. The typical expressions of Teresa's Christological experience, like "Most Sacred Humanity" and "divine and human together," indicate the cultural synthesis she achieved in a time, like the sixteenth century, when humanism began to go its own secularized way and spirituality stepped back from involvement with human life.

Many traits of her personal synthesis related more to the cultural vision of today's Church than to the cultural tendencies of her own age. Her unified vision of spirituality, of religious and ecclesial life, and of the gospel's role in filling human values with divine grace makes Teresa our contemporary.

After these general remarks we can say that the presentation of the "cultural, human and Christian values" of St Teresa coincides with the presentation of her *spirituality*. Those values can only be understood in the light of the full range of her teaching. Naturally, we cannot explain that fully here. Instead we will try to present a summary digest of key words and salient values while keeping in mind some methodological keys to reading her writings.

A Discerning Attitude

The *Teresian cultural* fact or event includes her person and the geographical and historical context in which she lived. It gave much to Teresa and received much from her as well. Faced with the ecclesial and social situation of her age, Teresa did not assume an attitude of neutrality. She accepted its contributions, rejected others, and enriched it. Her attitude was one of critical openness toward her world and her history, and we see her as someone relating to the real world but with a discerning attitude that was capable of accepting good, rejecting the bad, and of contributing to the betterment of situations. It is a lesson of *cultural creativity* for our own task. We need a discerning attitude toward our Church and our culture that is free of nostalgic attachment to the past, and not given to hazarding a future that does not yet exist. We need a discernment that can take up or reject influences, that can itself influence the Church and society today for the good, that prevents us from fleeing them or of taking refuge in sterile criticisms of them or in a perennial nostalgia for a past that no longer exists and values that have had their day.

Building Syntheses

In this Teresian cultural event we find a whole series of unified syntheses which are characteristic of the saint, e.g., the unity between her experience and doctrinal reflection on her experience, and her pedagogy or mystagogy in handing on truths and attitudes; the way she created a *lifestyle* that was able to incarnate the spiritual values which she esteemed and exalted so that they did not become merely abstract values or dead-ended doctrines; there is a Teresian style of prayer, of communion, of friendship, of silence and solitude, and of recreation and relaxation; her life unifed *love of God and of neighbor*, prayer and apostolic zeal, liturgical and personal prayer—*a desire to transcend dualisms* is so characteristic of the saint that it is a main feature of her spiritual synthesis; finally the way all these rich values are lived in *equilibrium* is a characteristic feature of her spirituality and style.

Development

Finally, we would point out that the interior key to the development of this unified wealth of Teresian values consists in several things: More than all else, we find reference to the *person of Christ,* and to his personal values, experience and doctrine.

This led to a *fundamental* recovery of the *evangelical values* of Christian, religious, contemplative and ecclesial life. *Prayer* is to be taken as a unifying value. It is a fundamental Christian expression of life involving friendship, filiation and communication with God. It is an existential *filter* for interior and exterior experiences and the place for discernment of events. It is both an attitude and an exercise whose value demands demonstration in *practice* and not just lip service. Then there is the conviction that on this *way of growth* exists a necessary ascetic moment, but that all spiritual pegagogy ought to tend to openness to and a prompt disposition for the action of God, that is, *to mystery and to the mystical dimension of Christian life*. Without it, dichotomies cannot be overcome, firm virtues cannot be acquired, unity is lacking in life and there is no fresh apostolic creativity. These things can only come from the action of God. He makes contemplatives be persons "present and anxious to serve" and who no longer do human work but instead do the work of God.

What we have said serves as a premise to our remarks on the various cultural, human, and Christian values which follow. We must realize that they are not listed like so many separate entries in a catalogue, a *sum* of objects. Rather, they form an organic whole that flowers spontaneously from the interior of a person who is unified in essentials and walks the path of progressive discernment through prayer. This organic unity comes about, in other words, when we *let ourselves be shaped* interiorly by the action of God who makes us friends "of his own condition" and brings about in us—as he did in Teresa—this great synthesis of values. We could call it *God's culture*, and it must become the *Church's culture*. There must be the same organic unity of life and attitudes of Christians as we face a world, a society and a history which are part of a *divine plan*. Contemplation as a unifying force is the ability to enter into this cultural world. Or, if you wish, our task is not ourselves to create this synthesis of culture with its human and Christian values; our task is to *contemplate it* in Christ and to welcome it with eyes fixed on God. We must receive it from God's salvific will: it is his project and his will for contributing to the *re-creation* or creation of those values.

For this reason the cultural key of the Teresian Carmel is *contemplation*. Our very name carries the connotation of a mission of contemplation in the Church's mind. Our task is to render conditions favorable for a culture of contemplation, in the genuine sense of that word, as a doctrinal and practical "resonance" of our Teresian and Sanjuanist tradition. We are faced with a principle which has been defined, almost as if it were a prior condition for any type of cultural work, "the contemplative dimension of life." (Card. C. Martini) It is an attitude that urgently needs to be recovered and will require all the forces of the Teresian Carmel on the doctrinal level, on the level of personal and community practice, on the level of ecclesial apostolate, and on the level of our communities' lifestyle.

I am convinced and wish to stress that the rediscovery of the human, spiritual and doctrinal Teresian values has not as yet found concrete expression in the lifestyle of most of the groups of the Order. It has not yet led to experiences that have something stimulating and enlightening to offer God's People and turn all the places in which we live into places of *ecclesial welcome* and witness to these values which we affirm *in theory*.

Only by remembering that in Teresa of Jesus and John of the Cross values are drawn from life and are incarnated in life can we finally realize that which is perhaps the object of nostalgic desire on the part of many: a deepening of the lifestyle of our communities on the liturgical level, on that of prayer and of community life, together with a growth in the depths and heights of our manner of being. And here we open the most important chapter, in my opinion, of the march of the next few years toward the Centenary of St John of the Cross and toward the year 2000: How can we, without nostalgia for a past that no longer exists, incarnate in the Carmel of Teresa and John of the Cross a style of life that will be both the *wellspring* of a creative "rereading" of its own values and at the same time an *effective witness* of the human and Christian values which pertain to our "spiritual patrimony?" How can we do this so as to be able to share these values, in an open communion of both receiver and giver, wtih all God's People?

CULTURAL VALUES

Among cultural values we wish to draw attention to some elements which will demonstrate the *vital experience* and *adequate influence and transmission* of values which afterward we will see in their human and Christian facets.

Teresa's Cordial Openness to the Social and Ecclesiastical Realities of Her Times.

She was not ignorant of them nor was she scandalized by them. She faced with realism both the evil and good in her social and ecclesial situation and brought to bear upon them discernment and a moderating Christian influence.

A Universal Awareness

Though a cloistered nun, the saint had a universal awareness and lived always in spiritual communion with all the realities of her world. She knew Castile and Spain, was aware of the schisms of the Church in Europe, knew about the wars between Spain and France and between Spain and Portugal. She had knowledge of the evangelization of America — an adventure with its lights and shadows. Nor was she ignorant of the Jewish and Islamic worlds. She lived her times with a universal awareness because she saw in everyone "his (God's) children and my brothers." (Cf. C, 5, 2, 10-11)

Contact with the Cultural Values of Her Epoch

A friend of learning and of the learned, St Teresa kept contact with the literary, humanistic, and spiritual values of her epoch. She knew the cream of the crop of theologians of the moment, as can be seen from the long list of her confessors in Testimony 58. She also came into contact with the currents of spirituality of her epoch: Franciscan, Dominican, Jesuit. She had a great longing for a deeply biblical culture as can be seen for her esteem for those, who like Dr Vazquez, knew Scripture. This is confirmed by her cry in C, 7, 3, 13: "Who would know the many things there must be in Scripture to explain this peace of soul!"

In Search of a Unified Synthesis

St Teresa wanted to join learning and experience, theology and spirituality. She occupied a position of mediation in the polemic that divided theologians and "spirituals." Her cordiality toward representatives of spirituality and theology, then entangled in domestic polemics (e.g., Dominicans/Jesuits, Dominicans/Franciscans) indicates a will for unity and unification that transcends polemics surrounding the unique truth of God.

Essential Values of the Christian Experience

We must recognize that both in her life and in her subsequent influence in the field of spiritual theology, St Teresa emphasized Christian experience in the light of scriptural discernment and theology. It is the science of experience and invitation to a culture that is incarnated in life and bursts forth from life that creates styles of life.

To Enrich and Be Enriched through Communication

If the saint could affirm that *charity grows when it is communicated* (L, 7, 22), one could also affirm that culture grew in her through adequate transmission. The opportunity of communicating her experience created a language, various symbols, and various means of transmission. Her copious dialogue with the learned enriched her cultural possessions. The principle of *communication* as an attitude of giving and receiving in a universal dialogoue is, after all, a fundamental lesson of the saint.

Mystagogical Sense

The saint's culture is intrinsically a culture of life; it is born from life and leads to life. It is a mystagogical transmission that seeks to communicate, create, and solicit experience in the various resonances that it can have in each person and each place.

Channels of Transmission or Watercourses for Culture

In the saint we find a series of channels by which culture is enriched, viz., reading, study, contact with learning and the learned, dialogue with the major theologians and spirituals, experience of life open to communication, prayer in which the Lord teaches the truth. At the same time she is teaching us through her very attempts to find channels for *communicating* culture, over and above her search for culture itself as a synthesis of truth and of life. She writes her books, employs her imaginative language; she creates a language; she makes use of various literary genres — like poetry, letters, exclamatory writings. She translates spiritual life into a *style* of life, into a way of being, into an aesthetic of the very house in which she lives. She translates spiritual values into celebrations and domestic represenations.

HUMAN VALUES

In the last decades we have heard a lot about "Teresian humanism." Without doubt we are dealing with a necessary and joyful recovery of a facet of the saint which on the other hand has always been recognized: her humanism, her attractiveness.

In the synthesis of human and humanistic values of St Teresa, we must recognize that we are dealing with an appreciation of all that is human and not simply a superficial appreciation. This appreciation begins with the *evangelical root* of human values and with a confrontation of them with the mystery of the Sacred Humanity. Teresa's experience and teaching attest to the truth that charity humanizes according to the measure of Christ Jesus. If it is true that every human value demands a *conversion* to the gospel, then through that conversion the value is purified and assayed. The saint says: "The more holy the more sociable." This process leads to fulfillment in a humanism that imitates Christ in a charity that knows no limits or frontiers.

We have no need here to develop at length a theme well known in Teresian literature. There even exists a good anthology of Teresian texts in the book *Camino del Amor* (*Pathway of Love*) La Estrella, 1982, pp. 343-404. But we will underscore in outline form some of the better-known headings:

— Appreciation of common sense as a requirement for a vocation and for a balanced spiritual life;
— Esteem for truth, for simplicity, for genuine sincerity;
— Striving after true freedom of spirit;
— Attention to the person on the journey of the spiritual life;
— Appreciation for the cultivation of the genuine value of human and Christian friendship;
— Discretion and gentleness in dealings and in government;
— Fortitude and determination in the face of adversity and in the field of total self-donation to God;
— A profound sense of gratitude to persons;
— Sincere expression of affection and of sharing in the joy and sorrows of life;
— Cultivation of joy, of recreation, and affability, and of human agreeableness;
— Esteem for work and diligence;
— Sober harmony in the arrangements of the house and especially in all that refers to divine worship;
— Passionate defense of marginalized groups of her times: the poor, women, *Indios* (native Americans);
— Concern for peace expressed in criticism of violence and personal interventions for the prevention of wars;
— Valiant interventions in favor of the truth and for shedding light on errors or judgments regarding persons and events: letters to the King or to the General of the Order;
— The fundamentally religious meaning of everything that is human since every person is made in the image and likeness of God and is a "dwelling place" of God;
— Esteem for ascesis though joined with charity;
— Criticism of the human titles of society, of nobility and of the "mayorías" who held sway in the monasteries of her time.

CHRISTIAN VALUES

Once again we affirm that the human values (found in St Teresa) are exquisitly Christian and appear like a human and social flowering of the gospel and as a witness to a humanity permeated by the gospel.

By now considering some "Christian" values, we wish to refer to some characteristic elements of Christian life which St Teresa manifested in her spiritual synthesis.

In this regard we will pick out some nuclei of values according to a certain hierarchical division.

Christ

Before all else, there is the *Person of Jesus Christ* in his divinity/ humanity as the personal synthesis of all values and as the absolute value to which one must be conformed. St Teresa offers us a rich range of Christological titles which show that her fundamentally Christocentric attitude is the key to interpreting all her books and doctrine. She calls him: Master, Spouse, Lord, Friend, Model, Life, Dwelling. Christocentrism distinguishes the progressive way of Christian life in all its facets, according to a fundamental progression of Christian life: quest, encounter, conversion, discipleship, revelation, life in Christ, and service to Christ.

Prayer

The second place is held by the *fundamental value of prayer* which is the fundamental evangelical life expression around which Teresa forms her synthesis of Christian life: prayer/friendship, prayer presence/intimacy. It is a value which is being discovered today as the basic response to the God who reveals himself and speaks as a friend. (*Dei Verbum,* 2) Teresian prayer is Christocentric in inspiration (as the Master prayed), in its relationship to him, and because of the progressive path of Christological transformation.

Mysticism

In the third place, Teresa emphasizes the *mystical vocation of the Christian* and even of every human, that is to say, to an alliance and to a "koinonia." Fundamentally everyone "depends" on God and is already set apart by his vocation to communion with God. (*Gaudium et Spes*, 19) This is the initial thesis of the *Interior Castle.*

This fundamental conviction — the invitation to "mysticism" to a living out of mystery, or to Christianity as "mysticism and mystery" — about the doctrinal conviction of the Holy Mother is rounded out by gratuitous initiative of God: in the hope that God must act first, that no one by his own efforts may enter into this experience of God, but, on the contrary, we must be disposed and ready for God's gratuitous action and grace.

Service

In the foruth place, St Teresa attests to the *unity of life,* and *the mystical dimension of ecclesial service* forms part of her store of basic ideas. The entire last chapter of the *Interior Castle* (7, 4) offers this synthesis of Teresian thought. The life of prayer, of sanctity, and mysticism are translated into being "like Christ" and into "living like him" in the unity of love of the Father and of service to others. For this reason Christian life and the life of prayer with their intensified moments of activity or contemplation are situated in (like the life of Christ himself) an "ecclesialization" of prayer and of service in a unity of life. In the end that means living in the Church and serving the Church.

Love

In the fifth place, the saint emphasizes in a synthesis of authentically evangelical and pauline flavor the supreme value of *charity* as the criterion and measure of all progress in the spiritual life, of every authentically Christian manner of living, over and above any other virtue which might even be dangerous if not accompanied by charity. (Cf. W. 4-7; C, 5, 3; C, 7, 4; Solil.

2, etc.). Consequently, the charity of the saint bears two fundamental names: *communion* and *service.*

This simple enumeration of the final goals providing basic
motivation or inspiration in Teresian spirituality show us clearly
the channels of culture which the Teresian Carmel must pro-
mote in the Church within the strong and balanced synthesis
which Teresa offers: Christocentrism, prayer, vocation to a
mystical life, unity of life in service to the Church, affirmation
of charity as communion-service. It is the final synthesis of the
book of the *Interior Castle* (7, 4).

FUNCTIONAL VALUES NECESSARY
TO REACH THE GOAL

For the sake of the ultimate aforementioned values, we find
in the Teresian synthesis an insistence on some Christian virtues
which characterize the life of prayer. These virtues have a *func-
tional* characteristic to the extent they do not exist as ends and
are not the absolute measure of perfection. Nevertheless they
are *necessary* and are the compulsory steps of Christian perfection which cannot be realized except by means of a basic evangelical attitude which is founded on these virtues and is expressed
in them.

These virtues, in St Teresa as in St John of the Cross, have an
ascetical character when there prevails in them the element of
generous, although always limited, human effort. They have a
mystical character when they are lived with the consciousness
that God is the one who rouses these profound attitudes in the
new man, the friend of God, shaped by him in the evangelical
virtues which no longer can be either simple efforts or sometimes an evangelical "caricature," but must be an "interior confirmation" to the attitudes of Jesus Christ himself.

I wish to note, finally, that the virtues which the saint teaches
in the *Way of Perfection* always have this triple dimension in
which their full value and balance come together: they are *Christocentric virtues* — inspired by the words and attitudes of Christ,

made by him and which "conform" one to him; they are *communitarian* virtues — as premise for or emanation of love they have the grace of building up communion and they stand surety for it; they are *ecclesial* virtues — they express the holiness of the Church which is always evangelical holiness.

These are the Teresian virtues and they are well known to all:

— interior and exterior poverty;
— abnegation or affective detachment;
— humility, which is to walk in the truth;
— fortitude or determined determination;
— corporal and spiritual ascesis (mortification);
— trust and hope;
— self-knowledge which is the source of true humility.

In this context it is worth remembering as well the series of attitudes which give shape to theological *charity*, with the entire range of requirements of service, of mercy, of goodness of heart, of effective "love of benevolence," of constancy in personal attitude. The magisterium of the saint is very rich, as can be observed from a rapid reading of chapters 4-7 of W and of C, 5, 3.

CONCLUSION

As I have already had occasion to underline in the fundamental points in the introduction, this synthesis regarding the cultural values of the Teresian magisterium must needs be a summary reading in the light of the needs of today for the Order and for the Church. To sum up, it seems to me worthwhile pointing out the following *three fundamental tasks.*

A Doctrinal-Theological Synthesis Which Creates an
Awareness and Keeps It Alive in the Church Today

The cultural, human and christian values of the Holy Mother and Holy Father and other representatives of Carmel form the richest part of what *Perfectae Caritatis* 2 calls the "heritage" of a

religious institute. It must be developed in order to create a consciousness of our charism and heritage in the Church in the face
of dispersion or in the face of the prevalence of foreign elements
or elements of little significance.

A Pedagogy and a Style of Life

There is an urgent need to translate the Order's pedagogy
and initial and ongoing formation into *styles of life* able to incarnate, transmit, enrich those spiritual values. A recovery of
values at the level of doctrine or of consciousness does not mean
to say that we have already recovered a form of life or a style of
life. This is the direction that our efforts ought to take, and along
these channels we must carry initial and ongoing formation in
the upcoming years.

Channels of Apostolic Transmission

With the wealth of our heritage there is no justification for
our presence in the Church if we do not place that heritage in
fruitful communion with all the present-day experiences of the
people of God. It follow that we must rethink our apostolate
along two essential lines:

— regarding *contents* of our evangelical message in the light of
   our spiritual patrimony and our original charism;
— regarding the channels of transmission that are most adequate
   in a creativity along the lines of *pastoral ministry in spirituality.*

Only in this way can we make all the wealth of the Teresian
Carmel into service stimulating and creating a culture in the
Church of today.

ST JOHN OF THE CROSS: CULTURAL, HUMAN AND CHRISTIAN VALUES

Federico Ruiz

Federico Ruiz has written many articles and books on St John of the Cross. Last year the publishing house of the Discalced Carmelites in Madrid issued his new book Mistico y Maestro, San Juan de la Cruz. *He is a professor of theology in Rome.*

St John of the Cross is our best quide in setting forth a plan of life and work for us. He is this at all times, but especially now as we seek to renew our identity. Three reasons for this stand out among others: (1) because he is the Father of the Teresian Carmel and the one entrusted most with its formation: From the very first days at Duruelo he was entrusted with intellectual and spiritual formation offices in Carmel, i.e., master of novices, rector of colleges, director of friar and nuns. He had special grace and talent for this work; (2) because of the perennial value of the mystical-theological-pedagogical synthesis which he left to the Church and to Carmel: Though his output was slim, it has lasted, and it continues to provide us with a valid model and point of reference for today; and (3) the generalized acceptance which St John of the Cross and his writings are finding today in the Church and outside: This tells us powerfully what men and women of today expect and ask of the Teresian

Carmel. St John of the Cross meets present-day needs, and by following in his footsteps we will meet them as well.

Let us admit from the start that much of his appeal is owed to factors that were uniquely his own: natural gifts, special grace and the enlightening experience of his mystical sanctity. Even so, there is much in him that we can model ourselves on and take inspiration from, since he is the most complete and fully-realized example of *carmelitanismo* among the friars.

The fact that St John of the Cross sought to live in an unassuming way and kept a low profile caused a great many of his personal and cultural merits to go unnoticed by his contemporaries. At a time when people sought titles, offices, and important connections in order to be somebody, St John of the Cross lived as a simple friar. He gave no thought to leaving a mark in the tense, partisan politics of the Carmel of his day, "seeking only to obtain for everyone his morsel." (*Dictamen* 19)

St Teresa appreciated his personality. She saw him as holy, wise and a teacher of God's mysteries. She knew some of his counsels and poems, but even she did not have the time or distance from him needed to discover his genius as poet, mystic and theologian. She did not know any of his great works: *The Ascent, The Dark Night, The Canticle* or *The Living Flame.*

Even after the publication of his writings, the true human personality of John of the Cross and his culture remained largely unnoticed. His tough demands tended to eclipse his deep humanism. His lyrical and devotional style overshadowed his gifts and learning. And because his books were dedicated to Carmelite friars and nuns, the universally human and Christian import of his interpretations went unnoticed.

I will develop the subject for our reflection in an outline fashion under five headings. The body of the exposition will consist in discussing the three levels of value that form our subtitle (human, cultural, and Christian). As an introduction I will present some clarifications regarding an essential trait of the saint: the *unity* existing between his life and his vision. As a conclusion I will discuss his *mystagogy*, his mystical teaching, which gives content, tone, and formulation to our sanjuanist heritage.

UNITY BETWEEN THE SAINT'S
LIFE AND WORDS

Unity is one of the most notable and characteristic traits in the life and work of St John of the Cross. It bears on the essence of the subject of the values which I will discuss shortly. But we need first to study it by itself since it is a precious lesson and heritage for us.

The profane and religious sciences — history, literature, psychology, theology, philosophy — are daily uncovering more, and more important, values in the saint's work. He has contributions (that bespeak genius) to make to these fields and to many more. To judge by the pace of recent studies, the rate of discovery is increasing rapidly.

And yet, St John of the Cross presents himself to each of these various investigative viewpoints in one and only one guise: the figure of the contemplative Carmelite and Christian and mystic who drew deeply on life experiences and expressed them powerfully. In St John of the Cross it is not possible to disengage one aspect of his life and work from another, and study only the writer or the thinker, or the poet or the theologian, or treat any of that independently of his contemplative religious identity as one dedicated to formation and to spiritual direction. The different accomplishments of his life and writings form an organic whole that cannot be divided.

The fact is, the saint did not leave his mark on so many independent fields foreign to his contemplative vocation by studying each separately. After careful literary studies in Medina del Campo and philosophical-theological studies in Salamanca, he went on to Duruelo where he focused his attention on his vocation as a Discalced Carmelite. From then on it is his only vocation and only life-task. It is the heart of his personal and community life, his services in pastoral ministry and government. It is this unifying center that enabled him to be of interest even to those who do not share his faith.

Jean Baruzi has written a precious page on this outstanding fact: the vocational unity of John of the Cross and the universality of his work and message. He is a contemplative Carmelite, enchanted by his vocation: he lives it and finds his inspiration in it, he learns it and teaches it among his Carmelite brethren. His gaze is fixed on Christ, the Beloved, whom he follows by the narrow path throughout his mystical journey. Each step in this process and each word expressing it are verified and nourished with a biblical text. He is a Christian, a Catholic and a Carmelite. And at the same time, we feel that this man, unawares, embraces the whole range and depth of faith and of humanity through the extraordinary quality of his experiences and of his words.

This is a very significant lesson for the Teresian Carmel in its present task of renewal: because it does not lose sight of the spiritual source of Carmelite life and of the leading function of these spiritual values in its service to the Church, this open and unifying approach allows one to cultivate various fields of religious thought and contemporary culture, while avoiding that dispersion that leads to loss of identity as well as the opposite danger of excessive uniformity in thought, in awareness and in work.

Such a unity is kept alive by means of a hierarchy of values which John of the Cross constantly upholds in his spirit and in his way of living. We might group them roughly according to the following levels: (1) the personal and community life of the religious together with all its requirements; (2) the jobs in government and formation which he was given throughout his life; (3) spiritual assistance to nuns and seculars; (4) his activity as a writer in the service of the three foregoing levels. This hierarchy or set of priorities allowed the saint to carry on his work in studies or in writing, without it ever conflicting with the requirements of his religious life or of the services asked of him in government and construction which had to occupy so much of his time.

HUMAN VALUES

I place this category of values first because they serve as the foundation for the growth and manifestation of those that will follow. We could speak of a "sanjuanist humanism" or of "John of the Cross the Man." Either would be valid, but the second seems to me to include more and be more concrete.

He develops the aesthetic and literary dimension of Christian humanism. For example, "A single thought of man is worth more than all the world . . ." (*Sayings of Light and Love*, 32) He develops its philosophical dimension: love, beauty, the harmony of regenerated humankind or in its first state of original justice. Mankind as the image of God . . .

To be sure, the values of greatest interest to us are those that John himself incarnated in his person and in his life and recommended to his disciples.

Among those that he himself lived, we find a great variety of aspects: (1) contemplation of nature, (2) friendship, (3) pain and privations, and (4) manual work.

These last two expressions of his lively humanism deserve a special remark as they are often overlooked, even though they both leave a strong imprint on his personality and guide his vocational preferences and his work.

The saint's humanism can be seen in the way he suffered *pain* from the beginning of his life until its end: *pain* as a value, not as a misfortune. John of the Cross grows in his suffering. We note this inclination in his loving care for the sick. In his youthful days in Medina he had turned from the trades in order to dedicate himself to the care of the contagious sick. As superior of a house, he would take direct charge of the care of the sick, their food, their medicine, and their cleanliness. Of his years in Baeza a neighbor would say, "I hardly ever saw him in the square or in the city; if he should happen to go out it would be to visit the hospital."

Another special expression of his humanism is *manual work*. His involvement with nature was not limited to the quiet contemplation of landscapes, rivers and woodlands. He was given to hard, regular and prolonged physical work, not just now and then or for the physical exercise. Physical work formed a part of his obligations. And when it came to things like sweeping and scrubbing, which were services to the community, John of the Cross was always the first to lend a hand.

But he freely chose, in addition to these community duties, personally to take on hard, prolonged work. In Duruelo, in Alba de Tormes, in Granada and in Segovia he spent months doing heavy labor on the construction of the houses. And at Segovia he spent long periods quarrying stone for the construction and enlargement of the *convento*.

We conserve some very significant testimony regarding his conduct on his visits to the nuns at Beas. He came from El Calvario, Baeza, Granada. He spent some days there, hearing confessions, instructing, consoling the nuns. While the community followed its horarium, John kept himself busy. One of the nuns declared:

> He took great care to flee idleness and when he was free for a time he would write or ask for the key to the orchard and go there to weed it or do similar work. Sometimes he kept busy making partitions or flooring in our convent. And if he should have a companion, he would come in to help him. If not, he would ask some of the nuns to help him. He also liked to dress the altars and did so with great neatness, silence and cleanliness.

This is the humanism of John of the Cross. He does a bit of everything: hears confessions and instructs, writes, digs in the orchard, decorates the altars, and builds partitions and flooring.

These likings of his reveal his deeply humanistic attitudes and sentiments. The witnesses have adverted to it in many other ways as well. In virtue of the *unity* mentioned before, divine values shine in his human conduct. As one witness says succinctly: "God Our Lord gave him a *holy* way of *being* which was respected by everyone." That is the mixture of the divine and human which St John of the Cross received and acquired.

Another of the fundamental values lived by the saint and recommended to others by him was the "human virtues." Even though called human, they are not the "wild" fruit of nature's bounty but a divine gift and the harvest of careful cultivation. In the difficulties through which the primitive Teresian Carmel had to pass, he was given many an opportunity to practice them to a heroic degree and to recommend them to others with a particular insistence.

In the *Maxims*, collected by Father Eliseo from the oral teachings of the saint in the houses where he was superior, there is a surprising insistence on the "human virtues": sincerity, nobility, courage, respect, gentleness, politeness. He firmly condemned such vices as ambition, artifice, that boorishness and fierceness which are marks of barbarians, as well as lying and adulation. The insistence of the saint on these attitudes and of Father Eliseo in recording them, shows that they were in increasingly short supply and in danger of being lost.

His humanism is one of fraternal common life that is gentle and in accordance with his vocation. His *Precautions* set out requirements, but not hardships. These human virtues are nourished and acquired by force of love and mortification.

CULTURAL VALUES

In this section we will consider the values of the cultural environment which John of the Cross makes his own, as well as the intellectual and effective ability with which he develops and personalizes them. From now on we must keep in mind the principle of the vocational *unity* of John of the Cross. All his knowledge and all his experiences are directed toward his contemplative vocation.

This harmony came about in his life almost spontaneously. Only rarely do we find *breaks* in his life, and they lead to a reestablished equilibrium. The first of these took place at Medina del Campo when he left his literary studies in order to enter the novitiate. A new break follows in Salamanca when he leaves the study halls in order to retire to the solitude of Duruelo. His painful experience of the conflict between theological studies and his contemplative vocation in the environment of Salamanca will later suggest to him the motto which he will take as rector of the college at Alcala: *religious and student, but religious first of all.*

His writings give us a certain idea of the depths of his culture and education, depths hardly suggested by the testimony left us regarding his reading habits. If we may list for a moment the influences that seem strongest, we have:

— scholasticism, Thomism in particular;
— Augustinianism, followed in some points of theology and
    mystical doctrine;
— the mystics of antiquity and the Central European medi-
    eval mystics;
— recent and contemporary Spanish mysticism;
— information regarding authentic currents and misguided
    ones.

Just as interesting as his breadth of culture is the manner in
which he assimilated these influences: he does not cite authors
or books, nor does he copy texts. He barely mentions a Father or
a medieval theologian. From writers of his own times, he mentions St Teresa just once. We cannot help but be struck by the
contrast between the influences felt in his writings and the practical impossibility of naming particular authors or titles of works
that may have influenced him. St John of the Cross did not simply drink at the fountains of their wisdom; he drank up the
fountains.

The saint rethought and relived what they had to teach and
made them his own through a slow process of distillation. He
passed beyond perceptions and beyond doctrine regarding things
to reality itself and addresses directly God, Christ, man, the
theological virtues, prayer, suffering, beauty, etc. For this reason his writings leave us with an impression of fresh originality.
They touch on real things as they are in themselves, and are not
simply facts learned in someone else's writings.

This direct encounter with reality took place in his own life
and experiences, full as they were of divine manifestations and
painful darkness. He tested all that abundantly, and he could
also observe and evaluate the positive and negative experiences
of the many persons in his care. Certainly, in his ministry of spiritual direction his activity was to help, to impart his criteria and
share experiences. However, indirectly he was also learning and
testing the truth and efficacy of his convictions.

There is only one true point of convergence of his study and his
experience: Holy Scripture. He knew it almost by memory. And
what is more important, he spoke of the "Bible as lived — *Biblia*

experimentada." He knew it and identified himself with it in such a manner that its words and its acts became the history of his own life. This explains why John of the Cross had such frequent recourse to biblical language as the most personal and adequate vehicle for expressing his own experience.

Without going into detail about culture and the special manner in which John of the Cross acquired it, we may establish several corollaries of interest to us today:

(1) The cultivation of spirituality involves theological preparation and formal study if one is to avoid falling into those *devociones a bobas* — half-witted devotions — so detested by St Teresa. In his work of providing direction, advice and help to plain people, John made use of a first-class theological training.

(2) Varied and abundant culture was his, too. John read both ancient and modern authors. He was informed about the trends of hs age and knew how to discern the ecclesially valid from anomalies sprouting forth. He did not live only by his personal reflection or comment on the Bible in the abstract, on the fringes of historical involvement with his times.

(3) He did not make an exhibition of his learning by piling up citations and mixing sources. He selected, gleaned and took profit from what he studied, and was silent.

(4) His advanced professional preparations did not alienate him from the simple ministry of the formation of novices and students, of direction of religious, and of providing help to the many secular persons who came to him for enlightenment.

CHRISTIAN VALUES

The presence of Christian values in the work of St John of the Cross is especially evident in the interest in him found in so many different sectors of the Church, among believers living different lifestyles and having different focuses for their spiritual interests.

The universal appeal of the saint does not derive from abstract generalities that have no concrete expression and are independent of his immediate audience. The opposite is true. John writes concretely with definite situations in mind and concrete criteria applied to them. He names his audience explicitly and says they are contemplatives, and he takes decisive positions which seem applicable only to them.

His strength derives from many factors about which we cannot go into now in detail, but we can somewhat summarize them:

(1) The Bible nourished his theological discourse, his lyricism, his mystical experience and gave a Christian flavor to all his doctrine. Alongside the Bible we should mention other sources of a more general character which are the heritage of the entire Church. He found nourishment in Christian and ecclesial values, and it is quite normal that he should pass them on enriched.

(2) Typically Christian mysteries and themes: the Most Holy Trinity, the mysteries of Christ, following the cross, faith, hope and love, love and transformation, deep and transparent meditations, contemplation, the virtues, the nearness of God and darkness, etc. The reader finds himself on familiar ground, in spite of the newness of some of the saint's viewpoints and the unfamiliar language.

(3) The theological life was a lived synthesis of the Christian experience. In this regard the saint made a contribution of primordial importance in centering Christian life on a theological communion with God that is both active and passive and embraces everything from the first steps of a Christian to the final foothold on the mystic heights. Faith, love and hope accomplish everything in ascesis, in the dark night, and in mystical transformation. His appreciation of them finds reaffirmation in the Second Vatican Council, e.g. *Decree on Priestly Formation, 8.*

The saint's stance discloses something very significant. These works and these values which are fundamentally Christian were written by him for Carmelites. He addressed them to "some persons of our sacred Religion (Order) of the primitives of Mount Carmel, both friars and nuns, because they asked it of me . . ." (*Ascent*, Prologue, 9) That is to say, when the Carmelites asked him for Carmelite spirituality, he replied with a Christian synthesis. How should one explain this anomaly?

St John of the Cross never left a single special tract regarding Carmelite life or even religious life in general. Even though he was the chief master for the formation of the Carmelites and even though he carried out his work wholeheartedly, when it came to writing he wrote about the Church. Even more, it seems clear that his oral teaching did the same. We have plenty of witnesses to his methods: He spoke of God, of the mysteries of Christ and of theological life. His talks usually took up a biblical text from the Hebrew Scriptures and New Testament and were commentaries on them. It was his habit to explain the gospel first according to the letter of it and then according to the spirit.

This procedure is of obvious significance and emphatically orients the Carmelite. Our peculiar nature and spiritual strength are found in the way in which we live several Christian values with increased concentration and radicalness: the presence of the Holy Trinity and intimacy with God, patient and generous conformity to Christ's person, prayer and the goodness of the heart, nakedness and freedom in order to be able to walk by the narrow path.

How did John of the Cross manage to become, interiorly and exteriorly, such an unmistakably whole Carmelite and at the same time a universal Christian? He formed the primitive Carmelites according to his charism by having recourse to the essential teaching of the gospel. In doing so, and as a normal consequence, he is able to form every Christian with the essential elements of the Carmelite charism.

Although he was very concrete in the way he lived his conventual life, he never let himself be lost in tiny details. When he dedicated the *Precautions* to the nuns at Beas, he was at the same time writing and explaining to them the *Ascent* and the *Canticle*. He had no wish for them to live a religious life composed only of the "cautions" — he wanted them to take life from the gospel of faith, hope and love.

Ignorance of this feature of St John's work has led some to say recently that St John of the Cross is more a doctor of the Universal Church than a teacher of Carmelite spirituality and life. This statement misses the point on all levels: historical, hermeneutical and spiritual. As I have just indicated, his peculiarly Carmelite outlook and his universality are so interrelated that they draw their strength from one another and are mutually dependent.

MYSTAGOGY

I should make a final reference to what could be considered the method by which the saint personally assimilated these values and then transmitted them in his oral teaching and in writing. Although a corollary to the forgoing, it has such influential importance that it deserves separate treatment.

It was in him a true vocation. Although he was always reserved and quiet, he remained open and ever ready for spiritual conversation. He himself used to say that "although one should talk day and night about the Lord, he would not find it tiring and neither would those listening." To a traveling companion who invited him to see some recently-built palaces, the saint replied, "We are not going in order to see, but rather in order not to see." And they did not see the palaces. A witness adds the reason: "Because he spent most of his time in prayer and in communing with God our Lord and with his neighbors for the sake of prayer."

He had special personal talent for this work, but while noting that fact we must mention that we are dealing with an attitude and style that can and should be the norm of life and action of every Carmelite. This quality is not acquired by study or by technical preparation. It is not a technique of spiritual direction or of homiletics. It derives from one's personal manner of living from which it is inseparable. It requires discernment regarding one's own experience and a sapiential knowledge of the mystery of God as well as the joyful and painful experience of life's trials.

The mystagog is one who, having experienced and continuing to experience God and his mystery, guides another who is setting out on his way. His guidance does not consist in giving practical norms. Rather, the mystagog seeks to present to the ones helped the mystery of the living God and of communion with others in such a way that they may enter into direct contact with God. The art of the mystagog consists not in passing on his/her personal experience, but rather in using his/her experience to be able to present in all its life and warmth the mystery of a personal and prodigiously generous God who reveals himself gratuitously to whoever seeks him.

For the kind of preferential apostolate entrusted to the Teresian Carmel, this modality of communication is the most adequate. Spiritual themes have little value if all they pass on is abstract themes and problems. That approach does not go beyond information, instruction and theoretical pastoral and theological knowledge. It fails to become life and wisdom.

If today the words of St John of the Cross are alive and produce results, it is because they come from the center of his being. His first disciples were aware that:

> The words of God that sprang from his mouth were not the cold words of the scholar but rather words that set the heart on fire with a desire to improve one's life and to seek God.

St John of the Cross continues to be a good model to inspire us with the force of his personality, with his depth of learning, with his rich original experience, and with the living power of his words.

THE TERESIAN CARMELITE: AN OVERVIEW

Tomás Alvarez

Tomás Alvarez is a respected exegete of the writings of St Teresa who has published his own critical edition of her works in Burgos, Spain. For many years he held educational and administrative posts for the Discalced Carmelites in Rome.

This present synthesis ought to have been written in the light of the series of analyses that were presented in the preceding addresses on the subjects of culture, inculturation, the situation of Carmel in today's Church, and the cultural values of St Teresa and of St John of the Cross . . . but these materials were not available to me. Therefore, I see my task as that of framing some suggestions. To give them some order I have decided to take an historical approach, that is to say, to view today's Carmelite as depending on a past which conditions him. He lives his present under the impact of change and of renewal, and he is responsible for his future. And I will talk about this historical Carmelite not so much as an "ideal Teresian Carmelite" cut from the cloth, and according to the pattern, of the theology of our charism. Rather, I regard him as the flesh-and-blood Teresian Carmelite of today who bears the imprint of a past that has shaped him, and I will talk about him as he grapples with the future of Carmel and of the Church.

THE TERESIAN CARMELITE SINCE HIS FIRST BEGINNINGS

The Teresian Carmelite first appeared in this world during a time of *renewal* in the Church and religious life. It was the age of the Tridentine Reform or Counter-Reformation. But he parted from the "thrust" or "vectors" which characterized that "ecclesial and religious renaissance" and found his identity instead in two or three decisive factors: the typological power of his Founders, the weight of their spiritual magisterium, and the crucible of the crisis of growth of the Order.

The Founders as Typological Examples

First of all, we have St Teresa, la *Santa*, with her humanism, her religious experience (mysticism) her pluralism and far-seeing vision; then St John of the Cross, poet (and humanist), teacher and theologian, with his deep experience of God and of life. They are two complementary "types" who have decisively shaped the group with their impact, perhaps also at the risk of being excessively idealized and thus distorted as role models for the Carmelite and his community in the search for their vocational identity.

Their Doctrinal Legacy

First, the *Santa*, then St John of the Cross: Neither of them left a legislation that would fix the "observance" of the masculine Carmel; they left an interpretation of the gospel which was suited for shaping us as religious; a doctrine which was able to generate a new spirituality for the group and begin a life-giving movement. Both left a spiritual/doctrinal heritage sound enough to give rise to a proper or "specific" pastoral ministry in the Church as well as inspire clear new directions in the world of culture (literature, theology, dialogue with secular culture and with the sciences). But the Carmelite family would become aware of all this only slowly and by degrees. Sometimes more, sometimes less. We have no statistical picture of the use of Teresian/Sanjuanist books by the group of first-generation friars, but we know that they never ceased to be read; nor was their influence entirely checked.

The First Great Growth Crisis

Almost immediately the determinative value of the Founders as "types" was called into question. Most of all the *Santa*. As for St John, his example was manipulated or turned to false purposes. Soon the Teresian Carmel found itself divided, nearly definitively, into two congregations and other fragments. This division would have deep repercussions for its identity. The concept or ideals that had inspired the Founders were discounted and their place taken by more observance, less humanism and a diminished sense of intimacy with God. Other rejections of cultural influences followed: the friars held themselves aloof from the universities. The Teresian ideal of missions was called into question. The group withdrew into itself. Sensitivity to the needs of the Church and the world, felt so much by Teresa and John, withered away. All of these changes became official, not merely in the laws of the Order but above all in its historiography, and historiography is the major influence in shaping the "memory and consciousness" of a group. These dregs, perhaps, have not yet been entirely drained away.

All of this was revived with the Restoration of the Order at the end of the last century and beginning of our own. The Order recovered its unity. It also recovered the contents of the old historiography which provided a kind of collective memory for its developing self-consciousness. The Order recovered the missionary ideal as the heritage of the entire Teresian Carmel and this led to an opening of new horizons. (For centuries our Carmel had been absent from Africa and only barely present in America and Oceania.) But the closed attitude toward universities continued and with it the resulting cultural limitations. Periodicals appeared, but they were aimed principally at the cultural "space" inside the Order, not toward the universe outside. Some of these would succeed in breaking loose and reaching out toward more universal values. Probably a summary judgment of our literary and scholarly production would lead to this same affirmation of limitations. The same could be said of our libraries. And there were no cultural centers in the strict sense.

It is impossible that this cultural heritage should not leave its imprint on our present; or that it should not affect the consciousness of the group as far as its culture is concerned, especially in its scholarly and intellectual aspect.

TODAY'S TERESIAN CARMELITE

He is more aware of his own identity. The impact of the Council roused him to action as have the secular cultural factors that have so rapidly changed the fact of modern people and of religious. But even so, today's Carmelite continues to work, as it were, on two different "currents." He carries forward the burden of four centuries of history, but he is also asked to meet the needs of the present moment. It is quite normal that a group should have a certain retrospective attitude to a four-centuries-long history, but it would be expected that such a backward glance would stimulate creativity in meeting present-day challenges of life. One cannot reach a balance between these two forces or an awareness of one's identity on the basis of memories. We cannot restore the past. We live in a present. From that past we have received role models or "types," a spiritual cultural "baggage," and the experience of both successes and limitations. All these can serve as the basis for useful reflections for us today.

Types of Life or Role Models

We are well aware of how sensitive modern men and women are to the magic of role models, especially contemporary ones. St John and St Teresa stand out as role models of Carmelite life, and their humanism and prophetic mysticism make them perennially valid models. But because they are models, there is a danger of misrepresenting them. Fully of their age, they reflect passé elements of their ancestral culture. But the chief danger lies in the fact that because of the extraordinary quality of their human and Christian life, our group psychology may tend to idealize them, to distort them, and so limit their power to shape our lives as Carmelite individuals and groups and to call us into question. Saint John of the Cross ought to have an especially prophetic function or mission in our family and be a catalyst for the development of new role models that are chronologically and culturally more our contemporaries. We need to ask ourselves why those recent "types" for our life that appeared in the nineteenth and twentieth century, many of whom are truly valid — it is enough to recall the names of Fathers Herman Cohen, Palau, Kalinowski, Père Jacques, Marie Eugène, Juan Vicente, et al. — why have they not prospered among us. Why is it that we tacitly refuse them a place alongside St John as models for us? Is it that we do not need models who have incarnated the Carmelite Teresian identity in our new world with its values, its dialogue and ecclesial services? Is there not something fundamentally wrong in the fact that the modern "typical Carmelite" or role model that we normally invoke are exclusively women: St Thérèse of Lisieux, Blessed Elizabeth, Edith Stein . . . ? And what about the men?

Our Ideario

By this word I mean the doctrinal/spiritual heritage which we have received from our saints, from St Teresa down to the teachers of our own age. It is a treasure (*"tantum doctrinae thesaurum,"* as the Popes themselves have stressed). But, at the same time, it presents the group with a risk, precisely because the very quality and richness of their thought and because the spiritual guidelines of our Masters propose a model of life and a human and Christian manner of being that far outdistance the mediocrity and vulgarity which the life of every institutionalized human group seems to lead to. There follows a credibility gap between their "message" and the average level of our life. At the risk of falling into the well-known dichotomy between "having and being," I would still say we have adapted well to possessing this doctrinal heritage to the point that we can theorize about it and share it with the Church, but without incorporating it into life. Fortunately we can answer that in the last third of this century the Teresian Carmel has made great advances in becoming aware of its doctrinal legacy and the lived heritage it has received from St John and St Teresa, and its recent teachers as well. This is true in the novitiates and in ongoing formation as well as in the official reflection of the Order. However, it would be worthwhile taking stock of the extent to which the practical incorporation of the message in our life has kept pace with our theoretical knowledge and study of it.

Limits

We have already noted some limitations inherited from the past. In part we have overcome them. For example we have: our opening toward intellectual work and the normalization of academic studies for our young people; the establishment of some centers of higher studies; dialogue with the ecclesial magisterium of the last Popes fostering a growing awareness of the pastoral mission that we have in the Church; concentration on spiritual culture and on the pastoral promotion of the spiritual life as the preferential service of the Teresian Carmel. However, our foothold in certain qualified sectors of Church life remains precarious, for example, in the ecclesiastical sciences and in university centers. There are scarce possibilities of inter-disciplinary dialogue, for example, with various specialists or with the disciplines that have an interest in studying our saints. We do little in the field of communications media, even though they are indispensable for keeping us abreast of and involved with modern life, and in order to get out the Christian message. And there have been few initiatives in the field of pastoral ministry or renewal of pastoral methods.

In general, the Teresian Carmelite at this historic moment after the Council has made notable efforts to become aware once again of the values contained in the charism of his Founders, but he has not made a comparable effort to realize those values in present-day life. Much of the effort in that direction has been directed toward legislative renewal, but today laws are not wellsprings of vitality to which religious groups turn for their renewal, because laws cannot formulate the operative options, the practical choices, of the group. Creativity depends more on initiatives from the grass-roots level and from the impulse given by new blood; or in dialogue between these and the hierarchy.

PREPARING FOR THE TERESIAN CARMELITE OF TOMORROW

In response to this retrospective overview, historicist traditional posture, we will have to favor and encourage creativity, prophetism, and the will to dialogue with men and women and the culture(s) of today and tomorrow. Regarding these points, I want to propose only a few modest reflections.

First Suggestion

Renew and intensify that which is often called "interior inculturation" (trans: interiorization of values). Culture in the strict sense is not to be found only in large-scale expressions as in major ethnic groups or in privileged periods of cultural expression. On a more modest scale, culture can grow in and shape the life of human groups on all levels and in the most rudimentary groups. We find culture in tribes, in regions, in philosophical schools, in religious families, etc. In the tiny "collectivity" that St Teresa of Jesus and St John of the Cross drew together around themselves (1562-1591) a specific cultural expression took shape with a style of life, and "ideario," with its aesthetic preferences (at the least, a clear sensitivity to poetry), and (above all) a spirituality. And this culture was incarnate not simply in a group or school but rather in a movement that they started . . . "Interior inculturation" for us today would mean that we would have to cultivate these seminal values insofar as they are able to generate a group cultural "module," a lived spirituality, a human style of life together, an intellectual or scientific sense of direction, and pastoral priorities. It is a process that does not stop at tracing the outlines of past "modules," but rather recreates them within the contextual framework of the culture of men and women to-day. These are practical attitudes which together go against the grain of our tendency to study Carmelite spirituality like a branch of history or a cultural exhibit or specimen in a museum or archive. If the *Way of Perfection* and *Spiritual Canticle* and the *Story of a Soul* . . . do not serve to shape within a group a taste for the spiritual, a human style of common life, and our outlook on reading the gospels, they will remain mere "objects of study" and will not become sources of life and culture for the group. This is true not only of the three works mentioned above. It is true of the entire complex of our family's spiritual and doctrinal heritage. It is true of everything that might help to reconstitute from the inside a "group religious culture" or enable one to dialogue in proper terms with the culture of the environment. In our case, we will have to think through the questions of the effective role which our laws (*Rule* and *Constitutions*) must have among us, and what is the proper role of that other group of spiritual motivations: the role models, the spiritual *ideario*, the experience of God as witnessed to by our saints, the human and evangelical virtues that characterize us, etc., that are the warp and woof of our spirituality and which must be the starting point of every effort at interior inculturation.

Second Suggestion

Intensify our exterior inculturation in dialogue with modern culture and with the cultural variants of the various peoples among whom the Order is present. Above all, in general terms, we should not excessively limit our cultural horizons (even our intellectual ones). To lock ourselves into specialization in spiritual theology, or pastoral ministry of prayer, or Sanjuanist studies, etc. would be a loss to the specializations themselves. That means we must strike a balance between a specific pastoral ministry in agreement with our charism and a widening of our cultural horizons. For these reasons we must decisively foster the formation of nuclei of "intellectuals" (would that we had them already!) in the Order as well as the specializations that fall within the wide range of ecclesiastical and humanistic disciplines (Bible, canon law, pastoral ministry, theology, history, philosophy, psychology, pedagogy, sociology, the exact sciences, the arts). These are specializations which will have a normal function of "raising the level of culture" for the entire group. Perhaps for this we will have to create the indispensable infrastructures that we still lack, including everything from centers of studies and specialized libraries through economic funds for our publications. In the second place, and in response to particular cultural situations: The secularism which characterizes modern culture demands of a religious order like our own a new sensibility to determined human values. In the contrary case our religious and spiritual categories would not say anything to the men and women of that culture. How, for example, can we bring the message of St John of the Cross to bear on a culture impregnated with the theology and politics of liberation? How can we succeed in getting through the seemingly impenetrable barrier of materialistic and Marxist ideology? How can we make it possible for our Teresian and Sanjuanist spirituality to come into a mutually enriching contact with the spirituality or cultures of the peoples of the East among whom the Order is present? In fact, it is easy to demonstrate how the presence of the Carmelite Nuns and their function as witnesses to contemplative life in geographic areas not specifically Christian is much more diffused than that of the Carmelite friars.

The inculturation of the religious and the Carmelite in today's world demands a special effort of "communication and adaptation." This involves special impact in every sector of the "mass media."

(1) Taking as a concrete point of reference the teaching of St John of the Cross (which so greatly determines our identity and our ministry), it is obvious that the saint formulated his teaching in assertions, categories and symbols of another cultural era. To repeat them without translating them is to weaken their relevance and usefulness. They must be rethought and rewoven into the fabric of our world, and that demands deep cultural coexistence on our part with the world (in philosophy, sociology, literature, arts . . .).

(2) One of the most striking characteristics of modern culture, of both intellectuals and the man in the street, is the immense power of the "mass media": newspapers, advertising images, audio-visual communication, TV. All of these offer intrinsic possibilities for evangelization, spreading doctrine, promoting currents of spirituality, etc. But they are means that use highly refined techniques that cannot be improvised on the spur of the moment. The mass media were objects of intense attention in the Council and continue to be so in the postconciliar Church. Today, it seems unthinkable to undertake serious pastoral projects without the use of these working tools. All the more so in view of how little attention we have paid to them. Fortunately, we do have a couple of specialists in the field of journalism and broadcasting. Should we not welcome them and look for suggestions from them? Should our Order not have some kind of press office for communicating with the press, with information agencies, with public opinion whenever it is necessary, without leaving everything to improvisation? What resources and new possibilities would the field of communication of information offer for the internal culture of the Order and for our programs of apostolic service?

(3) As is well known, in the postconciliar Church, many renewal "movements" carry out a special function alongside the official magisterium. And they decisively influence the progress of the Church and its process of inculturation in contact with the masses or with groups called together by the Spirit. It is on this same charismatic level of witnessing that we must situate our service to the Church: that is the prophetic aspect of our religious life. How can we witness to this precise grace which has been conferred on the Teresian Carmel without paying attention to the signs of the time, that is to say, without moving into this world of the poor among whom the Spirit is breathing today, bringing to life seeds of renewal for the good of the Church? If the Teresian Carmel is in fact a movement or a current of spirituality within the Church, then it will necessarily tend to exchange its contributions with the currents and movements present in the heart of the pilgrim Church.

CONCLUDING SUMMARY

Among the chief objectives for the promotion of a culture that would characterize the Teresian Carmel, I would single out:

(1) An effort toward interior inculturation (commitment to living and not simply to handing on the spirituality of the saints of our Order);

(2) An enlargement of the range of scientific (scholarly or academic) culture of the Order in both ecclesiastical and secular sectors (with more specialists and more attention to infrastructures);

(3) The development of sensitivity toward particular cultures and toward grass-roots renewal movements;

(4) Greater familiarity with the "mass media" as a tool for translating and transmitting "by osmosis" our spirituality to today's culture;

(5) Concentration on a pastoral ministry that agrees with our Carmelite Teresian charism.

TERESA THEMES

THE ECONOMIC CONCERNS
OF MADRE TERESA

Teofanes Egido

Teofanes Egido has contributed the first and larger part of this article to CARMELITE STUDIES 1. He continues researching the life and times of St Teresa: last year he published a critical edition of the transcript of the famous court case of the Cepeda family, El Linaje Judeoconverso de Santa Teresa *(The Judeoconverso Lineage of St Teresa).*

THE ECONOMIC CONCERNS OF MADRE TERESA

The amount of attention given to economic concerns in Teresa's writings is truly remarkable. This fact warrants, and even demands, that we pause to consider a theme which at first glance seems out of place among the personal topics concerning a woman who has been conveyed to us almost exclusively in terms of her mystical life,[1] but which is essential in a historical introduction to her works.

It is significant that the first of her writings to have been preserved should be a note which reproduces nothing more nor less than the customary formula of the time for extending an order of payment,[2] and that her last dated letter deals with the unsuitability of making a foundation in Pamplona "unless it is with an endowment," since in 1582 the alms were no longer as promising as in the past.[3] Finally, she died enduring the bitter sorrow caused by her relatives over questions of inheritance.[4]

151

During the dramatic period of her activity, Madre Teresa faced countless legal actions and financial worries, as well as foundations insured with generous endowments. She would suddenly find herself with unexpected money (which usually came for the legendary Indies), and just as often knew the repeated anguish of being penniless. She moved from a policy of founding in poverty (at the mercy of Providence) to a conviction that no new monastery should be founded without having its material resources well assured. She never tired of offering advice on a thousand proceedings and profitable investments, averting hardships, encouraging interconventual assistance and looking anxiously and expectantly toward Seville, hoping for the shipments that in those days obsessed all Castilians who, according to Pierre Vilar, were so much under the curse of gold.

Precious Metals as a Model of Spiritual Dynamics

A clear indication of Teresa's sensitivity to the economic factor is that, in order to make spiritual phenomena more comprehensible to her readers, she does not hesitate to resort to money and precious metals as a handy, everyday model from the material world, useful for examining the criteria of evaluation for supernatural realities. And we should not forget the connections which Teresa's ancestors had with the world of money.

The Madre had the good fortune to live in a Castile with a strong, stable monetary system; she handled, in large or small amounts, the most durable money, which had remained practically unaltered since the stabilization completed by the Catholic Monarchs [Ferdinand and Isablla] at the end of the previous century, in contrast to the instability of the rest of Europe in this regard at the same period.[5] Consequently, the denominations used by the saint for everything were the following: the golden *escudo* (equal, in the money of account, to 350 *maravedís*), though the most common gold coin continued to be the *ducado* (375 *maravedís*); the silver coin *par excellence* was always the *real* (34 *maravedís*), and the most common of the copper coins were the *cuarto* and the *ochavo* (4 and 2 *maravedís*), though, at least in her writings, she preferred to speak of the poor, ordinary *blanca* (½ *maravedí*).[6]

Thus Teresa often associates God and his works with gold, in terms which were very pleasing to those Castilians who were as anxious to possess that precious metal as they were ordinarily deprived of it. Among the works of God the soul was naturally outstanding, and in describing it she found no better recourse than to compare it to a medieval castle, "made entirely out of a diamond" (as it says in the *Interior Castle*), fashioned by the "divine glazier" from "gold of the greatest purity."[7] References to gold, jewels, and a whole array of precious stones flow from her pen when she attempts to explain things worked in the soul according to their importance in the dynamic of union, the great gift that cannot be produced by human effort, and "from that very fact we see that it is not of the same metal as ourselves, but fashioned from the purest gold of divine wisdom."[8]

By contrast, when discussing human works, especially those of poor Madre Teresa, she resorts to the metaphor of the least valuable coin, not to *blancas*, which she so often needed in real life, but to the copper *cornado*, archaic and perhaps no longer legal tender, as if she were speaking of an old, worthless coin.[9] "Here we will help with our little *cornado*," she says to Don Francisco de Salcedo, alluding to the prayers with which she repays his generosity.[10] Thus, when she carefully delineates her complete response to divine mercy in the autobiography of her soul, she has recourse once again to the *cornado*, meager payment for such exalted gifts.[11]

Everyday Income and Expenditures

The classical sources [of information on Teresa's life], as well as those more directly personal, make little attempt to capture the painful daily preoccupation with survival; nevertheless, it is worth dwelling upon such a vital aspect of everyday life, especially when one of the fundamental concerns of the foundress, as we shall see, was that her daughters and sons never lack sufficient good food, even if it meant sacrificing the abstinence, for example.[12]

Fortunately, the account book signed by the Madre in Medina del Campo during the short interval of her imposed term as prioress (August and September, 1571) has been preserved. It is a concise document, from a rather brief period, but explicit enough to enable us to follow the economic life of a monastery founded in poverty, without endowments, according to the saint's original ideal for her Reform.[13] Recorded day by day, the income and expenditures yield the final balance:

TABLE 1

INCOME AND EXPENDITURES OF MEDINA DEL CAMPO

(in maravedís)

1571	Income	Expenditures
August	5,171	17,003
September	12,780	10,719
TOTAL	17,951	27,722

The monthly ledgers, besides indicating that the Madre, the subprioress, and the procurator signed accounts that failed to balance, also prove the financial need and the obvious imbalance between income and expenditures, to the detriment of the former, despite the deceptive appearance of September. The surplus that month is due to an extraordinary donation by the merchant Juan de Medina, who surprised the community with the large sum of 20 *ducados* [7,500 maravedís] on the second Friday of September.

The basic item under *expenditures* is that constituted by the diet of bread, eggs and oil, generally complemented with fruit, fish (more expensive), rice and greens. Pedro the servant, the part-time workers, and the sick nuns above all, had their ration of good meat assured, even on Friday; the menu was occasionally enriched with the most varied spices and delicacies. Besides the food, any extraordinary expense could unbalance the budget: the cost of the trip for the superiors whom the Madre replaced, the foundress's own journey, the sending of special messengers, some repair to the roof or irrigating wheel, etc., greatly exceed the normal costs for food and sacristy.

With regard to the *income*, the items could not be simpler. They were based on the two sources specified by the Madre in the *Constitutions*: the product of the nuns' labor, and donations from the outside. "Let them help support themselves by the work of their hands" was a clear recommendation against the customs of her day, and she adds the further clarification that it must not be oppressive labor, but peaceful, "not elaborate work, but spinning."[14] In spite of this, and of eliminating workrooms in her monasteries,[15] the visitator must keep in mind the need for work and for the accounting of its productions, if only to flatter natural feminine vanity a little, as she will say in a splendid chapter [of her *On Making the Visitation (of the Discalced Nuns)*].[16]

With such conditions the economy of the house remained at the mercy of the market. Since the account books of the foundations in industrial centers (Segovia, Toledo) have been preserved, it is possible to measure the importance of the communities as partial auxiliaries of textile manufacture. Medina's record plainly reveals what one would have expected: that the income derived from labor was insignificant in comparison to the magnitude of the donations, the real support of daily Carmelite finances.

TABLE 2

INCOME FOR THE COMMUNITY OF MEDINA DEL CAMPO

(in maravedís)

1571	Labor	Donations
August	367	4,693
September	426	12,354
TOTAL	793	17,047

We repeat that an increase of a few maravedís [between August and September] is hardly significant in an account which is so deficient and shows no general pattern of improvement. What is clear is that normal expenditures could be handled thanks to this charitable income, as the similar case of Valladolid confirms.[17] But not all markets were as generous as Medina, where, according to the Madre's own testimony, they were also prodigal with donations in non-monetary gifts,[18] nor could the Carmelite convents withstand the competition of other monasteries in identical circumstances, or that of the army of urban poor, whether real or feigned.

At least this was the case for the first foundation. The Avilans were never very generous with San José, and when they learned that the greatest patron of the convent, Francisco de Salcedo, had the bright idea of leaving a tiny legacy to the nuns ("which is too little to provide anything to eat, and there is not even enough for supper"), the city "stopped giving the alms they used to give."[19] As a last resort they elected Madre Teresa as prioress.[20] The saint's observation is full of humor and realism: "They have made me prioress now out of pure hunger."[21]

The Problem of Dowries and Fixed Incomes [rentas]

In any case, if normal donations and the income from their own labor served to take care of daily needs, they were never sufficient to cover the cost of erecting new houses and the extraordinary expenses of later improvements, nor for paying any sizeable debts. The truth is that in such circumstances, and in the convents founded in poverty, generous benefactors abounded: the saint's brother Lorenzo, who had become wealthy; the opulent María de Mendoza; numerous merchants and the many characters whom Teresa gratefully mentions throughout her *Life, Foundations,* and *Letters.* But the dowries of the professed sisters were the principal and permanent contribution.

On this point, as in everything related to money, Teresa's opinion underwent a profound, not to say radical, transformation while her original program of reform was becoming modified by contact with the real world.

At first, shocked by her experience at the Incarnation, she was determined to eliminate all that could constitute an offense against the strictest equality in the community. For many years she had felt the tragedy of a system of religious life built upon the very social exigencies which created the problems it attempted to solve. It is not necessary to emphasize again the comfortable circumstances of some nuns and the misery of others in that monastery.[22] Such inequality was rooted in the difference in dowries. Because of this the reformer never hides her hostility toward dowries, which is not to deny that she gladly received those which were offered, remedies for needs from the first foundation to the last.[23] But, it was by no means part of her original intention to impose on her future nuns this require- ment which was universally demanded in both civil and religious life, much less to use the unequal dowries as justification for a regime of personal privilege.[24] She reasoned that the community, when refusing a candidate or denying profession to a novice, would be able to act without the constraints created by a com- pelling dependence on the income that would be lost.[25]

Nevertheless — and here too her previous experience was at work — it was necessary to face the risk that, lured by the equal- ity, some might enter who were "merely looking for a secure future."[26] To avoid this other danger, and because donations and labor would not suffice to combat the hunger which arose in San José or Beas, she established the principle that "giving no dowry is unsuitable," though she continued to preach that "if the nuns are very much of our spirit we need not be too concerned about the dowry."[27]

By 1576, a year of changes, the saint's mind had already be- come clear in this matter. Nuns who, of course, met the other requirements were gauged according to their dowries. She re- joiced that in Beas, which was very needy, "they have received a nun whose dowry came to seven thousand *ducados*," and because "two more are about to enter with the same amount."[28] She ad- vises María de San José, "by all means take the nun, because the dowry you say she has is not bad,"[29] and she cautions her not to accept a Portugese applicant too readily, "for I have learned that you will not get a penny from the family, and we are not now in a position to take anyone for free."[30]

In conclusion, by the final phase [of Teresa's life] entry with- out a dowry was already exceptional. The norm was to encourage this contribution, which was the privilege of only some members of the varied social spectrum, given the disposable wealth at the time of Philip II. If initially at San José in Avila "four poor orphans would support one another because they were taken without any dowry,"[31] the Reform lost this mutual-aid character after it spread; poverty came to be interpreted in a very Teresian manner; and her monasteries, instead of being a haven for the needy and lodgings for aristocrats (though neither were lacking), became convents principally supported by middle-class members.[32]

This "bourgeois" character was reinforced by applying the saint's requirements to the candidates: among these it was especially emphasized that illiterates should not be admitted, and that the novices "be capable of praying the Divine Office."[33] Given the known (or suspected) level of literacy at the time, the mass of countryfolk was automatically excluded from Teresian monasteries. The first profession books are eloquent in this respect; many of the *freilas* (lay sisters exempted from the dowry, who were expected to be "strong" for manual tasks) did not know how to sign their names (recall the interesting case of Anne of St Bartholomew), and a comparison of the geographic origins of almost all the Discalced nuns of 1581 reveals the telling scene of the choir nuns (with dowries), overwhelmingly of urban extraction, in contrast to the small minority of lay sisters, primarily of rural extraction.[34]

Teresa's discretion left wide margins for the application [of these requirements][35] which were suppressed five years after her death when members of the Chapter of Valladolid (1587) set "a fixed rate for the nun's dowries, something very foreign to our Holy Mother," as the disappointed but loyal María de San José testifies.[36] The economic foresight of the new General, the Genoan Doria, and the specification of the amount allowed the convents to face the impending financial crisis, but it closed Carmel to those (namely, the poor) who could not afford the considerable 500 *ducados* demanded.[37]

It was a similar story with *fixed incomes* [*rentas*]. To live off *rentas* was the desire of every powerful Castilian, and not only those of the sixteenth century. Whether this represented a medieval legacy, a rejection of Jewish or Moorish values, or the imposition of prevailing ideologies (because work was not respected as a source of wealth, or simply because money in land, in urban real estate, or in the most active elements of the royal estate was the most secure investment at a time of price fluctuations), it is certain that the concerned "projectists" of the day failed in their brave struggle to orient people toward more productive investments, when they came up against something which had turned into a symbol of social prestige and wealth.[38]

As we have seen in treating her social attitudes, St Teresa did not share in this obstinate tendency.[39] Coming from a *judeoconverso* background (a social stratum closely tied to the world of "despicable" work), and convinced of the demands (and security) of poverty, she opposed current custom and, contrary to the practice of other monasteries, planned her own on the economic foundation of work and donations, to the scandal and fear of many, but to the satisfaction of the *espirituales*.

Let us not forget that this break with tradition was not easy, nor was it considered when Doña Teresa de Ahumada planned the foundation of San José ("it was not my intention . . . that the house have no income; on the contrary, I would have desired the possibility that nothing be lacking").[40] The final chapters of the *Life* throw light on the inner struggle between her realism and the plans for a new poverty. In the end, her particular understanding of the "primitive" Carmelite *Rule*, divine locutions, the apparition of St Peter of Alcántara exhorting her "in no way [to] decide to receive an income,"[41] and (why not?) her certainty that the reformed life would be more secure against upsets if such material concerns were left to "the Lord of money and of those who earn money" [*Way* 2, 2], broke down all opposition, and she decided to obtain a brief from Rome "so that this monastery could exist without an income."[42] Thus San José in Avila was born and lived (with many difficulties, to tell the truth) without an income, that is to say, without the financial backing of money derived from fixed interest on capital which founders placed in the many opportunities for state, municipal, or private investment; so did the monastery of the rich market town of Medina del Campo, though with much greater ease.

The struggle came when her vision of founding in wealthy urban centers turned sour, and she found herself faced with the contingency of considering places without such economic resources, where donations were risky and there was scant hope of making anything off the small product of the nuns' labor. This happened in Malagón, the third foundation. With certain resources in grain and cattle, and a population of some 600 inhabitants, it was the exact opposite of the financial, industrial, or commercial cities which the Madre had in mind. Nevertheless, this village was the domain of a layperson,[43] viz., Doña Luisa de la Cerda, her great friend and collaborator; and the foundress could not totally refuse the hints (demands) of the eminent aristocrat.

The decision to found there involved two problems. One was secondary: the difficulty of observing the abstinence of the *Rule* (from which the community was promptly dispensed). The other was more far-reaching: the necessity of relying upon an income, "since the town was so small" [*Foundations* 9, 2-3]. St Teresa resisted Doña Luisa's "great importunity," but on this occasion the determined lady found enviable allies in the scholars led by Fr Báñez.[44] If before the Madre listened to the *espirituales* and the grim St Peter of Alcántara, now she was persuaded by the prudent judgment of the theologians, who were well-armed with the decrees of Trent and anxious not to curb the expansion of a spiritual force by difficulties whose solution had been foreseen by the Council.

This shows that the saint listened to whoever seemed fitting to her; and Malagón was the first of a series of monasteries erected upon an economic platform of fixed and secure incomes. Shortly before this date, in the *Constitutions* of 1568, she had ordained: "Let them live always on alms and without any income [*renta*]."[45] In 1576 she had already changed to a sensible arrangement of income and expenditures for houses with endowments, as a lesser evil than the indebtedness and inequality of the Incarnation.[46] In one of her letters which exudes the most clarity, flexi-

bility, and realism, written in 1581 at the end of the process and
prior to the Chapter which was so important for her Reform,
she recommends to Gracían a radical modification on this point
previously so close to her heart. This eloquent text reveals how
far she had come since 1562: "In our *Constitutions* it says that
the houses should be founded in poverty and cannot have an income [*renta*]. As I now see that all are on their way to having
one, see if you think it is good to delete this and everything about
it in the *Constitutions*, so that those who see it will not think they
have become lax so quickly; or let the Father Commissary say
that, since the Council permits it, they may have it."[47]

This was her thinking. Teresa's foundational practice in this
respect is well-defined and follows clear standards expressed
time and again by the Madre. After the period of hesitation, her
norm reveals how she was affected by the specter of the economic
and human scene she had encountered while living in the Incarnation:

> In the case of monasteries founded with an income, my goal al-
> ways was that they have enough to keep the nuns from depen-
> dence on relatives, or on anyone, and that food and clothing
> and everything necessary be given to them in the house, and
> that the sick be very well cared for. For when necessities are
> lacking, many troubles arise. In founding many monasteries in
> poverty, without an income, I never lack courage or confidence;
> I am certain that God will not fail them. In founding them with
> an income that is small, everything fails me; I find it better that
> they not be founded. (*Foundations* 20, 13)

Thus, anyone who reviews the contracts for the foundations
of Malagón, Alba de Tormes, and Soria will be amazed at the
accumulation of details that the saint demands, how she ties up
all the loose ends and how exacting someone can be who never
worries about minutiae. For the same reason she raises numerous
objections to the viability of Caravaca, Beas and Villanueva de
la Jara.

It can be said, in spite of everything, that the foundations
with an income were always the exception, repeated but only

justified by the economic poverty of the place where the convent was located and required by the most serious pressures and imperatives. Thus, she never became reconciled to the idea of erecting monasteries with incomes in rich cities, even if it meant resorting to a thousand stratagems and to fictitious contracts, as happened in Seville and even more clearly in Burgos. This privilege was reserved for populations of a specific character:

> The places where I did agree to make foundations with an income were small and required that either I found the monastery with an income or not at all since without one there would be no means of sustenance. (*Foundations* 24, 17)

The consequences for her program are shown in the following table:

TABLE 3
INITIAL ECONOMIC BASE OF THE
TERESIAN FOUNDATIONS

FOUNDED IN POVERTY		FOUNDED WITH AN INCOME	
Foundation	Year	Foundation	Year
Avila	1562	Malagón	1568
Medina del Campo	1568	Pastrana	1569
Valladolid	1568	Alba de Tormes	1571
Toledo	1569	Beas	1575
Salamanca	1570	Caravaca	1576
Segovia	1574	Villanueva de la Jara	1580
Seville	1575	Soria	1581
Palencia	1580		
Burgos	1582		

Credit and Investment

Although Teresa's convents had few opportunities to accumulate capital for investment during the brief period of her life in which she was making foundations, by 1582 a certain reality was already taking shape: alongside monasteries that "lived off fixed incomes [*rentas*]" as comfortably as Soria, there existed others indebted to an alarming degree, such as Avila and even Seville. Some resorted to ordinary forms of credit to liquidate their financial deficits, and to deal with the growing costs of buildings or transfers; others took advantage of contemporary methods for putting their surplus funds into profitable investments. The Madre had to take care of all this, worried or calm, but always immersed in a sea of red tape, of narrow- or wide-ranging operations, of complicated contracts whose clauses had to be read and re-read in every detail so that what occurred in Seville might not be repeated, when (through haste or an honest misunderstanding) the guarantor, Don Lorenzo de Cepeda, had to avail himself of sanctuary in order to avoid prison over a dispute about taxes.[48]

These transactions obsessed Teresa and everyone involved in them to such a point that at odd moments they appear as another model of spiritual phenomena. Such is the case in the *Way of Perfection*, when to underline the authentic, lasting value of humility and obedience in contrast to the debatable worth of delights, graces, and raptures, she can think of no better comparison than the following: "This understanding [of self based on humility and obedience] is like current coin (*moneda que corre*), like unfailing revenue, like having a perpetual annuity (*juros perpetuos*) and not a sum that's paid only once (*censos al quitar*); for these other experiences come and go."[49] And, in effect, she needed to become entangled and disentangled from *juros* and *censos* in order to counsel her less experienced daughters, with an agility which would naturally surprise those who do not allude to these fundamental preoccupations in their classical biographies [of her].

Whatever form they took because they were interest derived from capital based nearly always on the income of the State, the "devilish annuities (*juros*)" (as Carande calls them) were on the one hand the Austrian monarchy's[49a] most formidable instruments of credit, and on the other hand the most secure form of investment (along with landholdings), notwithstanding all the uncertainty lent them by royal intrigue and speculation. Given the growing financial needs of the monarchs, and in spite of exhausting the resources of the public treasury's ordinary revenues, they toyed like mad with paper money, which led to increased hoarding of precious metals and assured many of comfortable but unproductive "living off of fixed incomes [*rentas*]," splitting dividends.

The Madre frequently had to deal with these papers as a fortunate creditor. Thus, among the annuities [*rentas*] granted to Malagón by Doña Luisa de la Cerda, the most secure is undoubtedly the one obtained in this way. The same occurs in Alba de Tormes, Seville, etc.[50] The interest rate of this bond on the public debt was usually about 7%; but since it was possible to do better, when St Teresa met someone as well acquainted with these matters as Fr Doria and a benefactress as generous as Doña Beatriz de Beamonte, she obtained a splendid annuity, as she records in the *Foundations* with special gratitude to the Genoan financier.[51]

Together with the form of paper currency just mentioned, that of *censos* ("private" bonds) was the most widely circulated in Castile. A means of credit for municipalities as well as individuals, this original mortgage on rural or urban property (and on other goods) obliged the purchaser to the concession of some interest (also about 7%) on capital credited by the seller. Temporary and perpetual mortgages, under more or less fraudulent terms of agreement, contributed to the indebtedness and progressive exploitation of the rural population, which saw in these advance payments from the aristocracy, the Church, and the moneyed bourgeoisie, the only opportunity to finance better production, to try breaking new ground or else become further ruined in the attempt.

Madre Teresa also had to deal with these mortgages [*censos*] as protagonist, beneficiary, debtor, and counsellor. When Lorenzo bought the estate of La Serna, his sister did not conceal her pleasure, but neither did she hide her misgivings at seeing him saddled with "heavy mortgages [*hartos censos*]" in order to liquidate the enormous cost of the transaction (14,000 *ducados*).[52]

With everything else, she had to struggle with municipal mortgages [*censos*] under a whole variety of forms. Pieces of property belonging to an entailed estate [*mayorazgo*] were sold with all of the complicated formalities of a case such as Medina,[53] while others in identical circumstances bypassed the stringent legislation, as happened with the Salamanca houses of Pedro de la Banda, a tightfisted and irascible gentleman who sold them in order to redeem a mortgage owed on some pasture land.[54] The structure of the Segovia foundation determined that it be made with a mixed perpetual rent [*censo perpetuo*] of money and kind (2,900 *maravedís* and 14 chickens annually), which was payable to the rigorously exacting local council, and which the community would have to redeem at 375,000 *maravedís*, etc.[55]

Generally, Teresa was wary of these mortgage bonds, and only had recourse to such a form of credit in real emergencies, as in Segovia; in order to pay for the rest of the excellent houses of Diego de Porres "it was necessary to assume a mortgage, and from that point on the house was expressly and officially mortgaged; from the feast of St James onward there was a payment at the rate of 14 of the said 1,800 *ducados*."[56] In Seville another such case occurred; her correspondence with the brilliant prioress repeatedly indicates the concern caused by the burden of those mortgages [*censos*] and the slowness in redeeming them, "since you have the money to do so."[57]

Her constant norm was not to burden herself with these debts, especially when she foresaw the immediate purchase of the house, in order to avoid useless expenses.[58] If such a course became inevitable, it was necessary to pay off the mortgage as soon as possible, for the simple reason that "it would be a very great good to lighten the burden."[59]

Moreover, the movement of these negotiable values is revealed when a complicated affair of *censos* versus *censos*, and redeeming *juros*, is initiated. In Toledo, the *censos* and *juros* of La Palma resolved a situation which was cleared up thanks to the tranfer of the *censos* and *juros* of the good merchant Avila.[60] In Segovia, the redemption of mortgages against the foundation was accomplished by those in favor of Doña Ana Jimena and Doña

María de los Barros, as well as by the anticipated help of "a very good income [*censo*] from a sister, amounting to 630 *ducados.*"[61] The foundation of Caravaca was erected on the basis of a very unequal portfolio: a collection of small and moderate annuities [*censos*] which the benefactresses provided, along with other usable or marketable objects.[62]

Examples could be multiplied, but we prefer to spare them. The Madre's practice is very clear: when she had her choice — and she did not always have it — she preferred hard cash to bonds placed on public or private debts. At least she felt an acknowledged aversion to the latter, since not all of those involved had the same promptness nor the same resources in paying the interest charges. She says this clearly to her brother: "And do you think there is no work in collecting mortgage payments [*censos*]? One is always involved in distraints. You see that it is just a temptation."[63]

And it would likewise be a temptation for us to continue delving into such fruitful areas, which the mystical doctor's writings illuminate, and the knowledge of which is indispensible for an integral grasp of her work. It is understandable that the supernatural phenomena associated with an extraordinary personality like Teresa's should have dazzled and diverted the interests of Teresianists to less mundane points than those here considered. But it would be dishonest to present her enchanting pages from perspectives which obscure the indispensible material reality of one who herself laments that "at a time when I considered money and business hateful, the Lord wanted me to be involved in nothing else."[64] (Trans. M. Dodd and S. Payne)

NOTES

TRANSLATOR'S INTRODUCTORY NOTE: This is a translation of the fourth and final part of Teofanes Egido's "Ambiente Histórico" in *Introducción a la Lectura de Santa Teresa*, ed. Alberto Barrientos (Madrid: Editorial de Espiritualidad, 1978), 43-103. A translation of the first three parts appeared in *Carmelite Studies*, vol. 1, 122-82, under the title of "The Historical Setting of St Teresa's Life."

This concluding section has taken longer to prepare, partly because there are no exact English equivalents for many of the economic terms Egido employs. "Rentas," for example, are endowments, bequests, or other legal arrangements entitling the owner to certain set revenues paid at predictable intervals. We have generally translated this term as "fixed income," since the *dependability* of these revenues was what most concerned Teresa and her contemporaries. "Censos" refers to bonds on public or private debts, and has ordinarily been translated here as "mortgages."

Egido's quotations from St Teresa are taken from the E.D.E. edition of her works, i.e., from Santa Teresa de Jesús, *Obras Completas*, 2d ed. (Madrid: Editorial de Espiritualidad, 1976). Thus, in references to the saint's correspondence, Egido lists first the date and heading as they appear in the E.D.E. edition, followed by the number of the paragraph from which a particular passage is taken. We have preserved (and sometimes corrected) this numbering for the sake of anyone who might wish to consult the original Spanish.

With the exception of her correspondence, all translations of Teresa's writings are from *The Collected Works of St Teresa of Avila*, trans. Kieran Kavanaugh and Otilio Rodríguez, 3 vols. (Washington, DC: ICS Publications, 1976–1985), unless otherwise noted; all other translations are ours. The numbering of chapters and paragraphs in the E.D.E. and I.C.S. editions is usually the same. Finally, we have added several translators' notes, to clarify certain obscurities in the text and to point out which of the secondary works cited are available in English translation. We appreciate the expert advice given us by Dr Jodi Bilinkoff and Fr Kieran Kavanaugh.

1. This void has been partially filled by the work of Luis Ruiz Soler, *La personalidad económico administrativa de la Santa Madre Teresa de Jesús* (Zarauz, 1970), although he gives more space to the administrative than to the economic dimension.

2. All editions of the correspondence begin with this piece, dated in Avila, August 12, 1546.

3. Letter to Catalina de Cristo, September 15-17, 1582.

4. Efrén de la Madre de Dios and Otger Stegginck, *Tiempo y Vida de Santa Teresa*, Biblioteca de Autores Cristianos, vol. 283, 2d ed. (Madrid: Editorial Catolica, 1977), 966-68.

5. For the stability of the Castilian coinage compared with the rest of Europe, see F. Braudel and F.C. Spooner, "Prices in Europe from 1450 to 1750," in The Cambridge Economic History of Europe, vol. 4: *The Economy of Expanding Europe in the Sixteenth and Seventeenth Centuries*, ed. E.E. Rich and C.H. Wilson (Cambridge: Cambridge Univ. Press, 1967), 458.

6. Current monetary equivalencies are impossible to establish except by resorting to a comparison of purchasing power. By way of a very elementary

orientation it can be said that specialized laborers (carpenters, plasterers) earned a salary of 80 *maravedís* in 1515, 170 in 1562, and 204 in 1582. A day-laborer would earn about half of this, i.e., 34, 60 and 102 *maravedís* during the same periods. With this wage he had to face the primary expenses of basic goods, which increased in the following proportions throughout the sixteenth century (using the years 1511, 1549 and 1560 as the points of reference): 7.3, 21.7 and 43 *maravedís* for a liter of oil; 2, 14 and 28 *maravedís* for a liter of wine; and 1.7, 3.4 and 6.8 *maravedís* for a kilo of bread. More complete data may be found in *Historia social y económica de España y América*, ed. J. Vicens Vives, vol. 3 (Barcelona, 1961), 43ff. Even more detailed is Earl J. Hamilton, *American Treasure and the Price of Revolution in Spain*, Harvard Economic Studies, vol. 43 (Cambridge, MA: Harvard Univ. Press, 1934).

7. C, 1, 1, 1. Letter to P. Gaspar de Salazar, December 7, 1577.

8. C, 4, 2, 6. TRANSLATOR'S NOTE: The translation here is our own.

9. The *cornado*, a copper coin of former times, did not survive the stabilizing of monetary parity by the Catholic Monarchs [Ferdinand and Isabella]. See *Historia social y económica de España y América*, vol. 2, 99; Felipe Mateu y Llopis, *La moneda española* (Barcelona, 1946), 170.

10. Letter to Don Francisco de Salcedo, July 6, 1568.

11. L, 21, 5.

12. See the explicit data in this regard in the letter to Don Cristobal Rodríguez de Moya, June 28, 1568, 9.

13. Archives of the Carmelite Nuns of Medina del Campo. Silverio, in *Biblioteca Mística Carmelitana* [hereafter cited as *BMC*], ed. Silverio de Santa Teresa, vol. 5 (Burgos, 1933), 370–74, edited only part of these accounts, the full knowledge of which I owe to the help of Fortunato Anatolín.

14. *Constitutions*, 9. TRANSLATOR'S NOTE: The translation here is ours.

15. *Constitutions*, 8; *On Making the Visitation* [*of the Discalced Nuns*], 10.

16. *On Making the Visitation* [*of the Discalced Nuns*], 12. She advises the visitators of her nuns: "And it is very consoling to the nuns when they are at work to know that it will be seen by the visitator. Even though this is not an important matter, we women who live so enclosed a life and whose consolation is found in pleasing the visitator should be treated at times with a sensitive understanding of our weaknesses."

17. In fact, according to the amount sheet which has been preserved (Blue Book, Archives of the Discalced Carmelite Nuns, fol. 139v, the existence of which was pointed out to us by José Vicente Rodríguez), the community's incoming revenues in July 1578 were similar in proportion to those of Medina: 6,742 *maravedís* in alms (in this case almost entirely from Doña Ines and Doña María de Mendoza), and only 340 from their own labor.

18. In July itself, just a few days prior to the time embraced by the transcribed accounts, she speaks of "a great gift in the way of food" (Letter to P. García de San Pedro, July 1571, 2). At the beginning of the foundation she notes that "others gave us many alms for food" (F, 3, 14).

19. Letter to Don Lorenzo de Cepeda, December 15, 1581, 8; to María de San José, November 8, 1581, 4; to Gracián, October 4, 1580, 7. Compare the worried tone of the letter to Don Alvaro de Mendoza, September 6, 1577.

20. "By almost all the votes," the profession book testifies significantly in this regard; see the edition of the *Escritos de Santa Teresa*, ed. Vicente de la Fuente, Biblioteca de Autores Españoles, vol. 55 (Madrid, 1861), 569.

21. Letter to María de San José, November 8, 1581, 3. And full of anguish, she begs: "All of you pray to God for me that I can give the nuns here something to eat, for I do not know what to do (Ibid, 29).

22. The situation is clear enough from the data offered by Otger Steggink, *La Reforma del Carmelo español: La visita del General Rubeo y su encuentro con Santa Teresa 1566-1567*, Textus et Studia Historica Carmelitana, vol. 7 (Rome: Institutum Carmelitanum, 1965). The monastery of Avila was no exception. Bennassar has been able to prove that circumstances were the same in San Quirce in Valladolid; see Bartolome Bennassar, *Valladolid au siècle d'Or* (Paris: Mouton & Cie., 1967), 100 and idem, *L'homme espanol: Attitudes et mentalités du XVIe au XIXe siècle* (Paris, 1975), 67-68. Vázquez de Prada observes that these conditions were fairly widespread; see "La Reforma Teresiana y la España de su tiempo," in *Santa Teresa en el IV Centenario de su Reforma carmelitana* (Barcelona, 1963, 58). TRANSLATOR'S NOTE: The second of the books by Bennassar is available in English as *The Spanish Character* (Berkeley: Univ. of California Press, 1979).

23. Two providential dowries—along with money coming from the Americas —solved the initial economic problem of the Reform. See the letter to Don Alonso de Cepeda, December 23, 1561; and F, 31, 42.

24. "Insofar as I can remember I have never refused to accept anyone because of lack of money, provided I was satisfied with all the rest" (F, 27, 12-13); see also the letter to P. Domingo Báñez, February 28, 1574. This is even clearer in *Constitutions*, 21 and *On Making the Visitation* [of the Discalced Nuns], 28.

25. "Thus I beg God to give you light. You are very fortunate that you do not receive dowries, for it can happen that in monasteries where they are accepted the nuns, so as to avoid giving back the money—which they no longer have—leave the thief in the house who steals the treasure from them; which is a great pity (W, 14, 4; this corresponds to 20, 1 in some editions of the Valladolid autograph of the W).

26. W, 21, 1; 14, 1.
27. Letter to María Bautista, January 21, 1577, 3; Letter to María de San José, May 6, 1577, 10.
28. Letter to P. Ambrosio Mariano, October 21, 1576, 26; Letter to María de San José, October 5, 1576, 15.
29. Letter to María de San José, July 11, 1577, 5.
30. Letter to María de San José, September 26, 1576, 3.
31. L, 36, 6. TRANSLATOR'S NOTE: The translation here is ours.
32. See Antonio Dominguez Ortiz, *El Antiguo Régimen: Los Reyes Católicos y los Austrias* (Madrid, 1973), 236.
33. *Constitutions,* 21. TRANSLATOR'S NOTE: The translation here is ours.
34. This can be seen in the appendices to Vicente de la Fuente's edition of *Escritos de Santa Teresa,* 364.
35. Note the range of dowries brought to Malagón, mentioned by Efrén-Steggink in *Tiempo y Vida,* 388.
36. María de San José, *Ramillete de mirra* (Burgos, 1966), 400.
37. From this date onward a dowry of 500 *ducados* is reflected more universally in the profession books that we have examined (Valladolid, Palencia, Medina del Campo).
38. Noël Salomon, *La vida rural castellana en tiempos de Felipe II* (Barcelona, 1973) 252. TRANSLATOR'S NOTE: The "projectists" [*tratadistas*] were a group of tract-writers of the period who proposed plans for economic and administrative reforms.
39. Saint Teresa reflects concretely on the collective psychosis regarding *rentas* and their connection with "honor" [*la honra*] (in the W, 2, 6, for example. Many people came to her monastery asking the nuns to pray that they might acquire *rentas* (see W, 1, 1).
40. W, 1, 1.
41. L, 35, 3; 36, 20-21.
42. L, 39, 14.
43. Salomon, *La vida rural castellana,* 355, 357.
44. Ibid. Note the mobilization of the theologians of Alcalá in the consultations on this matter (Archives of the Carmelite Nuns of San José, Avila, no. 29 of the catalogue of Lucinio del Santísimo).
45. *Constitutions,* 9.
46. *On Making the Visitation* [*of the Discalced Nuns*], 10, 13.
47. Letter to Gracián, February 21, 1581, 9. "In founding [monasteries] with an income that is small . . . I find it better that they not be founded (F, 20, 13). "The price of things keeps on increasing so much that one needs an income of about 300,000 (*maravedís*) in order not to be poor" (undated letter which Silverio places toward the end of 1579). Nevertheless, she

retains the wish in her heart: "Given my choice, I would not want to see the houses already founded in poverty with an income (*renta*)" (Ibid). TRANSLATOR'S NOTE: The two latter fragments appear as nos. 439 and 440 in the enumeration of the letters found in the second edition of the *Obras Completas*.

48. F, 25, 9. TRANSLATOR'S NOTE: The incident mentioned here arose over the wording of the purchase deed for a new house in Seville, which Lorenzo was helping the nuns to buy, and concerned the payment of a sales tax known as the *alcabala*. Apparently Don Lorenzo and the other guarantors failed to read the fine print, for although they had understood beforehand that this tax was to be paid by the sellers, the contract itself clearly states that the purchasers were liable. A lawsuit ensued, and when the nuns refused to pay the tax, the sellers attempted to arrest the principal guarantor, Don Lorenzo, who managed to escape by taking advantage of the "right of sanctuary" at Los Remedios, the monastery of the Carmelite friars in Seville.

49. W, 18, 7; this corresponds to 19, 5 in some editions of the Valladolid autograph.

49a. TRANSLATOR'S NOTE: The rulers of Spain during this period (Charles I, Philip II) were members of the Hapsburg dynasty, which had originated in Austria.

50. The investment capital (principal) yields 30,000 *maravedís* in Malagón, 150,000 in Alba, and 98,000 in Seville; see *BMC*, 5:376; 6:159-60, 233.

51. "At twenty-five per thousand" [*de a 25 el millar*] (F, 30, 4). See our edition of the *Foundations* in *Obras Completas*, 2d, chap. 30, note. 4. Regarding the complicated system of securities, see Ramón Carande, *Carlos V y sus banqueros*, vol. 2, 90ff. TRANSLATOR'S NOTE: Some commentators indicate that "twenty-five per thousand" would equal 2.5%; apparently sums were expressed in proportions of one thousand rather than one hundred to avoid extra decimals.

52. For interesting data confirming the Saint's economic perspective on this undertaking, see: Letter to María de San José, October 5, 1576, 3, Letter to Lorenzo de Cepeda, January 2, 1577, 10; Letter to María de San José, December 10, 1577; and Letter to María de San José, February 8-9, 1580, 14.

53. *BMC*, 5:357ff.

54. F, 19, 7-10; *BMC*, 6:143ff.

55. *BMC*, 5:191.

56. Ibid., 186.

57. Letter to María de San José, June 18, 1576, 3; Letter to María de San José, December 21, 1579, 12.

58. Letter to Gracián, December 4, 1581, 1.

59. Letter to María de San José, September 7, 1576, 7.
60. *BMC*, 5:414ff.
61. *BMC*, 6:187; and Letter to María Bautista, September 11, 1574, 3.
62. Ibid. 270-79.
63. Letter to Don Lorenzo de Cepeda, January 2, 1577, 10.
64. Letter to Don Lorenzo de Cepeda, January 17, 1570, 12.

DAME JULIAN OF NORWICH AND ST TERESA OF JESUS: SOME OF THEIR COMPLEMENTARY TEACHINGS

Adrian James Cooney

Father Adrian J. Cooney is a member of the I.C.S. He draws on his experience and research as an instructor of English on the college level for this fascinating study of parallels between Julian of Norwich and St Teresa.

Interest in one mystic ordinarily leads to the study of others. Teresa of Avila's position is unrivaled in the history of women mystics; and she contributes significantly to the development of Western mysticism. Dame Julian of Norwich, Norfolk, England, a fourteenth-century mystic, is less well known. Today, however, her teaching is becoming increasingly better appreciated. The purpose of this essay is to explore Teresa's writings and those of Julian on the following subjects: God, man, and Christ's reconciliation.

JULIAN AND TERESA: TWO ERAS, ONE FAITH

There is little that we know of the life of Julian of Norwich. Nowhere, so far, are we informed where she was born; nor are

173

we given her family name or other details of her life. There is strong evidence, however, of her being well acquainted with some of the great Benedictine writers; and some believe she was a Benedictine nun of the nearby monastery of Carrow who had received permission to become an anchoress.

Part of Julian's life was manifestly spent as an anchoress in a cell attached to the Church of St Julian in Conisford at Norwich. While it is disputed whether or not Julian was living in this anchorhold or at her own home when she became seriously ill, we do know from her own writings that her revelations began on May 13, 1373. She first wrote them down in what is now generally designated as the short text; then, subsequently, she expanded this into what is now called the long text.

The two volumes of *A Book of Showings to the Anchoress Julian of Norwich*[1] edited by Edmund Colledge, OSA, and James Walsh, SJ, give the Middle English version of her accounts. These volumes are the basis for my own Modern English translation which is used throughout this essay when portions of Julian's writings are incorporated. After each quote a concise note gives its origin as either from the short or long text; the number of the Revelation follows; then, the page numbers locate the passage in Colledge-Walsh's Middle English version. Wherever quotations used are part of commentaries by other authors, these are in each case so indicated and identified.

In their preface to their scholarly work, Colledge and Walsh propose: "Only after the completion of the long text, we believe, did she occupy the anchorhold of St Julian's Church and embrace the solitary and enclosed life."[2]

In 1934 the American medievalist Hope Emily Allen discovered Margery Kempe's *Book*. Margery describes in this work her visit to Julian and makes clear where the anchorhold is located. Also, Margery gives an account of the wise and prudent direction that the anchoress gave her during that visit lasting a few days. The title "Dame," used before Julian's name, is found in Margery Kempe's autobiography. Margery, speaking of herself, tells us:

> . . . Then she was bidden by our Lord to
> go to an anchoress in that same city,
> named Dame Jelyan . . . [3]

When Julian was

> ...thryttye wynters alde and a halfe...

(thirty and a half years old), she became seriously ill; and this grave illness occurred in

> ... the yer of our Lord a thosand and thre
> hundered and lxx111 the xiii day of may...

(the year of our Lord a thousand and three hundred and seventy-three on the 13th day of May). From this we can establish that Julian was born in the latter part of 1342.[4] That she was alive at least for part of 1416 is evidenced by a legacy of 20 shillings left to "Julian, recluse at Norwhich," as James Walsh, SJ, records in his *Revelations of Divine Love of Julian of Norwich*.[5] He tells of an earlier bequest, dated May 19, 1404, which reads:

> To Julian, an anchoress at St Julian's Church,
> Norwich, 12d. and 8d. to Sara living with her.

("Sara" is regarded as a servant who took care of the meals, errands, and other duties. It was a common practice for an anchoress to have a servant or servants.)

It appears that Julian died sometime during 1416 since another anchoress occupied the anchorhold in the latter part of that year. The evidence for this comes from the bequests of John Plumpton and of Lady Suffolk cited by R.M. Wilson in his article "Reviewing Robert K. Stone's *Middle English Prose Style: Margery Kempe and Julian of Norwich*."[6]

While her writings give so few biographical details, Julian does share with us some of her experiences, as well as the revelations she received. In the following account, Julian tells us of the desires that she had before the Revelations:

> I desired three graces by the gift of God. The First was to have recollection of Christ's Passion. The second was bodily sickness, and the third was to have of God's gifts three wounds. For the first came to my mind with devotion; I thought that I had great feeling in the Passion of Christ, but still I desired to have more by the grace of God. I thought that would I have been in that time with Mary Magdalen and with the others that were Christ's

lovers, that I might have seen bodily the Passion of our Lord that he suffered for me, that I might suffer with him as others did that loved him . . . Notwithstanding all this true belief, I desired a bodily sight, wherein I might have more knowing of the bodily pain of our Lord our Savior, and of the compassion of our Lady and of all his true lovers that were living at that time and since; for I would have been one of them and suffered with them . . . For the second, it came to my mind with contrition, freely without any seeking, a willful desire to have as God's gift a bodily sickness, and I would that this bodily sickness might have been so hard as to the death, so that I might in the sickness take all my rites of Holy Church, expecting myself that I should die, and that all creatures that saw me might think the same, for I would have no comfort of the fleshly nor earthly life . . . For the third . . . I conceived a mighty desire, praying our Lord God that he would grant me three wounds in my lifetime, that is to say the wound of contrition, the wound of compassion, and the wound of willfully longing for God. (Short, Chapter 2, pp. 201-206.)

Her prose style, despite all her attempts to convince us of her being illiterate, a frequently used device employed by her contemporary writers, betrays a skill that can be compared to Chaucer's prose work *Consolation of Philosophy*, a translation he is believed to have made about 1380 of Boethius' *De Consolatione Philosophiae*. Julian was recording her revelations at that time.[7]

A careful reading of the short and long texts shows that Julian was a woman of profound understanding and learning. Far from being the unlettered poor woman that she so often describes herself as, she rivals both the anonymous author of *The Cloud of Unknowing* and Walter Hilton, the masterful spiritual director and writer of *The Scale of Perfection* who were both her contemporaries.

Julian uses a number of rhetorical figures conveying her thought effectively. Among these are alliteration, synonymous phrases, repetition, antithesis, admonition, argument, definition, exclamation and exposition, metonymy, personification, and transition; these are but some of the forty-seven examples found in her writings.[8]

While some of her teachings may at first surprise us and even seem to be unorthodox, we discover in analyzing all her texts that they are in keeping with the teachings of the Church and represent an authentic development within Christian mysticism. Colledge and Walsh make clear in their introduction to the Middle English text that "no one of her teachings in any way conflicts with her assurance that all which she was shown, and all that prayer had taught her of its meaning, is in total accord with every other truth which God has revealed to men."[9]

Julian's visions are related to Christ's Passion; and she derives from them an understanding of the extent of God's love and his reconciling humankind to him through these sufferings. Julian writes:

> For he is everlastingness and he made us only for himself and restored us by his precious passion, and ever keeps us in his bless-ed love; and all of this is of his goodness. (Long, Revelation 1, Chapter 5, p. 303.)

Julian emerges from her writings as a woman of both outstanding learning and exceptional dedication. These characteristics enabled her to address the Church and present the Revelations in a way that would make them acceptable. Those who have carefully studied her writings are unable to find the least trace of contrivance or deceit. Many questions arise because of the want of biographical details, especially concerning her education. Some regard her as a great scholar, knowledgeable in Latin, rhetoric, the works of William of St Thierry, and, above all, the Scriptures. In concluding their introduction to their presentation of both Middle English texts, Colledge and Walsh write:

> Whether it was Carrow or somewhere else which gave her training is inessential. She had been schooled in "the Abbey of the Holy Ghost."[10]

During the fourteenth century, English mysticism was informed by the national trait of individualism that caused many to live an eremitical rather than a cenobitical life. Julian of Norwich was among the numerous men and women who sought this way of life. Some of the others known today are Richard Rolle who became a hermit in Yorkshire, and an Austin friar, William Flete, who traveled to Lecceto, Italy, and lived in a hermitage there; there was also the anonymous Durham monk who lived as a hermit on Farne Island. Both the unknown author of *The Cloud of Unknowing* and Walter Hilton, the author of *The Scale of Perfection*, wrote for those, like Julian, living in solitude. Unlike the Celtic solitaries of that time, there was in evidence a prudent restraint in ascetical practices and conditions that were a part of Irish monastic and eremitical traditions. Julian's writings are singularly free of the mention of any severe penances; and, from what we can learn, her life was ordered principally to assure her of as much time as possible for contemplative prayer and taking part in the liturgies. The anchorhold was built against the church and the recluse could observe all the ceremonies through an opening.[11]

Before presenting Julian's teaching, it is helpful to have a description of the sixteen revelations. Julian presents this in her first chapter in the Long Text; and I will list these in Julian's words but without giving the entire presentation of each revelation. The opening words are Julian's:

This is a revelation of love which Jesus Christ, our endless bliss, made in sixteen showings of which the *first* is: Christ crowned with thorns; the *second*, the discoloration of the fair face of Christ; the *third*, our Lord God Almighty is all wisdom and love; the *fourth*, the scourging of Christ's tender body; the *fifth*, the Passion of Christ overcomes the fiend; the *sixth*, the Lord rewards all his blessed servants in heaven; the *seventh*, to experience well-being is to be touched and illumined by grace, to experience woe is a temptation but with spiritual understanding we are preserved in love just as in the time of well-being; the *eighth*, Christ's last suffering and death; the *ninth*, the delight the Blessed Trinity has in the hard Passion of Christ, and Christ's wish for our solace and mirth; the *tenth*, the Lord reveals his blessed heart cleft in two by love; the *eleventh*, spiritual showings of his dear worthy mother; the *twelfth*, our Lord God is all sovereign being; the *thirteenth*, our Lord God wills that we have great regard for all his deeds and of the excellence of man's creation and our blame turned to honor; the *fourteenth*, our Lord God is the ground of our beseeching and also, rightful prayer and true trust; the *fifteenth*, that we should suddenly be taken from all pain and woe and have our reward in joy and bliss; and the *sixteenth*, the Blessed Trinity, our Maker, who dwells endlessly in our soul in Christ Jesus and preserves us out of love; and we shall not be overcome by our enemy. (Long, Chapter 1, p. 281-284.)

In analyzing some of Julian's major concepts relative to the spiritual life, it is helpful to keep in mind the reflection that Julian gives at the end of the account of the Revelations:

Thus was I taught that love is our Lord's meaning. And I saw full surely and in all that before God made us, he loved us, which love was never diminished nor ever shall be. And in this love he hath made all things profitable to us, and in this love our life is everlasting. In our making we had beginning, but the love in which he made us was in him from without beginning. In which love we have our beginning, and all this shall we see in God without end. (Long, Revelation 16, Chapter 86, p. 733.)

Teresa of Avila was born on March 28, 1515, almost two hundred years after Julian's birth. Unlike Julian, we know many facts about Teresa's life not only from her autobiography, letters and the other writings, but from the accounts of others, especially the Carmelite scholars who have provided for us detailed accounts of her life, teaching and work. Her position in spiritual theology has long been recognized; and her work in reforming the Carmelite Order has given her a singular place in history. It is needless to sketch in this essay Teresa's life; it is well known by all interested in mysticism within the Western tradition.

In 1582 Teresa died, in 1614 she was beatified, and in 1622, with Ignatius of Loyola, Francis Xavier, Isidore, and Philip Neri, she was canonized. Pope Paul VI in 1970 gave her the title of Doctor of the Church; and Teresa became the first woman to be honored with this title.

How obscure Dame Julian's life appears in comparison; however, these great mystics complement each other in their teaching. While their roles in history are different, both enjoy a popularity today unrivaled by the past. It would be absurd to belabor the obvious differences between their centuries, the fourteenth and the sixteenth. Assuredly, there are a number of contrasts just as there are some similarities, particularly when countries have a highly developed culture. The Spain of Teresa's day was far different from the Medieval England that was Julian's. Indeed, the Spain Teresa knew had changed significantly since the fourteenth century. The Renaissance in Spain was well established in Teresa's time, and its profound influence was felt in every part of society. This is seen dramatically in the designs of the buildings erected in Spain during this time. The classical tradition flowered into a baroque that freed artists and artisans from their earlier restraints; and this is as evident in Spain as it is in Italy and other countries of Western Europe. Even those unaware of its impact were influenced by this change.

What is significant in both the life of Julian and of Teresa is that in their spiritual writings they responded to the special needs of their day as viewed in the perspectives of both theology and philosophy. While it appears that Julian was unaware of John Wycliffe's criticism of religion as he saw it practiced in fourteenth-century England, she taught a positive approach to faith in Christ free of all the castigating and extremes in his preaching.[12]

Despite Teresa's confusion between the followers of Martin Luther and John Calvin, she was aware of the radical transformation accomplished by grace as opposed by both Calvin and Luther who uphold a merely imputed justification.[13] There are many beautiful passages found in both Luther's writings as well as Calvin's; but they must all be placed within the general context of their teaching. Calvin writes:

> The whole of man from head to foot is thus as it were drenched
> in a flood of wickedness so that no part has remained without sin
> and so everything which springs from him is counted sin.[14]

Teresa's writings are extensive, profound, and practical. If we find her wanting in the more speculative approach such as witnessed by both Julian and John of the Cross, she stands in an unrivaled position in her profound knowledge and ability to express herself through similes and metaphors that illustrate her understanding and experiential knowledge in the spiritual life. Unlike Julian's writings, however, Teresa's present many difficulties both for those translating her works into other languages as well as those attempting to understand many passages in her original texts. She wrote with great rapidity and, more often than not, without any pause to reflect on what she had already written.[15]

It is necessary to limit the study of her writings to a few of her outstanding teachings on God, man, and their reconciliation, the three themes this essay embraces. Each concept could become an extensive thesis, and, indeed, would merit that evaluation; but this essay, because of its obvious limitations presents only a glimpse of what could and should be developed further.

As the quotations from Teresa are, like Julian's, integral to this essay, the reference giving its location will appear immediately after each excerpt, not in a footnote. All quotations are taken from the first English translation by Kieran Kavanaugh, OCD, and Otilio Rodriguez, OCD, published by I.C.S., of Washington, D.C. The reference will give the number of the volume of *The Collected Works of St Teresa of Avila*, the name of Teresa's work, and then Chapter, section, and page numbers.

As in the study of Julian, it is impossible to restrict a number of Teresa's quotations to a specific subject since they touch on many matters. A good example is found in this passage from her *Life*:

> . . . pay no attention to the kinds of humility . . . in which it seems to some that it is humility not to acknowledge that God is giving them gifts. Let us understand most clearly the fact: God gives them to us without any merit on our part. And let us thank His Majesty for them, because, if we do not acknowledge we are receiving them, we will not awaken ourselves to love. And it is very certain that while we see more clearly that we are rich, over and above knowing that we are poor, more benefit comes to us, and even more authentic humility . . . Let us believe that he who

gives us the blessings will give us the grace so that when the devil begins to tempt us in this way we shall understand and have the fortitude to resist — I mean, if we walk with sincerity before God, aiming at pleasing him alone and not men. (Vol. 1, *Life*, 10, 4, p. 75.)

How skilled Teresa is in going to the heart of that false humility that mocks the nature of the soul's purpose and God's grace. The necessity of accepting at the same time both one's sinfulness and the surety of God's mercy revealed through grace is contrary not only to the teaching of Luther and Calvin but also to those Catholic writers who choose to focus on humankind's depravity rather than its potential for holiness.

This delicate balance of humility and ambition is developed by Teresa in the following passages:

It seems clear to me the will must in some way be united with God's will. But it is in the effects and deeds following afterward that one discerns the true value of prayer; there is no better crucible for testing prayer. It is quite a great favor from our Lord if the person receiving the favor recognizes it, and a very great one if he doesn't turn back . . . It is good to try to understand how we can obtain such a favor; so I am going to tell you what I have understood about this.

Let's leave aside the times when Our Lord is pleased to grant it [delight in prayer] because he wants to and for no other reason. He knows why; we don't have to meddle in this. After you have done what should be done by those in the previous dwelling places: humility! humility! By this means the Lord allows himself to be conquered with regard to anything we want of him. (Vol. 2, *The Interior Castle*, 4, 2, 8-9, pp. 325-326.)

A passage that recalls Julian's description of God and, more specifically, of Christ as "Mother," is given in *The Interior Castle*. Teresa attempts to describe the spiritual marriage:

. . . the feeling is so powerful that sometimes the soul cannot avoid the loving expressions they cause, such as: O Life of my life! Sustenance that sustains me! and things of this sort. For from those divine breasts where it seems God is always sustaining the soul there flow streams of milk bringing comfort to all the people of the castle. (Vol. 2, *The Interior Castle*, 7, 2, 6, p. 435.)

In an earlier passage on the same subject of the union with God that takes place in the seventh dwelling place, Teresa writes:

When the soul is brought into that dwelling place, the Most Blessed Trinity, all three Persons, through an intellectual vision, is revealed to it through a certain representation of the truth. First there comes an enkindling in the spirit in the manner of a cloud of magnificent splendor; and these Persons are distinct, and through an admirable knowledge the soul understands as a most profound truth that all three Persons are one substance and one power and one knowledge and one God alone. It knows in such a way that what we hold by faith, it understands, we can say through sight — although the sight is not with the bodily eyes of the soul, because we are not dealing with an imaginative vision. Here all three Persons communicate themselves to it, speak to it, and explain those words of the Lord in the Gospel: that he and the Father and the Holy Spirit will come to dwell with the soul that loves him and keeps his commandments. (Vol. 2, *The Interior Castle*, 7, 1, 6, p. 430.)

In her *Spiritual Testimonies* Teresa tells us:

The imaginative visions have ceased, but it seems this intellectual vision of these three Persons and of the humanity of Christ always continues. This intellectual vision, in my opinion, is something much more sublime. Now I understand, as it seems, that those imaginative visions I experienced were from God, for they disposed the soul for its present state. Since it was so miserable and had so little fortitude, God led it as He saw was necessary. In my opinion, when visions are from God, they should be greatly prized. (Vol. 1, *Spiritual Testimonies*, 65, 3, p. 364.)

Teresa in introducing the image of the castle and her commentary on the first dwelling places stresses the soul's beauty and sacredness; and she finds in the concept an ideal means for teaching this truth:

> There came to my mind what I shall now speak about, that which will provide us with a basis to begin with. It is that we consider our soul to be like a castle made entirely out of a diamond or of very clear crystal, in which there are many rooms, just as in heaven there are many dwelling places. For in reflecting upon it carefully, Sisters, we realize that the soul of the just person is nothing else but a paradise where the Lord says he finds his delight. So then, what do you think that abode will be like where a King so powerful, so wise, so pure, so full of all good things takes his delight? I don't find anything comparable to the magnificent beauty of a soul and its marvelous capacity. Indeed, our intellects, however keen, can hardly comprehend it, just as they cannot comprehend God; but he himself says that he created us in his own image and likeness.
>
> Well, if this is true, as it is, there is no reason to tire ourselves in trying to comprehend the beauty of this castle. Since this castle is a creature and the difference, therefore, between it and God is the same as that between the Creator and his creature. His Majesty in saying that the soul is made in his own image makes it almost impossible for us to understand the sublime dignity and beauty of the soul. (Vol. 2, *The Interior Castle*, 1, 1, 1, pp. 283–284.)

It is of interest to observe that Teresa began her writing of the first redaction of her *Life* early in 1562 according to the internal evidence found in this work. This first redaction was read with interest by the censor García de Toledo after she presented it to him in June 1562.[16] He then returned it to her at the end of 1563 with a request for further details that would add to the clarity of the text. In addition to these, Teresa added a more extended and detailed presentation of her whole spiritual life and not just the state that she was in at the time. Specifically, Teresa responded by adding chapters 11 through 22 in which she develops an allegory that is a treatise on prayer. Her *Life* was in the hands of the Inquisition in 1577, and her confessor, Fr Jerome Gratian, urged her to write the work we know as *The Interior*

Castle.[17] Almost fifteen years had passed and Teresa, at 62, had been experiencing and understanding for five years a high degree of mystical prayer.[18]

In *The Interior Castle* there is a greater experiential knowledge and a consequent awareness of this as she herself professes in the second chapter on "The First Dwelling Places":

> . . . although in other things I've written the Lord has given me some understanding, I know there were certain things I had not understood as I have come to understand them now, especially certain more difficult things.

Typical of her humility, she quickly adds:

> The trouble is that before discussing them, as I have said, I will have to repeat matters that are well known; on account of my stupidity things can't be otherwise. (Vol. 2, *The Interior Castle*, 1, 2, 7, pp. 290-291.)

Julian in her long account of her Revelations tells us near the close of Chapter 86, the final chapter:

> For twenty years after the time of the showing save for three months, I received an inward teaching, as I shall say: It belongs to you to take heed to all the properties and condescensions that were shown in the example though you may think it mysterious and indifferent to your sight. (Long, Revelation 14, Chapter 51, pp. 520-521.)

And in the closing chapter of the long text, Julian writes:

> And from the time that it was showed, I desired often times to know in what was our Lord's meaning. And fifteen years after and more, I was answered in a ghostly understanding, saying thus: What would you know the Lord's meaning in this thing? Know it well, love was his meaning. Who showed it to you? Love. (What showed he to you? Love.) Wherefore showed it to you? For Love. (Long, Revelation 16, Chapter 86, pp. 732-733.)

Both Teresa and Julian had achieved greater understanding

during the years following their earlier writings. The spiritual growth each attained enabled them to understand better the graces they had received and to find better ways of sharing this wisdom with others. Julian always speaks of her accounts as being for every Christian; and Teresa wrote for her spiritual daughters and others who looked to her for guidance.

GOD: TRIUNE, INCARNATE AND VICTORIOUS

John of the Cross recognized the excellence of Teresa's account of spiritual betrothal and marriage. In his commentary on *The Spiritual Canticle*, Stanza 13, he reminds the reader that he has promised in the prologue his intention to give only:

> . . . a brief explanation of these stanzas, such a discussion will have to be left for someone who knows how to treat the matter better than I. Then too, the blessed Teresa of Jesus, our Mother, left writings about these spiritual matters, which are admirably done and which I hope will soon be printed and brought to light.[19]

(John has reference to the treatment of raptures, ecstasies, and other elevations and flights of the soul enjoying this high state of spirituality.)

We are wanting an evaluation such as that John of the Cross gives to Teresa's writings by anyone of Julian's contemporaries; however, Paul Molinari's analysis of the theological and mystical teaching in the short and long texts expressed in his introduction to his work, *Julian of Norwich, The Teaching of a 14th Century English Mystic*, merits quoting: ". . . the longer version gives a much more complete account of the same experience augmented by further supernatural communications and Julian's reflections, and possibly elements due to her reading, to instructions received by others, and so on."[20]

Teresa happily chose the imagery of the castle to represent the soul; we find a similar usage in Julian's Revelations in writing about God and man. She says:

He made man's soul to be his own city and his dwelling place, which is the most pleasing to him of all his works. (Long, Revelation 14, Chapter 51, p. 525.)

A more developed statement of this is made by Julian in her short text:

But then lay I still awake, and then our Lord opened my ghostly eyes and showed me my soul in the middle of my heart. I saw my soul as large as it were a kingdom; and by the conditions that I saw therein, I thought it to be a worshipful city. In the middle of this city sits our Lord Jesus, very God and very man, a fair person of large stature, worshipful, highest Lord . . . And my soul is blissfully occupied with the Godhead, that is sovereign might, sovereign wisdom, sovereign goodness. (Short, Revelation 9, Chapter 22, p. 268.)

For Julian, it was impossible to separate Christ from the Trinity. She wants us to understand this, and in the fourth chapter of her Revelations she writes of her first revelation:

. . . suddenly the Trinity filled full my heart most of joy, and so I understood it shall be in heaven without end to all that shall come there. For the Trinity is God, God is the Trinity. The Trinity is our maker, the Trinity is our keeper, the Trinity is our endless joy and our bliss, by our Lord Jesus Christ and in our Lord Jesus Christ. And this was shown in the first sight and in all, for where Jesus appears the Blessed Trinity is understood as to my sight. (Long, Revelation 1, Chapter 4, pp. 294–296.)

We find in Teresa a similar approach as is seen in the passage from *The Interior Castle*, 7, 1, 6 (as quoted on page 183 of this article).

Teresa's concept of Christ always acknowledges his union with the Eternal Logos. Speaking of the indwelling of the Lord, she refers to the sufferings endured by Christ and the desires that the soul should have:

The desires these souls have are no longer for consolations or spiritual delight, since the Lord himself is present with these souls and it is His Majesty who now lives. Clearly, his life was nothing but continual torment, and he makes ours the same; at least with the desires, for in other things he leads us as the weak, although souls share much in his fortitude when he sees they have need of it. (Vol. 2, *The Interior Castle*, 7, 3, 8, p. 440.)

It is through the Passion and Death of Jesus Christ that man is saved from his sins. Both Julian and Teresa were conscious of this and it was the *saving* death of Jesus that is an important part of their spiritual teaching and their reflections on his Passion. This is evident in Julian's Revelations; and it is well known how much emphasis Teresa put on the sufferings of the Lord and the part they had both in her conversion and in the subsequent development of her Christology.

While both mystics dwell on the various stages of prayer, specifically what is called "contemplative prayer," it must be seen that this advancement is all part of the ongoing reconciliation of humankind to God. Indeed, the entire spiritual life from its beginning to its fulfillment can be understood properly only in terms of this redemption.

Julian's revelations begin with a vision of the suffering Christ:

. . . suddenly I saw the red blood running down from under the garland, hot and fleshly, plenteously and lively, right as it was in the time that the garland of thorns was pressed on his blessed head. Right so, both God and man, the same that suffered for me. I conceived truly and mightily that it was himself that showed it me without any means. (Long, Revelation 1, Chapter 4, p. 294.)

In her commentary on the ninth revelation, Julian dwells on the joy and bliss that Christ had in the Passion; and she speaks explicitly of the Trinity and the sufferings of Jesus:

All the Trinity wrought in the passion of Christ, ministering abundance of virtues and plenty of grace to us by him; but only the maiden's son suffered, whereof all the blessed Trinity enjoys. And this was shown in these words: Are you well paid? By that other word Christ said: If you are well paid, I am well paid, as if he had said it is joy and liking enough to me, and I ask nothing else of my travail but I might pay you. (Long, Revelation 9, Chapter 23, pp. 391–392.)

There are many references found in Julian's work on the matter of salvation, and some of these are of exceptional beauty and relevance; but it is obvious that this study must limit itself. Unfortunately, Julian has been misunderstood by some of her commentators; among those who question her orthodoxy in her teaching on sin is Dom Roger Hudleston who translated Julian's writings and analyzed them.[21] Julian writes:

And God showed that sin shall be no shame, but an honor to man, for just as to every sin there is answering a pain by truth, right so for every sin to the same soul is given a blessing by love. Just as every sin be punished with divers pains if it be grievous, right so shall they be rewarded with divers joys in heaven for their victories, as much as the sins have been painful to the soul on earth. (Long, Revelation 13, Chapter 38, p. 445.)

Well aware of the possibility of her teaching being misunderstood and even interpreted as a making light of sin, Julian writes:

. . . now because of all this ghostly comfort that is before said, if any man or woman be stirred by folly to say or think: if this be true, then were it good to sin to have the more merit, or else to count less of sin, beware of this stirring. For truly, if it comes, it is untrue and of the enemy. (Long, Revelation 13, Chapter 40, p. 456.)

Julian shows her perception of what is the perfect disposition toward sin:

For the same true love that touches us all by his blessed comfort, the same blessed love teaches us that we shall hate sin only for love. And I am sure by my own feeling, the more that each natural soul sees this in the courteous love of our Lord God, the more loathed is he to sin, and the more he is ashamed. (Long, Revelation 13, Chapter 40, p. 456.)

Rather than making light of sin, Julian gives us a profound insight into its horror:

> For if it were laid before us, all the pain that is in hell and in purgatory and on earth, death and other, than sin we should rather choose all that pain than sin. For sin is so vile and so much to be hated that it may be likened to no pain which is not sin. And to me was shown no harder hell than sin, for a natural soul hath no pain but sin; for all is good but sin, and nought is evil but sin. (Long, Revelation 13, Chapter 40, pp. 457–458.)

As Julian brings her account of Revelation 13 to a close, she writes of Christ's love for us and his mercy and grace, and closes this chapter with a strong statement on love:

> No more than his love is broken to us for our sin, no more wills he that our love be broken to ourself nor to our every Christian; but nakedly hate sin and endlessly love the soul as God loves it. Then should we hate sin like God hates it, and love the soul as God loves it. For these words that God said are an endless comfort: I protect you full truly. (Long, Revelation 13, Chapter 40, p. 459.)

In Teresa's account of an intellectual vision she received while at Avila, probably in 1571, we have a contrast between a soul in grace and one in sin:

> Once while I was in prayer, the Lord showed me by a strange kind of intellectual vision what a soul is like in the state of grace. I saw this (through an intellectual vision) in the company of the most Blessed Trinity. From this company the soul received a power by which it had dominion over the whole earth. I was given an understanding of those words of the *Song of Songs* that say: *Veniat dilectus meus in hortum suum et comedat*. I was also shown how a soul in sin is without any power, but is like a person completely bound, tied, and blindfolded; for although such a person desires to see, he cannot, nor can he walk or hear — and he is in great darkness. Souls in this condition make me feel such compassion that any burden seems light to me if I can free one of them. I thought that by understanding this condition

as I did — for it can be poorly explained — it wasn't possible for me to desire that anyone lose so much good or remain in so much evil. (Vol. 1, *Spiritual Testimonies*, 20, pp. 329-330.)

Julian in her reflection on her fourteenth revelation writes, as does Teresa, of the soul united with God through grace:

And for the great endless love that God has to all mankind, he makes no distinction in love between the blessed soul of Christ and the least soul that shall be saved. For it is full easy to believe and trust that the dwelling of the blessed soul of Christ is full high in the glorious Godhead, and truly, as I understood our Lord's meaning, where the blessed soul of Christ is, there is the substance of all the souls that will be saved by Christ. (Long, Revelation 14, Chapter 54, p. 561.)

It is unfortunate that more attention has not been given to Julian's development of her teaching, specifically on sin. She does not make light of sin, and she is writing for those whom she describes as follows: "I speak of such men and women that for God's love hate sin and dispose themselves to do God's will." (Long, Revelation 16, Chapter 73, p. 667.)

Julian knows well the obstacles that occur among those preoccupied with past sins who consequently suffer from a lack of faith in God's mercy. Today, much of psychotherapy attempts a healing of the guilt complex, often with little, if any, success. Julian's teaching is as valid today as it was in the fourteenth century and provides an understanding of the proper attitude toward sin. At the close of Chapter 73, she writes:

For love makes might and wisdom full meek for us; for just as by the courtesy of God he forgives our sin after the time we repent, so wills he that we forget our sins as against our stupid heaviness and our doubtful dread. (Long, Revelation 16, Chapter 73, p. 670.)

Julian intends that her readers understand well that her teaching on sin is directed to those who will to serve God and may be hindered by preoccupation with their past sins; and she wishes at the same time that they attend to this teaching on sin:

... I know well the soul that truly takes the teaching of the Holy Ghost, it hates sin more for the vileness and the horribleness than it does all the pain that is in hell. For the soul that beholds the kindness of our Lord Jesus, it hath no hell but hell's sin, as to my sight. And therefore it is God's will that we know sin and pray busily and work willingly and seek teaching meekly so that we fall not blindly therein; and if we fall, that we rise readily. For it is the most pain that the soul may have, to turn from God at any time by sin. (Long, Revelation 16, pp. 684-685.)

The following passage illustrates Julian's acceptance of the teaching of the Church on eternal punishment. With reference to the devil, and to the damned, she writes:

I saw the devil is reproved by God and endlessly damned. In which sight I understood that all creatures that be of the devil's condition in this life and their ending, there is no more mention made of them before God and all his holy ones than of the devil, notwithstanding that they be of mankind, whether they have been christened or not; for although the revelation was shown of goodness in which was made little mention of evil, yet I was not drawn thereby from one point of the faith that Holy Church teaches me to believe. (Long, Revelation 13, Chapter 33, pp. 427-428.)

In her *Life*, Teresa shows a remarkable strength in dealing with these evil forces:

I took a cross in my hand, and it seemed to me truly that God gave me courage because in a short while I saw that I was another person and that I wouldn't fear bodily combat with them; for I thought that with that cross I would easily conquer all of them. So I said: "Come now all of you, for, being a servant of the Lord, I want to see what you can do to me ..." These enemies don't know how to attack head-on, save those whom they see surrender to them, or when God permits them to do so for the greater good of his servants whom they tempt and torment. May it please His Majesty that we fear Him whom we ought to fear and undersand that more harm can come to us from one venial sin than from all hell together. (Vol. 1, *Life*, 25, 19 & 20, p. 169.)

Teresa gives an account of what took place while she was at prayer one day. How graphically she describes this experience:

> . . . while I was in prayer one day, I suddenly found that, without knowing how, I had seemingly been put in hell. I understood that the Lord wanted me to see the place the devils had prepared there for me and which I merited because of my sins. This experience took place within the shortest space of time, but even were I to live for many years I think it would be impossible for me to forget it. The entrance it seems to me was similar to a very long and narrow alleyway, like an oven, low and dark and confined; the floor seemed to me to consist of dirty, muddy water, emitting a foul stench and swarming with putrid vermin. At the end of the alleyway a hole that looked like a small cupboard was hollowed out in the wall; there I found I was placed in a cramped condition. All of this was delightful to see in comparison with what I felt there. What I described can hardly be exaggerated. (Vol. 1, *Life*, 32, 1, p. 213.)

Teresa continues her description of this terrifying vision:

> I experienced a fire in the soul that I don't know how I could describe. The bodily pains were so unbearable that though I had suffered excruciating ones in this life and according to what doctors say, the worst that can be suffered on earth (for all my nerves were shrunken when I was paralyzed, plus many other sufferings of many kinds that I endured, and even some, as I said, caused by the devil), these were all nothing in comparison with the ones I experienced there. (Vol. 1, *Life*, 32, 2, p. 213.)

In Julian we find a passage typical of her positive approach even in the face of evil itself:

> God showed that the fiend has now the same malice that he had before the Incarnation, and also that he works as hard, and as continually sees that all the souls of salvation escape him gloriously by virtue of his (Christ's) precious Passion. And that is his sorrow; and full evilly is he ashamed, for all that God suffers him to do turns us to joy and him to shame and pain. And he has as much sorrow when God gives him leave to work as when he

works not. And that is because he may never do as evilly as he would, for his might is all locked up in God's hand. (Long, Revelation 5, Chapter 13, p. 347.)

Both mystics express their awareness of sin. Each, however, reveals a unique approach to this subject. Neither can be accused of making light of sin; rather, Julian and Teresa reveal the power of Christ over all evil forces; they put sin in its proper perspective theologically and psychologically.

Julian reflected on her *Revelations* for many years during which she received interior lights. These were unlike those given to her in 1373; they were rather graces she attributes to the Holy Spirit that "enlighten her mind and enflame her will" in deepening her knowledge and love of God. In commenting on this, Paul Molinari, SJ, writes: ". . . they were participation in God's light and love proper to the souls who have reached a high stage of union with God."[22] Since Julian gave many years to the development of her insights, it is important to study what she wrote in her later account. It presents a more in-depth interpretation of the revelations she received. In this essay there is a concentration on the spiritual aspects of these accounts rather than an attempt to present her recognized ability in speculative analysis and her literary skill.

For Julian all progress of the soul is an ascent to God and a movement away from the preoccupation with self. In the following prayer, Julian gives expression to this:

God, of your goodness give me yourself, for you are enough for me, and I may ask for nothing that is less than that may be full worship to you. And, if I may ask anything that is less, ever I am in want; but only in you I have all. (Long, Revelation 1, Chapter 5, p. 302.)

Another passage illustrates her concept of God and our relationship to him:

God the blessed Trinity, who is everlasting being, right as he is endless from without beginning, so right it was his endless purpose to make mankind, which fair nature was first prepared for his own Son, the second person; and when he by full accord of all the Trinity, he made us all at once. And in our making he knit us and oned us to himself, by which oneing we are kept as clean and noble as we were made. By the power of the same precious oneing, we love our Maker and take pleasure in him, praise him and thank him and endlessly enjoy him. And this is the working which is wrought constantly in every soul which will be saved, and which is the godly will. (Long, Revelation 14, Chapter 58, p. 582.)

In writing of God and humankind's relationship to him, she develops the theme in different ways, especially in her reflecting upon the intimacy that the soul enjoys with the Lord. As Julian describes this relationship of humankind to God she says:

And thus in our making, God almighty is our loving Father, and God all wisdom is our loving Mother with the love and the goodness of the Holy Ghost, which is all one God, one Lord. And in the knitting and the oneing he is our very true spouse and we his loved wife and his fair maiden, with which wife he was never displeased; for he says: I love you and you love me, and our love will never divide in two. (Long, Revelation 14, Chapter 58, pp. 582-583.)

GOD AS MOTHER

Julian is not the first to speak of God as our Mother; indeed, we find many passages in the Old Testament that reveal this concept used as a simile to express the love of God for mankind. Of the many that may be quoted, there stand out these verses in Isaiah:

What, can a mother forget her child that is still unweaned, pity no longer the son she bore in her womb? Let her forget; I will not be forgetful of thee. (Is 49:15)

Another verse:

I will console you then like a mother caressing her son. (Is 46:13)

It should be noted, however, that Julian goes beyond this scriptural use of contrast and simile and attributes motherhood directly to God. This was a tradition well established by St Anselm of Canterbury (1033–1109), and he should be regarded as specifically fostering devotion to the Lord, our Mother. Julian, however, as Molinari states: ". . . explicitly attributes the Motherhood to the Second Person of the Blessed Trinity."[23] The contemplation of the divine Logos in the bosom of the Trinity was a well known practice, and therefore, some of the mystics of the Middle Ages speak of using this concept in prayer. Julian develops this theme as she shares with us her revelations.

In Julian's *Revelations*, the concept of "motherhood" is used often; and in her logical development of her insights she uses the idea of the "Motherhood of Christ." Frequently when Julian writes about God, she is speaking specifically of the Second Person of the Holy Trinity. She writes:

> . . . in the second person, in knowledge and wisdom we have our keeping, and regarding our sensuality, our restoration and our saving, for he is our Mother, brother, and savior . . . (Long, Revelation 14, Chapter 58, p. 584.)

She continues her explanation of this attribution of motherhood to the Second Person of the Holy Trinity throughout Chapters 58 and 63; and Julian makes references to it constantly until Chapter 83 is completed.

The ability to present her reflections clearly is evident in the following passage in which the role each person of the Holy Trinity plays in our life is characterized:

> . . . all our life is in the three: in the first we have our being, and in the second we have our increasing, and in the third we have our fulfilling. The first is nature, the second is mercy, the third is grace . . .

> . . . the high might of the Trinity is our Father and the deep wisdom of the Trinity is our Mother, and the great love of the Trinity is our Lord; and all these we have in nature and in our sub-

stantial making. And, furthermore, I saw that the second person, which is our Mother, substantially the same dear worthy person, is now become our Mother sensually, for we are double by God's making, that is to say substantial and sensual. Our substance is the higher part, which we have in our Father, God almighty; and the second person of the Trinity is our Mother in nature in our substantial making in whom we are grounded and rooted, and he is our Mother of mercy in taking our sensuality. And thus our Mother is to us in divers manners working, in whom our parts be kept undivided; for in our Mother Christ we profit and increase, and in mercy he reforms us and restores, and by the power of his Passion, Death and Resurrection oned us to our substance. (Long, Revelation 14, Chapter 58, pp. 585–586.)

Julian introduces the concept of the Second Person of the Holy Trinity as the "Mother of Mercy" in whom we have our reforming and our restoring, and in whom our parts are united and all "oned to our substance"; it is developed by Julian because of its relationship to the sufferings of Christ in his Passion and Death. This approach makes it possible for Julian to say:

We know that all our mothers bear us to pain and dying. Ah, what is that? But our true mother Jesus, he alone bears us to joy and endless living, blessed may he be. Thus he sustains us with him in love and travail, into the full time that he would suffer the sharpest thorns and grievous pains that ever were or ever shall be, and died at last. And when he had finished, and thus borne us for bliss, yet not all this could make fulfillment of his marvelous love. And that he showed in these high and surpassing words of love: If I might suffer more, I would suffer more. He could not die again, but he would not stop working.

Wherefore it behooved him to find us, for the dear worthy love of motherhood had made him a debtor to us. (Long, Revelation 14, Chapter 60, pp. 595–596.)

It is obvious that Julian is reflecting on the mystery of the Holy Eucharist as she continues the theme of Christ's motherhood. She writes:

The mother may give her child to suck her milk, but our precious Mother Jesus, he may feed us with himself, and does full courteously and full tenderly with the Blessed Sacrament, that is the precious food of true life; and with all the sweet sacraments he sustains us full mercifully and graciously . . . (Long, Revelation 14, Chapter 60, pp. 596-597.)

In recalling the tenth revelation, Julian shows her skill in using the imagery of motherhood:

The mother may lay her child tenderly to her breast, but our tender Mother Jesus may lovingly lead us into his blessed breast by his sweet open side, and show us therein part of the Godhead and the joys of heaven, with ghostly sureness of endless bliss. (Long, Revelation 14, Chapter 60, p. 598.)

So convinced is Julian of the uniqueness of Christ's motherhood that she tells us:

This fair lovely word "mother" is so sweet and so natural in itself that it may not truly be said of none nor to none but of him and to him who is the true Mother of life and of all. (Long, Revelation 14, Chapter 60, p. 598.)

Julian goes on to explain why this is true:

To the property of motherhood belong nature, love, wisdom, and knowledge; and it is God. (Long, Revelation 14, Chapter 60, pp. 598-599.)

Jesus fulfills the role of mother beyond infancy and early childhood. Julian describes his ongoing mothering:

The natural loving mother that wants and knows the need of her child, keeps it full tenderly, and the nature and condition of motherhood will. And ever as the child grows in age and in stature, she changes her work but not her love. And when it becomes older, she suffers that it be chastised in breaking down its vices to make the child receive virtue and grace. (Long, Revelation 14, Chapter 60, p. 599.)

Thus he is our Mother in nature by the working of grace in lower part, for the love of the higher. And he wills that we know it, for he will have all our love fastened to him; and in this I saw that all debt that we owe by God's bidding to fatherhood and motherhood is fulfilled in true loving of God, which blessed love Christ works in us. (Long, Revelation 14, Chapter 60, p. 600.)

... in our ghostly forthbringing he uses more tenderness without any comparison, by as much as our soul is of more price in his sight. (Long, Revelation 14, Chapter 61, p. 600.)

Julian's constant emphasis on the title "Mother Jesus" stresses the importance of confidence and at the same time the detachment from self that is necessary for spiritual growth. Molinari calls attention to the significance of Julian's teaching as expressed in the quotations that speak of Christ as Mother. He develops an analysis of the Lord's "Motherhood" or "working" in our "ghostly forthbringing."[24]

Today there is an awareness of the maternal aspects as useful images in describing God's relationship to us; and it is consistent with recent theological and sociological developments. While all Christian theologians recognize that God is neither male nor female, some find that motherhood and more basically the feminine concepts in general offer a rich store of metaphors and similes especially in the description of the depths of God's love, his forgiveness, and his gentleness, as well as many other attributes. Julian and a number of other mystics in the Western tradition have chosen to express their understanding of God's love through the use of both male and female characteristics; this is not an impinging on the male qualities of the humanity of Christ. With remarkable orthodoxy, Julian succeeds in presenting us with a deeper appreciation of the relationship that we have with our Savior, and indeed with the Holy Trinity itself.

The increasing interest manifested in the dialogue of Christians and the Eastern religions, especially with the Hindus and some Buddhists, has increased an awareness of the use of feminine imagery in conveying the depth of the mystery of the Godhead. Dom Jean Leclercq, in his preface to *Julian of Norwich, Showings*, quotes John Moffitt's statement in a paper submitted to the *Second Encounter of Christian Monks*, Bangalore, 1973:

It may be that Christians have little or no need for concepts such as these in their own approach to God. But it is not beyond the range of possibility that they may find them of the greatest help in developing a sympathetic approach to God as understood in non-Christian religions. I think it highly important that we try to understand the concept of God as Mother and all that it entails, not merely historically and as reflected in textbooks, but as it may be found today in living Hindu experience.[25]

Despite our appreciating the use of the concept of motherhood by mystics and other writers of our own tradition, we may ask why did Julian take hold of it so strongly and make use of it so frequently. While she is far from rejecting the more familiar masculine imagery used in describing the Trinity and even more, as noted, the reality of Jesus' masculinity, it would seem that as a woman she found that the feminine concepts enabled her to explore her own approach to life and make use of her thoughts and feelings. In her use of both masculine and feminine concepts we find her contributing to a deeper appreciation of God. Rather than replacing the concept of the fatherhood, Julian works for what Leclercq describes as an "integration of all that is best of what we can conceive and experience of God."[26]

Julian's desire to share with others the profound insights she had through her intimacy with God leads her to make use of the images proper to womanhood and to motherhood specifically.

Colledge and Walsh write in their introduction to their Middle English presentation of Julian's texts:

"God our mother" is infinitely more than a whimsical and exotic devotion. Julian came to perceive it as she penetrated the mystery of the Trinity and of the incarnate Word; and she may have been helped to expound it by those who before her had been led along the same line.[27]

Teresa bravely commented on passages of Solomon's Canticle, "The Song of Songs." We are aware that of all the books of the Bible, the "Song of Songs" came under special attention of the Spanish Inquisition. As Kavanaugh and Rodriguez note in their introduction to Teresa's *Meditations on the Song of Songs*, Fr Luis de León was brought before the Inquisition and was attacked because of his translation of "The Song of Songs" and this led to his being imprisoned between 1572-1575. In her commentary on but a few of the verses, Teresa speaks of their ideal application to the relationship of the Virgin Mary to God; but she herself chooses to make use of them in expressing the love that exists between Jesus Christ, the Beloved, and the soul, his Bride.[28]

Reflecting on the biblical text "Your breasts are better than wine, and give forth the most sweet fragrance" (Song 1:2-3), Teresa writes:

> And this is what the bride says here according to my interpretation, that the breasts of the Bridegroom give forth fragrance greater than that of precious ointments.
>
> But when this most wealthy Bridegroom desires to enrich and favor the soul more, he changes it into himself to such a point that, just as a person is caused to swoon from great pleasure and happiness, it seems to the soul it is left suspended in those divine arms, leaning on that sacred side and those divine breasts. It doesn't know how to do anything more than rejoice, sustained by the divine milk with which its Spouse is nourishing it and making it better so that he might favor it, and it might merit more each day.
>
> When it awakens from that sleep and that heavenly inebriation, it remains as though stupefied and dazed and with a holy madness. It seems to me it can say these words: *Your breasts are better than wine.*
>
> An infant doesn't understand how it grows nor does it know how it gets its milk, for without its sucking or doing anything, often the milk is put into its mouth. Likewise, here, the soul is completely ignorant. It knows neither how nor from where that great blessing came to it, nor can it understand. It knows that the blessing is the greatest that can be tasted in life, even if all the delights and pleasures of the world were joined together . . . It doesn't know what to compare his grace to, unless to the great love a mother has for her child in nourishing and caressing it.
> (Vol. 2, *Meditations on the Song of Songs*, 4, 3-4, pp. 243-245.)

Teresa herself tells us that this "comparison is appropriate." She notes in the paragraph immediately after her well developed use of this imagery that:

> The soul is so elevated beyond the ability of its intellect, that it is, in part, like an infant that delights in a caress but doesn't have an intellect by which to understand how that good comes.

Even while the soul is sleeping, Teresa tells us, because of:

> . . . the divine inebriation the soul is still functioning because it understands and does something. It understands that it is near its God, and thus it has reason for saying: *Your breasts are better than wine.* (Vol. 2, *Meditations on the Song of Songs*, 4, 5, p. 245.)

In *The Dark Night,* John of the Cross makes use of concepts of motherhood in describing the relationship of God to the soul. He writes:

> It should be known then, that God nurtures and caresses the soul, after it has been resolutely converted to his service, like a loving mother who warms her child with the heat of her bosom, nurses it with good milk and tender food, and carries and caresses it in her arms. But as the child grows older, the mother withholds her caresses and hides her tender love; she rubs bitter aloes on her sweet breast and sets the child down from her arms, letting it walk on its own feet so that it may put aside the habits of childhood and grow accustomed to greater and more important things.[29]

All of these images are made use of as similes rather than direct statements of the activity of God; but within the same paragraph the simile is put to one side, and the critical edition of the Spanish text of John states:

> *La amorosa madre de la gracia de Dios (Wis. 16:25), luego que por nuevo calor y hervor de servir a Dios reengendra al alma, eso mismo hace con ella . . .*[30]

What is important is that all the translators who have rendered this text in English have neglected to translate it as it should be. Specifically, as Father Kieran Kavanaugh agrees, the opening sentence of the passage beginning with "La amorosa madre de la gracia de Dios" *should* read in an English translation:

The loving mother of the grace of God re-engenders in the soul new enthusiasm and fervor in the service of God . . .

To continue making use of the English translation by Kavanaugh and Rodriguez, I would draw attention to the directness of John's statements:

With no effort on the soul's part, this grace causes it to taste sweet and delectable milk and to experience intense satisfaction in the performance of spiritual exercises, because God is handing the breast of his tender love to the soul, just as if it were a delicate child.[31]

In making use of the images of motherhood to describe the intimacy between the soul and God, both Teresa of Avila and John of the Cross are part of that tradition going back as far as Clement of Alexandria (150-215) who used the image of "the Father's loving breasts" and "the milk of the Father" to stress the tenderness of God. In the time of St Irenaeus we have the portrayal of the Holy Spirit as feminine; and there are a number of Cistercian writers of the twelfth century who, as Colledge and Walsh note, make use of the title "Mother Jesus" in describing the tenderness of God's affirming love. There are many other examples in St Augustine, St Anselm, St Mechtild, and by the author of the Ancrene Riwle. Among the writers of Julian's time, St Bridget of Sweden and St Catherine of Siena use concepts associated with motherhood in describing the intimate relationship of God and the soul. In Julian, however, we have the full flowering of this imagery.[32]

RECONCILIATION

The sixteen revelations can be studied from this simple approach: God, man, and their reconciliation. It would be possible to reduce Julian's teaching to a revealing of the "homely loving of God," as Molinari points out in his study. There are a number of approaches to her work; and among these are her use of Scripture, the sources of her inspiration in the writings of other mystics and the Fathers of the Church, the prevalent teaching in England at the time as illustrated in some of the major works of the fourteenth century, Julian's personality as revealed through her writings, and many more; but care must be taken in any study to preserve the unique character of her teaching and the form she gave it.

The style she uses is a simple one, and the language is free of dramatics and contrivances to attain an effect; yet her prose often verges on poetry. When the Middle English text is read, the images sing out, and there is a pervasive calm, an absence of tension and of all that often attends the outpouring of mystical accounts.

Throughout both the short and long texts there is an analytical approach supporting the narrative and allowing Julian to share her reflections and give a commentary on them.

Julian, a woman of her day, makes use of the courtly language then so much a part of the literary tradition; and she succeeds in using these concepts associated with the romances of the court in presenting her description of the relationship of God and man. Nonetheless, she was aware of the danger of employing this courtly imagery carelessly. She writes:

> . . . let us beware that we take not so recklessly this intimacy so as to leave courtesy. For our Lord himself is supreme intimacy, and he is as intimate as he is courteous; for he is true courtesy. (Long, Revelation 16, Chapter 77, p. 695.)

Julian tells us:

> . . . fifteen years after and more [since the revelations were given to her], I was answered in ghostly understanding saying thus: What, would you wish to know your Lord's meaning in this thing? Know it well, love was his meaning. Who showed it to You? Love. What showed he to you? Love. Wherefore does he show it to you?

For love. Hold yourself therein, you shall know more in the same. But you shall never know therein other without end. (Long, Revelation 16, Chapter 86, pp. 732-733.)

Another important concept found in Julian is her teaching on God's "homely loving"; and we may trace the word "homely" back to the Old English hām + ly which has the meaning "intimate"; and Julian makes use of this word in both the short and long texts. (In the translation of the Middle English text made by the author of this essay, "intimate" is used throughout to preserve Julian's usage as much as possible as well as to transmit her essential teaching. Colledge and Walsh have chosen to translate it as "familiar," which fails to convey the message of Julian.)

Among the better known passages of Julian's is this account of her first revelation:

> . . . in this sight I saw that he is all things that are good, as to my understanding.
>
> And in this he showed a little thing, the quantity of a hazelnut lying in the palm of my hand, as it seemed to me, and it was as round as a ball. I looked thereon with the eye of my understanding, and thought: What may this be? And it was answered generally thus: It is all that is made. I marvelled how it might last, for I thought that because of its littleness it would suddenly have fallen into nothing. And I was answered in my understanding: It lasts and ever shall, for God loves it; and so have all things being by the love of God. (Long, Revelation 1, Chapter 5, pp. 299 -300.)

In her typical way, Julian gives us a detailed analysis of this revelation:

> In this little thing I saw three properties. The first is that God made it, the second is that God loves it, the third is that God keeps it. But what beheld I therein? Truly the maker, the keeper, the lover. (Long, Revelation 1, Chapter 5, p. 300.)

At once she relates this to her own life and, in doing so, gives a lesson to all:

. . . until I am substantially united to him, I may never have full
rest or true bliss; that is to say that I be so fastened to him that
there be nothing that is made between my God and me. (Long,
Revelation 1, Chapter 5, p. 303.)

We find that Julian establishes the proper perspective that is
needed in this life. She emphasizes the role of Providence, as we
now describe God's ongoing direction of all that takes place. In
her commentary on her third revelation, we find this made
clear:

. . . therefore the blessed Trinity is ever fully pleased in all his
works; and in all this he showed full blessed meaning thus: See, I
am God. See, I am in all things. See, I do all things. See, I never
lift my hands from my works, nor never shall without end. See, I
lead all things to the end that I ordain them with; how should
anything be amiss? Thus mightily, wisely and lovely was the soul
examined in this vision. Then I saw that it behooves me to assent
with great reverence and joy in God. (Long, Revelation 3,
Chapter 11, pp. 340-341.)

In examining this, Molinari writes:

It is clear from . . . this quotation that Julian is considering
two aspects of the divine presence. The one is that which we
commonly call Providence, whereby God is present in history
and controls events . . . The other is that of God's presence in
every single creature whereby he gives it being and life. It is primarily this second aspect that Julian has in mind when she uses
her formula "God the Maker, the Keeper, the Lover."[33]

Another passage emphasizing the divine Presence in every
creature is found in Julian:

. . . God is all that is good, as to my sight; and God has made all
that is made, and God loves all that he had made. (Long,
Revelation 1, Chapter 9, p. 322.)

There is a remarkable resemblance between Julian's description
of her soul and the teaching of Teresa of Avila. Teresa writes:

... let us imagine that within us is an extremely rich palace, built entirely of good and precious stones; in sum, built for a lord such as this. Imagine, too, as is indeed so, that you have a part to play in order for the palace to be beautiful; for there is no edifice as beautiful as is a soul pure and full of virtues. The greater the virtues the more resplendent the jewels. Imagine, also, that in this place dwells this mighty king who has been gracious enough to become your Father; and he is seated upon an extremely valuable throne which is your heart. (Vol. 2, *The Way of Perfection*, 28, pp. 143-144.)

The presence of God within the soul is dynamic; and Julian, in describing her sixteenth revelation, writes of this divine activity:

He showed himself on earth in the sweet Incarnation and his blessed Passion, and in another manner he showed himself on earth, as where I said I saw God in a point; and in another manner he showed himself on earth thus, as it were on a pilgrimage, that is to say he is here with us leading us, and shall be until he hath brought us all to his bliss in heaven. (Long, Revelation 16, Chapter 81, p. 714.)

In some passages Julian may seem to be expressing a form of pantheism; a careful reading will reveal this is far from her intention. John of the Cross and some other Christian mystics are open to the same distorted interpretation. In *The Ascent of Mount Carmel*, Book 2, chapters 6 and 7, some would find a pantheistic approach; yet, John is careful in his writing, and the distinctions he makes should be understood. In Chapter 5 of Book 2 of the *Ascent*, John writes:

To be reborn in the Holy Spirit during this life is to become most like God in purity without any mixture of imperfection. Accordingly, pure transformation can be effected — although not essentially — through the participation of union.[34]

With the same care, the Mystical Doctor teaches:

When God grants this supernatural favor to the soul, so great a union is caused that all the things of both God and the soul become one in participant transformation, and the soul appears to be God more than a soul. Indeed it is God by participation. Yet truly, its being (even though transformed) is naturally as distinct from God's as it was before, just as the window, although illumined by the ray [of sunlight], has an existence distinct from the ray.[35]

Using the same imagery as is found in the Hindu Upanishads in the development of these late Vedic treatises on the nature of man and the universe, Teresa of Avila describes the spiritual marriage in what could be interpreted as evidence of pantheism; but, as in Julian's writings and those of John of the Cross, it is absurd to isolate texts from the context of the main body of a work. Teresa writes:

In the spiritual marriage the union is like what we have when rain falls from the sky into a river or fount; all is water, for the rain that fell from heaven cannot be divided or separated from the water of the river. Or it is like what we have when a little stream enters the sea, there is no means of separating the two. Or, like the bright light entering a room through two separate windows; although the streams of light are separate when entering the room, they become one. (Vol. 2, *The Interior Castle*, 7, 2, 4, p. 434.)

In another passage on the same theme of the spiritual marriage, Teresa writes:

It seems the Lord desires that in some manner these others in the castle may enjoy the great deal the soul is enjoying and that from that full-flowing river, where this tiny fount is swallowed up, a spurt of that water will sometimes be directed toward the sustenance of those who in corporeal things must serve these two who are wed. (Vol. 2, *The Interior Castle*, 7, 2, 6, p. 435.)

Julian devoted Chapter 54 to the theme of the union that is possible between God and the soul. The following passage is but one of the many that illustrates this truth:

And I saw no difference between God and our substance, but, as it were, all God; and yet my understanding took that our

substance is in God, that is to say that God is God and our substance is a creature in God. For the almighty Truth of the Trinity
is our Father for he made us and keeps us in him. And the deep
wisdom of the Trinity is our Mother, in whom we are enclosed.
And the high goodness of the Trinity is our Lord, and in him we
are enclosed and he in us. We be enclosed in the Father, and we
be enclosed in the Son, and we are enclosed in the Holy Ghost.
And the Father is enclosed in us, the Son is enclosed in us, and
the Holy Ghost is enclosed in us, almighty, all wisdom, all goodness, one God, one Lord. (Long, Revelation 14, Chapter 54, pp.
562–563.)

It would be difficult to find a text among the Christian mystics
of both East and West that would describe as well the relationship of the soul to the Trinity. There is the quality of a canticle
in this work, especially when it is read in the Middle English in
which Julian composed it. There are many similar passages in
her writings; and among these is that strikingly-beautiful opening of Chapter 54 used to describe Revelation Fourteen. The
truth of God making no distinction between "the blessed soul of
Christ and the least soul that shall be saved" illustrates dramatically Julian's appreciation of the mystery of the Incarnation in
its redemptive purpose. (Long, Revelation 14, Chapter 54, p.
561; quoted on page 191 of this article.) In this text we find that
encouraging spirit that marks Julian's teaching, especially that
awareness of the union with God that we possess through grace.
Obviously it is a positive and even optimistic spirituality that
Julian upholds; and it has value in enlightening the soul to what
it already possesses in Christ through his divine Presence. Rather
than fostering a preoccupation with self, often a danger for those
who have come to take seriously their spiritual life, it nourishes
confidence in the Lord and the freedom needed for spiritual
growth.

In Revelation Sixteen, Julian insists on the awareness of the
reverence that the soul must have in its relationship with God,
yet her major concern is that the soul would suffer more from a
want of intimacy than from its carelessness in its relationship.
Her caution seems to flow from an English sense of propriety,

and she does not dwell on it. The following quotation speaks eloquently in its simplicity of Julian's understanding of the longing the Lord has for the soul:

> . . . he wills that we hastily attend him, for he stands all alone, and waits for us continually, moaning and mourning until when we come. He hath haste to have us with him, for we are his joy and his delight, and he is our remedy of our life. (Long, Revelation 16, Chapter 79, p. 706.)

There is a want of evidence of restraint, indeed the Lord finds his joy in the soul and is described by Julian as in a pathetic state until the soul gives itself to him.

CHURCH

The major influence in the life of most Western mystics is the Church, and the principal mission of the Church is the work of reconciliation. Julian and Teresa in their writings reflect an understanding of this role.

All the Christian mystics give us a deeper understanding of the relationship between God and man. While their approaches are colored by many influences, even those that they are unaware of, they present in varying degrees their own interior development. Some are wonderfully articulate; Julian and Teresa are among these; others are restrained in their sharing their experiences and understanding.

As the Church develops its teaching and proclaims it officially, the spiritual writers and the mystics as well are inspired by it, and they ideally relate this teaching to their own lives. In Julian and Teresa we find this response not only to the ancient traditions of the Church Fathers but to the Church of their day, especially to the theologians who shared their knowledge through both writings and sermons.

Frequently throughout their writings these mystics affirm their submission to the Church; and both were sensitive to the dangers of straying from its official teaching. As in every age, the mystics are seldom understood by their contemporaries; but in the Middle Ages as well as in Spain during Teresa's time there was the danger of being accused of heretical teaching or worse. Julian says:

> ... in all things I believe as Holy Church teaches for in all things, this blessed showing of our Lord, I beheld it as one in God's sight, and I never understood anything therein that astounded me nor hinders me in the doctrine of Holy Church. (Short, Chapter 6, p. 223.)

Teresa makes many similar statements, but she had reason to be careful especially in all that she would write on the subject of prayer and the spiritual life. Her *Life* was in the hand of the Inquisition at the time she began her writing of *The Interior Castle*. Teresa writes in her prologue to this work:

> If I should say something that isn't in conformity with what the holy Roman Catholic Church holds, it will be through ignorance and not through malice. This can be held as certain, and also that through the goodness of God I always am, and will be, and have been subject to her. (Vol. 2, *The Interior Castle*, Prologue, 3, p. 282.)

Julian in speaking of Christ and the Church says:

> ... he wills that we take us mightily to the faith of Holy Church, and find there our dear worthy mother in solace and true understanding with all the blessed community. For one single person may oftentimes be broken, as it seems to the self, but the whole body of Holy Church was never broken, and never shall be without end. And therefore a surer thing it is, a good and a gracious one to will meekly and mightily to be fastened and oned to our Holy Church, that is Christ Jesus. (Long, Revelation 14, Chapter 61, pp. 607–608.)

Consistent with this statement, Julian gives a list of the three means that man has at his disposal in this life in fulfilling his purpose:

> By three things man stands in this life, by which three God is worshipped and we furthered, kept, and saved. The first is the

use of man's natural reason. The second is the common teaching of Holy Church. The third is the inward gracious working of the Holy Ghost; and these three be all of one God. God is the ground of our natural reason; and God is the teaching of Holy Church, and God is the Holy Ghost, and all the sundry gifts, to which he wills that we have regard, and accord us thereto. (Long, Revelation 16, Chapter 80, p. 707.)

Teresa, too, wrote of her understanding and love of the Church, and she identified the Church with Christ as did Julian. In the opening of *The Way of Perfection*, Teresa writes:

The world is all in flames; they want to sentence Christ again, so to speak, since they raise a thousand false witnesses against him; they want to ravage his Church . . . (Vol. 2, *The Way of Perfection*, 1, 1, p. 43.)

In her counseling, Teresa advises her daughters in Carmel:

. . . believe firmly what Holy Mother Church holds, and you can be sure that you will be walking along a good path. (Vol. 2, *The Way of Perfection*, 21, 10, p. 121.)

Owing to the havoc taking place through much of Europe at the time, Teresa shows her fear of all that the Protestant Reformation was bringing about, particularly the destruction of churches, the disrespect for the Blessed Sacrament, the loss of many priests, and the consequent want of the sacraments in many places:

Now, Lord, now; make the sea calm! May this ship, which is the Church, not always have to journey in a tempest like this. Save us, Lord, for we are perishing. (Vol. 2, *The Way of Perfection*, 35, 5, p. 176.)

The concern that Teresa had for the Church is mentioned in many passages and developed in various ways throughout *The Interior Castle*, but its significance is emphasized especially in the brief epilogue Teresa wrote on November 29th, almost six months after she began writing this work on June 2nd, 1577. In addressing her nuns, she says:

> I ask that each time you read the work, you, in my name, praise His Majesty fervently and ask for the increase of his Church and for light for Lutherans . . . If anything is erroneous, it is because I didn't know otherwise; and I submit to what the holy Roman Catholic Church holds, for in this Church I live, declare my faith, and promise to live and die. (Vol. 2, *Epilogue*, 4, p. 452.)

Julian seems remarkably free from any preoccupation with the problems facing the popes who were in both political and economic exile in Avignon from 1309 until the return of the Papacy to Rome in 1377; and the Great Schism that lasted from 1378 to 1417 that led to three divisions within the Church; even the events facing the Church in England which were the subject of so much concern for other Christians, including Geoffrey Chaucer, John Wycliffe, and William Langland, who were constantly attacking the abuses then rampant, are left without any written comment by Julian. M. L. del Mastro writes in his introduction to his translation of Julian's longer text:

> The anchorhold at Norwich might just as well have been in China for all the notice she takes of current sins and scandals, local persons and events, or the general and particular immoralities of the failed shepherds of a spiritually starving helpless flock.
>
> Julian is not callous. It is simply that for her purposes in this book, she is not a "noticer." Her business is not to observe and comment, harshly or gently, upon the foibles and failings of those around . . . but to observe God alone, to listen to Him and make her response, and to transmit the experience to her fellow Christians.[36]

How different it was for Teresa. In writing *The Interior Castle*, she was aware that the Inquisition might call for her manuscript; indeed, as she wrote this work on prayer, her *Life* was in custody of the Inquisitors; and it would remain with them until six years after Teresa died. In addition to her daring to write on the subject of mental prayer that many conservative theologians believed would lead to Protestantism, she was conscious not only that she was a woman but that her paternal grandfather had been punished because of his having been found guilty of Judaizing, and for that reason he moved his family from their native Toledo to Avila. Even her confidant and spiritual director, Fr Jerome Gratian, was unaware of her true lineage; and this is evident in his remarks made to Anne of St Bartholomew concerning his inquiring into the background of Teresa's family:

> You have told me of your lineage more readily than the blessed Madre Teresa de Jesus. When I had inquired in Avila into the lineage of the Ahumadas and Cepedas from whom she was descended, and who were among the most noble families of that city, she became very angry with me because of what I was doing, saying that it was enough for her to be a daughter of the Church; and that it grieved her more to have committed a venial sin than if she had been descended from the vilest and lowest peasants "villanos" and Jewish converts in the whole world.[37]

Teresa's many declarations of fidelity to the Church and of submission to its teaching are not unusual; but it is only in recent years that we have come to appreciate her anxiety, and, indeed, how well founded it was.[38]

Julian gives little if any evidence of fear of what the Church authorities might think of her writings. There is a want of evidence to show that her writings were well known during her lifetime; and it is possible that they were discovered long after they were written. Margery Kempe makes no reference to them; but Margery does illustrate that Julian's reputation for holiness and good counsel were known even if her writings were not.

Teresa wrote for her daughters who looked for guidance and at the insistence of her confessors. Julian recorded her reflections on the revelations she had received and made clear that they were for every Christian; she went to great pains to express them as well as possible and to fathom their depths even after she had given a good account of them shortly after they had taken place.

In Revelation Thirteen, Julian expresses her understanding of the Church:

> God showed fully the great pleasure that he has in all men and women that mightily and wisely take the preaching and the teaching of Holy Church, for he it is, Holy Church. He is the ground, he is the substance, he is the teaching, he is the teacher, he is the end, and he is the reward wherefore every human soul works; and this is known and shall be known to each soul to which the Holy Ghost declares it. (Long, Revelation 13, Chapter 34, p. 431.)

CONCLUSION

Both mystics had a deep love of the Church and were nourished by its teaching, they were both wise and prudent. They knew the importance of declaring this in their writings; and both were aware that within the Church there were those who had little appreciation for any one, especially a woman, claiming to have visions or even teaching others in spiritual matters.

Julian and Teresa reveal the possibilities of spiritual development within the individual. Their writings interpret for us the truths of the Scripture, especially the Gospels. Each has contributed significantly to the rich heritage of Western Spirituality, specifically to an understanding of the Christian's vocation to intimacy with God.

While we have very little biographical information about Julian, her message reveals her as a woman of great learning, wisdom and prudence, and above all, as one who celebrated her life in Christ. Although details abound concerning Teresa's life, the depth of her spirituality is shown to us by the revelation of self contained in her writings.

In these two women, so different in their cultural experiences, we find sisters in the Spirit. Both have developed their teachings after prayer and meditation on God's love and mercy as revealed to them in an intimate way. Julian and Teresa show confidence in God's leading them to that triumph over the powers of evil.

Julian finds the devil pitiable; and Teresa laughs at him. Both have a sublime insight into the Triune God and a deep appreciation of the redemptive power of Christ's Passion. In their writings we find the development of the much neglected scriptural insights into God's maternal aspects. In Julian this is a major theme; in Teresa, however, these feminine qualities have a more limited but nonetheless important usage in describing the intimacy between the soul and God.

Although Julian is apparently less concerned with the turmoil of her day, Teresa reveals intense anxiety for the Church and its sorrowful state during the sixteenth century. Both mystics emerge from their writings as followers of Christ, daughters of the Church, and witnesses to the Truth.

NOTES

1. *A Book of Showings to the Anchoress Julian of Norwich*, ed. Edmund Colledge and James Walsh, Studies and Texts 35, 2 vols. (Toronto: Pontifical Institute of Medieval Studies, 1978), 788pp. Hereafter cited as "C&W — Toronto."

2. *C&W — Toronto*, 1, 43.

3. *The Book of Margery Kempe*, a modern version ed. and trans. Sanford Brown Meech, Early English Text Society Original Series 212 (New York: Oxford Univ. Press, 1944), 33.

4. *Julian of Norwich's Revelations of Divine Love*, ed. Frances Beer (Heidelberg, 1978), 7.

5. Julian of Norwich, *The Revelations of Divine Love*, trans. James Walsh (London, 1961), 2.

6. R.M. Wilson, "Reviewing Robert K. Stone's *Middle English Prose Style: Margery Kempe and Julian of Norwich*," *Medium Aevum* 42 (1973):183-84.

7. *Julian of Norwich, Showings*, modern translation by Edmund Colledge and James Walsh, The Classics of Western Spirituality (New York: Paulist Press, 1978), 20. Hereafter cited as "C&W — New York."

8. *C&W — Toronto*, 2, 735-48: "Rhetorical Figures Employed by Julian."

9. *C&W — Toronto*, 1, Introduction, 196-97.

10. Ibid., 198.

11. See Alfred C. Hughes, *Walter Hilton's Direction to Contemplatives* (Rome: doctoral dissertation submitted to the Gregorian Univ., 1962), 24-26.

12. Julian of Norwich, *Revelations of Divine Love*, trans. M.L. Del Mastro (Garden City: Doubleday, 1977), 11–13. Hereafter cited as "Del Mastro."

13. In a lecture published in *The Proceedings of the Fifth National Congress of the Secular Order of Our Blessed Lady of Mount Carmel* (1965) by Spiritual Life Press, Washington DC, there is a treatment of Teresa's teaching and the Protestant Reformers entitled "St Teresa's Concept of Holiness" by the author of this essay.

14. Wilhelm Niesel, *The Theology of Calvin*, trans. Harold Knight (Philadelphia, 1956), 132 gives a reference to John Calvin, *Institutio Christianae Religionis*, III, 11, 9 — Corpus Reformatorum, 7, 448.

15. Teresa of Avila, *I.C.S. ed.*, 1, Introduction, 28–29.

16. Ibid., 18–19.

17. Teresa of Avila, *I.C.S. ed.*, 2, 263–64.

18. Ibid., 264.

19. C, 13, 7.

20. Paul Molinari, *Julian of Norwich: The Teaching of a 14th Century English Mystic* (London, 1958), 6. Hereafter cited as "Molinari."

21. Julian of Norwich, *The Revelations of Divine Love*, trans. and ed. Roger Huddleston (London, 1952), xxiii ff and 174–75.

22. *Molinari*, 72.

23. *Molinari*, 171, n.4.

24. Ibid., 175–76.

25. *C&W—New York*, Preface by Jean Leclercq, 10–11.

26. Ibid., 11.

27. *C&W—Toronto*, 1, Introduction, 196–97.

28. Teresa of Avila, *I.C.S. ed.*, 2, Introduction, 207–11.

29. N, 1, 1, 2.

30. San Juan de la Cruz, *Vida y Obras Completas de San Juan de la Cruz*, 10th ed., (Madrid: Editorial Catolica, 1978), 645.

31. N, 1, 1, 2.

32. *C&W—New York*, Preface by Jean Leclercq, 9.

33. *Molinari*, 158–59.

34. A, 2, 5, 5.

35. A, 2, 5, 7.

36. *Del Mastro*, Introduction, 13.

37. Jeronimo Gracián de la Madre de Dios, *Espíritu y revelaciones y manera de proceder de la Madre Ana de San Bartolomé, examinado por el P. su confesor*, ed. Silverio de Santa Teresa, Biblioteca Mística Carmelitana 17 (Burgos: Ed. Monte Carmelo, 1933), 259.

38. Teofanes Egido, "The Historical Setting of St Teresa's Life," *Carmelite Studies* 1 (1980):122–82.

JUNGIAN INDIVIDUATION AND CONTEMPLATION IN TERESA OF JESUS

Bonaventure Lussier

Bonaventure Lussier has a master's degree in spirituality from Catholic University of America. He resided at the motherhouse of the Washington Province of Discalced Carmelites—the Province ultimately responsible for the production of CARMELITE STUDIES—until recently; now he is at The Common, a retreat center in New Hampshire.

INTRODUCTORY REMARKS

In our day there is great interest in the spiritual development of past, well-known historical figures on the part of professionals such as Kelsey, Dunne, Fowler and others. The popularity of their works seems to demonstrate a desire on the part of the general public to read and learn from such material.

In this study I aim to trace the development of a woman, Teresa of Jesus, through maturation in her *Life*, by way of a modern tool, the depth psychology of Carl Gustav Jung, along with the reflections of modern Jungian women analysts, to see if Teresa's experience of contemplation shows she experienced a process that brings her to a wholeness that can be called individuation.

I will use the *Life* because it is the example of a work which allows us to follow through a personal spiritual development and because of its profound impact on Teresa herself as evidenced by three facts. First, it is her own account, as a mature woman, of the experiences of her life which brought her to maturity (contemplation). Secondly, she felt this work to be so important as a reflection of her growth process and life that she carried a copy of it wherever she went. Thirdly, as a result of her work and reflection on this *Life* she changed the way she addressed herself. She no longer refers to herself as Teresa de Ahumada but as Teresa of Jesus. This, we will see, represents for Teresa the deep transformation of her own personality, the realization of her Self, the attainment of union with God. Mutual illumination in the area of spiritual development is offered by two pilgrims on this personal journey, Carl Jung and Teresa of Jesus.

A METHOD AND SOME DEFINITIONS

I then intend to make a comparison of two expressions of a shared intuition. This intuition is the awareness that leads to self-knowledge and wholeness. Each of our two pilgrims, Carl Jung and Teresa, speaks from experience and has the common element necessary for self-knowledge and wholeness which I will refer to as awareness.

This awareness in Jung depends on the recognition, acceptance, integration and expression of the animus (in a woman), a part of the process of self-knowledge to wholeness, which is called individuation.

This awareness in Teresa comes about through a process of prayer called the four waters. This way she gets in touch with her self through awarenes and to an ever deepening self-knowledge and the whole of her person, symbolized by the union of human and divine and the maturing relationships she had with her spiritual masters.

I compare Jung's process of individuation (taking into account the role of the animus in the process of awareness to self-knowledge and wholeness as experienced by woman), with Teresa's expression of her experience of the role of prayer in the process of awareness to self-knowledge which enabled her to gain access to her own wholeness.

Ultimately, we wish to see that the intuition of awareness seen in Jung's individuation process and the intuition of awareness as seen in Teresa's union process are thematically similar in their end result, though expressed in the language of two different disciplines and ages.

By this method of exposition I intend to develop a comparison of similar themes in Jung and Teresa which will lead to the enhancement or deepening of the intelligibility of both. I would like to point out the influence of both Jung and Teresa as powerful seminal thinkers who have contributed enduring categories to depth psychology and to spiritual theology.

It is worth our while first to define the terms of Jungian depth psychology before we compare them to Teresa's parallel expressions. This is necessary not only because of the differences of language between Jung and Teresa, but also because these same terms are used in our modern culture in many different ways.

Ego

The ego is a cluster of functions within the person. It is that part of us that is conscious and controls or orders the information in and around us, and then acts. It is a complex function in that it takes the input received through the senses and the mental input of intuition, thought, the resultant feelings and the will, and integrates them into a composite image out of which a person may act.

As long as the ego relates to data and makes use of it, whether from the senses or the mind, that data remains conscious. The ego can control what is conscious or unconscious simply by responding or not responding to what is presented to the consciousness of the person. To respond to data is to keep it conscious, not to respond is to let the data fall into the unconscious. In sum, the ego acts by responding to conscious material when it arises (keeping the data conscious), or by ignoring it (rendering it unconscious). Either way the ego determines to some extent the actions of the person.

The ego can be referred to as the center of conscious awareness or "the center of the field of consciousness."[1] It is the tool of the conscious person.

In women the ego is the tool of expression of the anima (the soul she identifies with as a person). Both men and women are born with a soul (anima) but men develop the ego in such a way that it is divided from the soul, which for them becomes an unconscious inner reality. Women, on the other hand, identify closely with their soul, which is their instinctual nature, and are less easily separated from it by the development of their intellect.[2]

Both men and women have an ego, but for women the awareness of the ego, because of its close connection with the soul, is diffused.[3]

This concept of diffused awareness in regard to the woman's ego ought to be well grasped, for it is crucial to the later understanding of the animus as focal awareness for a woman.

To help us better understand these two concepts we will take a look at the work of the philosopher Michael Polanyi. He developed these types of awareness in relation to a process of discovery. He came to the realization that there is what he calls a tacit dimension (an unexplained dimension) which makes it possible for a person to go from a given experience of particulars to a meaningful concept of the whole.[4]

This view of knowing contrasts with the scientific explanation for the coming to discovery of his time (1891-1976) which held that the particulars put together properly, such as in an experiment, will result in a conclusion or discovery. Polanyi felt that this way of looking at discovery was sorely lacking in the recognition of the whole process.[5]

Jung himself realized this:

> . . . But even though the first step along the road to a momentous invention may be the outcome of a conscious decision,

here, as everywhere, the spontaneous idea—the hunch or intuition—plays an important part. In other words the unconscious collaborates too and often makes decisive contributions . . . *Reason alone does not suffice.*[6]

His new view of knowing posits three centers of knowing, the problem at hand, which is the object of a person's search; the clues which are present in the situation of which we are only subsidiarily aware; and the person who links the goal with the subsidiary clues.[7] The tacit dimension is that of which we know but cannot express, it is beyond our ability to articulate. This other dimension which he became conscious of required another term.

Polanyi knew that the awareness we were able to speak of was an ordered, logical awareness. This first type of awareness he called focal. The other awareness he called subsidiary. This awareness he referred to as knowing by, or relying on. It guides to the integration of a a coherent pattern, the whole picture, the total sense of the thing being considered or the relationship of the particulars together to form a whole.[8]

He called focal awareness an attending to. By this he meant that we place our attention on the particulars within a certain area out of which we wish to draw an insight.[9]

Together, and only together, subsidiary and focal awareness bring about an insight or discovery. With just one or the other a necessary component of the whole process is missing. With focal awareness a person is attending to the problem at hand but unable to see the total picture, the direction or overall pattern of the situation. On the other hand if a person has simply subsidiary awareness applied to a given situation then one is attending to the whole pattern or direction, but cannot focus in on a particular consequence or result of the overall picture. One is left with a general picture but no particular guided direction.

Polanyi saw that scientific discovery occurs in two steps: intuition and imagination. First there is a deliberate act of imagination looking for a hidden reality suggested by intuition's subsidiary awareness. Secondly there is a spontaneous effort of the creative intuition reaching for integration. Thus, the imagination is guided toward reality by following clues from its own personal intuition and for this there are no explicit rules to guide us to an insight because of the indeterminate nature of the reality itself.[10]

To develop further the concept of ego in woman the next step is to define it according to awareness. Instead of using Polanyi's term subsidiary we will use Irene Claremont de Castillejo's term "diffused." It is fair to substitute this term for the other because no accuracy of intention is lost. In considering Polanyi we are helped to understand that what is applied to the scientific approach to discovery is also true in other facets of one's being, especially our own reflections on and growing to Self.

We will use diffused awareness to identify the ego's function in woman, as Castillejo has suggested.

In Teresa it is difficult to know just when she talks about the ego as such because she is speaking from a classical tradition based on Augustine and Thomas Aquinas. Often she uses the same term to refer to various parts of herself which we would now separate and differentiate as to function. Despite this we can recognize that the ego is most often identified by the term "I" in Teresa's *Life*.

Archetype

The next several terms we will consider are archetypes. Archetypes are definite motifs, typical images and associations, determined as to their form (to a limited degree).

> The archetype in itself is empty and purely formal, nothing but a *facultas praeformandi*, a possibility of representation which is given a priori. The representations themselves are not inherited, only the forms . . .[11]

Archetypes are like picture frames within which a picture of particular feelings, images and attributes are attached. For example the archetype of mother can be felt as negative (devouring and castrating) or as a positive (containing, nurturing and grounding). The images that appear to the person through the active imagination or dreams can vary, but they will normally portray the feeling of mothering through an appropriate image.

They are patterns of development within the unconscious

that help us grow interiorly. We can compare them to negatives that need to be developed. They are found through images in the world around us which become roots for the unconscious. In other words, what we see with our eyes has its counterpart inside us through which the same feelings can be evoked. If a thunderstorm evokes the power and glory of God, then there is within us this same image which can be evoked by the unconscious when it wishes to draw the power and glory of God to our consciousness.

The archetypes are important because the conscious comes to know the unconscious through the images of the world which then symbolize the unlived life within, which we need to get in touch with in order to be whole.

Animus

Jung recognized that the animus in woman was related to her in a different way than the anima in a man. He felt it was a discriminative function for her.[12]

In a man the anima is a relationship function. Its purpose is to help a man be sensitive to the relationship of things that his ego has focused in on. One could say that it acts as his subsidiary awareness. In woman, on the other hand, the animus has a function of discrimination, distinguishing and discerning.[13]

When the animus is left in an unconscious state it remains a collection of unreflected, raw beliefs garnered from male figures with which the woman has had contact throughout her life beginning with her father. Because of their raw state these beliefs or opinions can be a good influence or a bad influence in the life of a woman.[14] Unreflected on and blurted out, just as they arise, they are unrelated and disjointed, following no logic and coming across as "gospel truth" without foundation, or they are projected on a male figure often denying the woman the ability to see the person as he really is.

As articulated opinions the animus material comes across as solid convictions that are hard to shake or as principles whose validity seems unassailable. If we were to analyze these opinions, we would immediately come upon unconscious assumptions whose existence must first be inferred; that is to say, the opinions are apparently conceived as though certain conditions or situations were present. But in reality the opinions are not relevant; they exist ready-made and are held so positively, and with such conviction, that the woman never has occasion to doubt about them. At the same time they do not fit the situation in which, or to which, she is addressing herself.[15] In this case the animus appears as a masculine character, which produces opinions that rest on "unconscious prior assumptions."[16]

On the other hand the aminus can act in a projection upon a masculine person outside of the woman herself. In place of the objective male person stands an opinion about him, overriding the person and any individual judgments about him.[17]

The animus then gives the woman the ability to recognize it through male figures in her life. Because of this one mustn't underestimate the importance of a woman's relationship with men. These relationships help her find her own animus. In fact we can say that they are crucial in her recognition of that animus.[18]

In summary, then, there are two ways that an animus can be recognized: as opinions or as projections on male persons.

Jung descirbes the animus in woman as serving the purpose of bringing forth the creative in the anima of a man.[19] This implies that a woman's animus has the purpose of seeding the anima of a man for creative results and puts into doubt the ability of a woman to be creative and whole on her own, bringing forth substantial creative results independent of a man. Jung has based this part of his understanding of the animus on his broader theory that the masculine principle is creative and the feminine is receptive. June Singer accuses Jung of a double standard: "It is evident that what is qualitatively different about The Creative and The Receptive is the Masculinity of the first and the Femininity of the second, and what is equally important is that both of these qualities are present in the intrinsic nature of each human being regardless of sex."[20]

In light of this, one would have to say that if Jung maintains the presence of both the masculine and feminine in each and every person whether male or female, then every person has receptive and creative qualities which when brought into harmony and developed result in wholeness and creative results. In the light of this we concur with Singer and can see Teresa's development as a possible result of her relationship with the men of her life but independent of them.

Wholeness can be achieved by a woman, independent of needing to fertilize man's anima. She has within her the masculine and feminine principles to come to wholeness in relationship with men, and does not need to be dependent on man for that wholeness. She can inseminate her own self with the animus rather than remaining dependent on a man.

Jung also maintained that the anima is a bridge between the conscious and unconscious in man and likewise the animus can be represented in the same way.[21]

Castillejo feels that a better image for the animus in a woman is that of a torch bearer. She develops the animus as a focal awareness.[22] (I touched on this when I developed the focal and subsidiary awareness of Polanyi's theory of discovery). This explanation of the animus is a very valuable tool for the understanding of the function of this masculine principle in a woman and is necessary for true wholeness on her part.

Focal awareness is the principle that compliments the woman's ego which is subsidiary in awareness, and makes it possible for her to be a whole person independent of the need for the focal awareness of a man's consciousness. She too has within herself the potential to be both subsidiary and focal, to be aware of and sensitive to rational being, and to focus in on and delineate specific aspects of reality.

The animus' main role is the power to focus. Woman's consciousness has a "diffused" awareness of its own but the animus provides the necessary polarity of that diffused awareness, the ability of focal awareness.[23]

The torchbearer must shine its light. Without the help of the conscious ego reflection it sheds the light of its torch on whatever is at hand, whether pertinent or not. The catch in the process of individuation for a woman is to balance this masculine focal awareness with her feminine diffused awareness of relationships so as to assure the positive relating of the unconscious focal awareness.[24] Then and only then can the animus shed its light on pertinent relevant matter from within the unconscious, making it available to consciousness and also giving the conscious mind the ability to articulate that which is known. It is a guide for her.[25]

For Teresa the animus can be recognized in her view of her father and the many men she had relationships with throughout her life, esepcially with her spiritual masters and Jesus Christ, who for the religious Christian is the most appropriate transcendent image of the animus' function.

Self

It is easy for us to get confused in the use of the term Self because we are tempted to think that when we talk about ego and animus we are talking about the woman's Self. However, in this article, in using the term Self, we are referring to the total balanced dynamic composite of differentiated parts of which the ego and animus are two among many parts. Jung defined the Self as the totality of all the parts in a balance of polarities acting as one united whole.[26]

A few of the polarities referred to are the conscious/unconscious, individuality/universality, temporal/eternal. All of these polarities are often referred to in the fundamental human polarity of masculine/feminine.

Because of the uniqueness and the limitlessness of the unconscious, which also includes the collective unconscious,[27] the Self can never be fully known. "I have suggested calling the total personality which, though present, cannot be fully known, the self."[28]

The process of individuation is to lead us to the discovery of the Self, to a whole balanced, dynamic personality.

... Is there anything more fundamental than the realization,
'This is what I am!' It reveals a unity which nevertheless is — or
was — a deversity. No longer the earlier ego with its make-
believe and artifical contrivances, but another, "objective" ego,
which for this reason is better called the "self."[29]

In the process of maturing we move from thinking that the
ego is the center of the personality to a realization that there is a
greater reality which unites all the disparate elements of the
psyche including the ego itself and that reality we call the Self.
"... That mysterious something in which the inner union takes
place is nothing personal, has nothing to do with the ego, is in
fact superior to the ego because, as the self, it is the synthesis of
the ego and the supra — personal unconscious."[30]

The Self is of greater importance than the ego or any other
part of the person because it is the sum of all the parts in a creative tension of inner polarities moving toward greater maturation. The psyche is in some sense equivalent to the Self for it too
refers to all parts of the person but only as those parts exist in the
person without differentiation, individuation or wholeness. The
parts in the psyche are undifferentiated for the most part. Some
parts may be known but overall there is no balance of the parts
nor an ongoing dynamic relationship, as one intends to include
when speaking of the Self.

When defined thus we can understand that the whole personality on its way to maturation through the process of individuation is the Self. Also one can see that the process of making
the Self conscious is an ongoing and never ending one, for we
can never exhaust the depths of the person to the point of knowing all. To do this would be to know, to the ultimate capacity,
and beyond, all the conscious, unconscious and collective unconscious materials involved in a persons's life.

This coming to the understanding of the Self as the center of
one's personality and the reconciling of the inner polarities
comes in the second half of one's life.

... conscious and unconsious, it is both together. Since it
transcends consciousness it can no longer be called "ego" but

must be given the name of "self" . . . The self too is both ego and
non-ego, subjective and objective, individual and collective. It
is the "uniting symbol" which epitomizes the total union of opposites. As such and in accordance with its paradoxical nature,
it can only be expressed by means of symbols . . . Hence properly understood the self is . . . an image born of nature's own
workings, a natural symbol far removed from all conscious intention . . . The integration of the self is a fundamental problem which arises in the second half of life . . . [31]

Teresa sometimes uses the term "self" to describe, later in her
life, the person of wholeness that she has attained through contemplation. Often, however, she uses this term to refer to the
sinful Self or the shadow of her life

Shadow

By the term shadow we mean those aspects of our own person
which we would just as soon deny because they are the negative
desires and feelings which are within us. It is the dark side of a
person, the opposite polarity to what is recognized as desirable
in our present life.

Teresa is highly sensitive to the shadow part of herself because
she has grown, by the time of the writing of her *Life*, accutely
aware of her inconsistencies and failings in comparison with the
perfect God within and outside of herself with Whom she relates
in the process of contemplation.

Self-knowledge

The common intuition of Jung and Teresa is that of awareness. Awareness is used in two ways: first with regard to the ego
and the animus as to their functions (ego functioning as diffused
and the animus as focal); second, in a broader sense of self-
knowledge, as source of the realization of the various functions
and parts within the psyche and the result of the proper use of
diffused and focal awareness in the Self.

It is the way by which we come to discover the unconscious

world. The more we are open to our awareness of the psyche and its parts the more self-knowledge we gain and the more we are able to utilize the inner powers of the psyche. ". . . The very fact that through self-knowledge, i.e., by exploring our own souls, we come upon the instincts and their world of imagery should throw some light on the powers slumbering in the psyche, of which we are seldom aware so long as all goes well . . ."[32]

Many are scared off by the immense power within for evil, not taking into consideration its opposite power for good. When we become aware of the negative aspects (shadow) within us and work to admit and understand them, we begin to understand the dynamic energy of the psyche for good and ill.

The shadow comes about when one brings energy to bear on a conscious part of the Self and is not aware or chooses to ignore the inner polarity of the conscious aspect where unconscious energy (libido) gathers to compensate. If this continues over a long period of time and the libido is not used consciously in a constructive manner, then destruction within or outside of the person results as the unconscious energy begins to make itself felt.

Self-knowledge leads the ego to admit its limitations and realize its dependence on other parts of the psyche and its subordination to the emerging Self.

In this way the person begins to realize that there is an utter dependence within—the ego has to relate and depend on the animus and has to deal with the shadow—and that one also has an interdependence on others in the world to which one relates. One is not isolated or alone. Added to this is the realization that the same process of recognition, acceptance and relating to is necessary in the world at large. With self-knowledge comes an awareness of how to relate to the world within which one exists. "Since knowledge of the world dwells in his own bosom, the adept should dwaw such knowledge out of his knowledge of himself, for the self he must seek to know is a part of that nature which was bodied forth by God's original oneness with the world."[33]

Not only does one recognize the world and its meaning as

source of the person but one begins to, with the delineation of the various aspects of personality and the discovery and development of the Self, embrace the world and love it again in a more proper, pure form.

> But again and again I note that the individuation process is confused with the coming of the ego into consciousness and that the ego is in consequence identified with the self, which naturally produces a hopeless conceptual muddle. Individuation is then nothing but ego centredness and autoeroticism. But the self comprises infinitely more than a mere ego. It is as much one's self, and all other selves, as the ego. Individuation does not shut one out from the world, but gathers the world to oneself.[34]

Through self-knowledge one can come to know God through the world He has created and especially in human beings as the image and likeness of God.

> We come to know the self as it appears to the perceiving ego; we come to approach the mystery of it through the clues that become apparent to the searching eye. In religious terms one could say something analogous, that we come to know God as he manifests himself in man and through man.[35]

In the early Christian tradition St Clement of Alexandria had pointed this out. Self-knowledge leads to knowledge of God and results in a self-transformation that makes one like him.

> To know oneself has always been, so it seems, the greatest of all lessons. For, if anyone knows himself, he will know God; and, in knowing God he will become like him.[36]

Teresa stresses self-knowledge and connects it inseparably with contemplation. She states that contemplation should never be without self-knowledge, that it sustains the search in prayer. This self-knowledge is a constant need that should never be forsaken. She did not have the differentiated psychological language that we have today and so she will use the word soul to refer to various archetypes that we have mentioned.

15. This path of self-knowledge must never be abandoned, nor is there in this journey a soul so much a giant that it has no need to return often to the stage of an infant and a suckling . . . Along this path of prayer, self-knowledge and the thought of one's sins is the bread with which all palates must be fed no matter how delicate they may be; they cannot be sustained without this bread. It must be eaten within bounds, nonetheless. Once a soul sees that it is now submissive and understands clearly that it has nothing good of itself and is aware both of being ashamed before so great a King or of repaying so little of the great amount it owes him, what need is there to waste time here . . .[37]

She is also sensitive to the fact that it is not enough to gain self-knowledge, but that one must begin the process of contemplation. One mustn't get stuck in one part of the process of prayer (that of gaining self-knowledge) but move forward to an ever growing awareness of Self, and through that, to service of all.

For Teresa the awareness of the various parts of herself leads to self-knowledge and out of this comes a wholeness in the light of Jesus as the totally whole God within and on which she models herself and unites that Self with him.

PROCESS

The process which depends on awareness as its functioning tool and as its continuing terminus in the Self is called individuation.

We look at the whole process of the growth of a woman from the totally unconscious united state of "being" in the womb, following conception, through various stages, tying in Teresa's experience of her own process, where possible, to the final stage of a differentiated and whole human being.

Individuation is a process by which a woman matures to the realization that she is a separate whole human being.[38] This process is dependent on the Self to initiate it. There are four

ways that it can be undertaken; first by a decision on the part of
the ego with the prompting of the Self; secondly through analysis; thirdly through contemplation; fourthly by an unconscious
decision to strive for any goal that reaches outside of the person's
selfish concerns.[39]

We can look at this process from the side of the ego as the expansion of its diffused awareness to include the focal point of
view or from the point of view of the Self which strives to regain
its original wholeness with a differentiated and differentiating
consciousness.[40] We have already seen this process through the
work of Polanyi. Here again is verified the move from (diffused)
subsidiary awareness to focal awareness in a woman's process
(and the reverse for men), as the balance necessary to achieve
the creative tension of the parts of the psyche needed for self-
discovery.

First Half of Life

The *first half of life* is actually outside of and before the formal process that Jung calls individuation and Teresa calls contemplation. This is the foundation period during which supports are being sunk for the building of the second half of life.

Within this first half of life there are two obvious stages
through which everyone passes; first the totally, wholly unconscious stage, in which one's whole experience is the development
of the physical make up of the body and the beginning of the use
of the senses, and secondly, the ego development.

1. Unconscious Whole

In the first stage the person lies "curled up, unconscious, in
the maternal womb."[41] This is a very good image of the person
at this point. Even after birth the child takes some time to distinguish between itself and other beings and things. It would
seem that this image still describes the basic inner disposition of
unconsciousness and dependency. "In the early phase of development the ego is in a state of unconscious identity with the objective psyche — the world of archetypes-within, — and with the
external world without, and therefore has little autonomy."[42]

The person at this point is a totality. There is no differentiation of the parts of the psyche and so one is completely in an unconscious state. There is no need for archetypes to convey groupings of feelings, (which will become important for woman later as her focal awareness), because she is in touch with all the unconscious psyche as a whole. The ego has not be distinguished from the whole and is unable to distinguish between the inner and outer reality.[43]

The various polarities within the person are experienced as a whole, though unconscious. There is no thought or reflection on the differences between its person and another's, inner and outer realms of reality, light and darkness, order and chaos, earth and water, fire and air, masculine and feminine, thought and feeling, intuition and sensation. If one were aware of these polarities or opposites one would be conscious because consciousness in psychology is defined as the ability to distinguish opposites.

In Teresa's *Life* we find no delineation of this first stage. We assume that this is because she is not aware of this unconscious time in her life. The material from this first stage is at the time of the writing of the *Life* unavailable to her. The most she tells us is what she most likely learned from her own family about the environment in which she was born.

2. Ego Development

This stage concentrates on the development of consciousness out of the primal state of "being" that is totally unconscious. In a woman this development of the ego can be seen in three areas of purpose: consciousness, understanding and activity.

Ego development is very important because the ego keeps a balance in dealing with the unconscious. It makes it possible to relate to the inner world of the unconscious and the outer world at the same time. If one were to have a weak or disabled ego the result would be neurosis or psychosis.

There is polarization at this point toward the feminine aspects and qualities of the person to the neglect and at the expense of the masculine polarity which we call the animus. When the woman's conscious feminine pole is heightened, libido is gained in the unconscious pole resulting in the storing of the energy in the animus. If this energy remains untapped or suppressed it will break out as irrelevant dogmatic opinions, (blurted out almost independent of the intention of the person), or as negative projections on another person or persons of the male sex.

Castillejo speaks of a mysterious source (nature's own being) from which all individuals derive their being. The difference between men and women with regard to this source is that women are never separated from it. An intimate contact with it is maintained throughout her life.

> Woman is vaguely aware of being herself in direct touch with the mysterious source, but her awareness is so diffused that she can seldom even speak of it. She needs, passionately needs, the animus' torch to light up for her the things which she already innately knows, so that she can know she knows them.[44]

Though the inspiration she gains is from the source, she needs a torch to throw light on the figure of the source and to focus on specific issues.

Second Half of Life

Properly speaking the *second half of life* (when a person is middle aged) is when the process of individuation begins. This process builds up the person as a balanced whole personality.

1. Animus Recognition

At this stage the woman comes to recognize the unconscious animus within the psyche as a power to be reckoned with.

The beginning of this stage is initiated when a crisis is caused by a breaking into consciousness of the unconscious animus. This is quite a shock to the ego which has been built up in the first half of life as the center of the person. It now has either to accept the fact that there are other elements to the person of which it is unaware and must deal with, or suppress them in an attempt to deny their existence and maintain the facade of being the central reality of the psyche.

Up to this point the woman's stress has been on the ego and the conscious life as feminine. The unconscious masculine, focal awareness of the animus has been ignored or unrealized and has been receiving compensating libido to guarantee the future possibility of its differentiation and inclusion in the Self.

The animus has built up enough energy to break out into consciousness and the effects of this breakthrough are not guided by the ego. This leads the animus to come forth as unreflected, undeveloped and negative. The animus acts as a focus gone awry. Its focusing power is not being utilized consciously and reflectively and because it must function, recognized or not, it throws its light and focuses on irrelevant material which could probably be useful in context but outside of that context is superfluous and damaging.[45] What is worse, at times the woman may appear to be right on target but is unknowingly leading the conversation down the wrong path.[46] Self-knowledge helps her to recognize the negative animus by means of the irrelevant nature of the statements that come forth.[47]

Another way in which the animus breaks forth into the conscious is as a projection on men in general or on a man in particular. This is the first place the animus is presented in such a way that it can be recognized for what it really is, a masculine archetype, a function within the woman.[48]

To be the victim of opinions and dogmatic, irrelevant statements can be attributed to sloppy thinking or malice, but for one to recognize the act of projecting characteristics on another and to learn through relationship that this projection is not true to the person on whom it is forced, is for woman the realization that one has put onto the person something from within the psyche, and a failure to recognize the true character of the person with whom she is relating.

The ideal is to recognize projection. The process of individuation brings the woman to recognize the animus projection, to cease projecting in the future (because the animus' libido is assimilated creatively by incorporating the insights gained from its focal awareness), to see the man for who he is and allow the man to be himself.[49]

The attitude in this searching out of the animus must be one of sincerity. This sincerity is a direct result of a woman's awareness of how serious this archetype is to the achievement of the Self. In a sense this sincerity is self-evident and has been taught to her ego via her nature. Her nature sees things in relationship and she has seen that all relationships rely on it. Without this sincerity relationships fail. She now must establish a relationship to the animus in order to take this aspect of her psyche as a part of the unfolding Self.

Teresa often writes about the determination that is necessary to proceed along the path of contemplation and knowing the Self. This seems to be the same element which is spoken of here.

We must keep in mind how serious she was about her relationships with men, especially her spiritual masters and her stress on their necessary role in helping her to discover her true Self.

In regard to the above crisis in this stage, we point out the episode in her *Life* when she became ill to the point of death. She was resisting the move to the interior life, self-knowledge and wholeness, and the only way the Self could awaken her to the reality of her unconscious was this crisis in her life.[50] She seems to sense that it was not the illnesses in her life that kept her from deeper prayer but that she was using these as an excuse not to enter herself. This crisis forced her to face that fact.

2. Acceptance

The very fact that one has gone through the crisis and has recognized the reality of the animus implies an acceptance in a passive sense. Here we are concerned with an active loving and acceptance of the animus as a vital and positive part of a woman's life and not in the passive sense.

A woman needs to embrace this archetype and begin to appreciate its value as her ego's compliment, the focal awareness of her psyche. With this act she differentiates its various aspects and learns how to relate to it in such a way as to put to good use its power to focus.

She must relate to the animus with her total diffused awareness of the situation or area she wishes to search out. Most especially she must relate her feelings, their intensity and their object.[51] With this information the animus will focus on relevant material, the matter at hand, and will not mislead her if she is sincere and open in her dialogue with it. To leave out any of her feelings is to run the risk of receiving irrelevant material from it.

> . . . He needs a human being to see the light he sheds. But shed his focusing light he must. To me, this is who he is.
>
> In this sense, and in this sense only, has he any concern in our becoming conscious, for the more conscious we are the more we use his torch; and the more he is an essential part of us, a comrade and a partner, the nearer we approach that impossible goal of individuation.[52]

3. Articulation

One has to be able to express in words, concrete images, or metaphors the truth of what the animus says.

There are two formal tools that one can use to articulate what the animus relates. The first tool is analysis, in which the person shares, in words or some other creative expression, the truth that has been related with a trained psychoanalyst who assists in clarifying the process by which the animus is contacted, its intent, purpose, goal and the means to gain further progress and achieve that which is related. For a woman this seems to center around the articulation of the stages of her animus' development.

The second tool is that of the "inner urge to find and obtain the truth."[53] Teresa would use the term contemplation to name that inner urge and process. Nowhere does Teresa state — in so many words — that contemplation is the "inner urge to find and obtain the truth." However, she does come to the discovery of the light within her, Jesus Christ, who is her truth and states that it came through the process of contemplation. She felt attracted to that process of contemplation in the second half of her life. She felt a call to search for her inner truth. She describes this at one point as the determination which she had to continue that search. We can call this determination "the inner urge to find and obtain the truth." (See note 72) She goes on to point out that the ultimate result of this process of contemplation is the truth. June Singer touches on this by saying:

> One way to confront the self is through analysis. One way to approach God is through prayerful contemplation. I am not so sure that in their essentials these two ways are so fundamentally different. At the beginning of analysis the patient brings his symptoms and places them in the lap of the analyst, very much like the child who brings his small problems before his picture of Jesus, making bargains with the Lord. As time passes, each relationship, the analytic and the religious, goes through several transformations. Gradually, in either case, one grows out of the egocentric position and into an awareness of the true nature of the relationship between that which is finite and temporal, and that which is infinite and eternal. In my own experience, and in that of certain of my analysands, as analysis progressed beyond the elementary stages, the common thread of the two apparently different kinds of goal-directed movement gradually become visible. The variation comes mostly in the language of metaphor, which is demanded when we speak of the unknowable.[54]

The articulation in contemplation is through various figures. Teresa found her understanding of the animus and its focal awareness so necessary for her prayer and work through her father, her spiritual masters and the person of her God, represented most often by Jesus. Each of these figures represent various aspects of her animus and at the same time the spiritual masters gave her a forum to articulate what she had experienced.

4. Application and Synthesis

To reflect on the need for application and synthesis of what one has learned from animus one has only to look at the characterizations given by Emma Jung. She gives four to describe the way in which the animus unites woman to her masculine side:

> Goethe makes Faust, who is occupied with the translation of the Gospel of John, ask himself if the passage, "In the beginning was the Word," would not read better if it were, "In the beginning was Power," or "Meaning," and finally he has him write, "In the beginning was the Deed." With these four expressions, which are meant to reproduce the Greek *logos*, the quintessence of the masculine principle does indeed seem to be expressed.[55]

This stage deals with action as a result of the integration of the animus. A woman is now involved in the ongoing balancing and living out of the dynamic tensions she has found within herself. She has now rediscovered the original contrasexual nature of the psyche and in embracing this reality finds herself whole.[56]

Given the necessary sincerity and resolve to continue this process a woman continues to experience an ever-expanding wholeness, a totality of the Self possible in being and action. The goal has been reached. She now integrates the diffused and focal awareness into the total awareness of all that is around and in her. Let us reiterate this goal with two quotes from Jung:

> Individuation means becoming an "in-dividual," and, in so far as "individuality" embraces our innermost, last, and incomparable uniqueness, it also implies becoming one's own self. We could therefore translate individuation as "coming to selfhood" or "self-realization."[57]

> . . . And that is the self, the wholeness of the personality, which if all goes well is harmonious, but which cannot tolerate self-deceptions . . . the goal of psychic development is the self.[58]

Stages of Animus Transformation

Now that we have delineated the stages of the process of individuation itself, let us step back and look at the stages of the animus transformation as experienced in the total life of a woman, using Teresa as an example.

There are four stages of animus development as developed by Ann Belford Ulanov.

1. Great Mother

The first stage is that of the Great Mother. It is the point in development when the child identifies with its mother. For a woman the experience of self as feminine is not separated from the experience of her mother as feminine. She identifies with her mother, rather than seeing herself as a separate identity relating to her mother.

A man remains an outside entity which she can experience but never entrusts herself to. He is an addition to her feminine world and at times is seen simply as a fixture in life or as a spouse. She has ideas about what men are like but she has no personal relationship to them.

Her femininity is an unconscious natural instinct for her during this time. Her animus is entrapped in the archetype of the Great Mother, which supplies her with general truths, standards, and hard and fast preformulated ideas that are considered facts which reality must fulfill. All this is necessary to fill the gap of a missing personal conviction based on experience and a reflective Self.

This would seem to have kept her free of the animus, but instead she is dependent on the masculine within herself because she has not developed or related consciously to it. As she becomes more and more unconscious of her animus the more it can act unnoticed and subversively.[59]

There is a possible hint of this stage in Teresa when she refers to her early prayer life. "... I sought out solitude to pray my devotions, and they were many, especially the rosary, to which my mother was very devoted; and she made us devoted to it too . . ."[60] This may reflect her early need to take on her mother's habits, attitudes, etc., which were constellated in this one statement. It at least reflects a realization that her mother had determined one form of prayer at one point of her life.

She does not express the role that men — especially her father — played for her in this part of her life. It didn't seem to be a concern for her when she wrote her *Life*.

2. Great Father

The second stage of animus transformation is that of the Great Father. The masculine is experienced as an anonymous, transpersonal, and overpowering thing. It is seen as separate from the ego, thereby making the ego conscious of its own limits.[61]

"... She is eternal daughter of a Spiritual Father, and, in its secondary personalization as the Oedipus complex, she is still emotionally attached to her actual father ..."[62]

Teresa does refer to early images of her father. She sees him as the protector who saves her from evil,[63] and as one who cannot see wrong in his girl.[64]

When she wanted to leave home and join the convent, her father became the possessor. She understands his natural attachment to her in retropsect. At the time she did not allow her father to interfere with what she felt to be right.[65]

This portrayal of her father seems to be the portrayal of the animus which through her outward father represents its possession and guidance of her will, not letting go until it runs its course. Teresa takes the initiative and responsibility for the direction of her life.[66]

She leaves the house of her father exteriorly, symbolizing the break with the Great Father stage, by leaving her family home to go to the convent without her father's permission.

When describing this separation she gives a great description of the feeling a woman has when breaking from the Great Father stage.[67] Again she describes this path of separation when her father dies.[68]

3. Patriarchal Marriage

In the third stage the animus takes on a personal, individual image which establishes an equal relationship with her, freeing her from her father. Thus a male person and friend has the role of consciousness, freeing her from the encompassment in the unconscious, or he is the inner animus, the unconscious made conscious within woman herself which takes on this role.[69]

This third stage is symbolized by the image of a patriarchal marriage, the type generally accepted in Western society. In this type of marriage the man gives up completely any functioning of his feminine aspect and the woman gives up any functioning of her masculine aspect. Each has to identify completely as a person with those characteristics which match their physical make up.[70]

Here we can look at Teresa's relationship with her father when he thought that she was teaching him how to pray, but in reality as Teresa describes it, she saw him as her teacher in that she was not practicing what she told him to do and he was progressing rapidly, standing as a reprimand to her.[71]

It was similar to a patriarchal marriage in that her father became the masculine image while actively pursuing prayer and she was content to let him do so without pursuing it herself. She would be content to let him pursue it and thus fulfill that part of her that wanted to journey inward. The crisis she experienced was the breakthrough of her animus which was being ignored. The Self wished to realize wholeness. Her animus, the father within her, wanted actively to pursue it.

This also can be seen in her spiritual masters. These spiritual masters were various priests and a layman to whom she went for direction in her prayer life. In the early ones she found that she went to them to be her guides or to shed light on her way. She speaks of them as checks on her growth so that it might be gradual and consistent.[72] They helped her to understand what was being experienced in the process.[73]

At this stage she does not trust the animus as the guiding principle within her. She even depends on her spiritual masters to give her the ability to express what she is going through, and she often refers to them as her light.[74]

All these references indicate that Teresa still sees the animus as out there in her father and in the spiritual masters and has not yet gone within. While she can recognize and embrace the abilities that lie within herself as the animus function, she still finds it in these men completely. These men, instead of acting as a corrective for her, are determiners, just as the head of the household is for the wife in a patriarchal marriage. She lets them determine her direction and exercise the masculine role of guide.

4. Confrontation and Individuation

In the fourth stage the dominating archetype is the Self and is marked by confrontation and individuation, self-discovery, and self-giving. It is marked by the positive animus.

The woman in this stage develops a new relationship to her animus. She no longer needs to project it out to men, but relates to it as an inward function of her Self. Individuation now involves her animus as mediator of the unconscious to her ego.

The ego now acts to assimilate the material formulated by the animus but can never take the animus itself totally in. The animus is autonomous and related, but never incorporated as a whole.

In Teresa's case we see this in her accounts of the relationships with her spiritual masters toward the end of her life. By this time she has changed: the woman who depended on men to direct her almost entirely, thus relieving her from developing her masculine animus, and who depended on them to make the decisions, now is a woman who is integrating the animus into her life to the extent that she now can dialogue with men, teach and direct them in areas according to her experience, all the while being able to disagree and go against their advice in agreement with her experience, reflection and insight. She is aware of her Self and recognizes the truth.

As an example of this there was the time when she came to the conclusion that a certain spiritual master was trying to push her too far too fast.[75] She simply resisted his counsel. She had enough self-awareness to know that his direction was untrue to her experience. She also at that time began to take a more active part in choosing her spiritual masters. Previously she seemed to have taken people as masters who were available or recommended and was not so interested in pursuing the matter aggressively.

In chapter twenty-three of the *Life* she arranges to see a certain holy man who she feels will be a good master and suited to her inner awareness of her process of growth in contemplation.[76] In this person she could recognize her own animus. She says "I began to have such a great love for him that there was no greater recreation for me than on the days I saw him . . ."[77] Her love for this man considered him a person sensitive to her process of prayer, and it also reflected her own inner focal awareness concerning that process. In fact she also speaks of him as giving her light, which is a key image of the animus as we have described it.[78] At the same time she recognizes that he cannot give her the ability to articulate what she is going through and so she finds that he is only one aspect of her animus, unable to provide her articulation as well as a sense of awareness of the process.[79] She trusts her feelings and is aware of her inner workings and experience so that they work together to comprise a self-knowledge that leads to a sureness about the validity of her experience. Rather than take the master's word for it she goes elsewhere to try to find expression for the experience. She finds that expression in a book.[80]

Her final consolation in this incident came through a Jesuit who was sent to her by her master who then was able to recognize and affirm what she already experienced, knew and articulated.[81]

Later Jesus' voice tells her that she is no longer to talk with men but with angels. In this she experiences an opening to the inner dimension of her own personality, not to mention the dynamic presence of that God within her as an objective Other.[82] The voice came from deep within her and was powerful. She says that because it was a new thing, a novelty, she feared it at first.

This was a turning point for her. She describes it as a complete change. "Thus it wasn't necessary that I be given any more commands . . ."[83] This is not to say that she eliminates the spiritual masters from her life, but that she now regards their role as counselors, rather than directors to whom she would look to determine her direction.

She tells of a time when she discovered that the word is within her. The animus (as we've seen) is often referred to as the word. This was after the books she had been reading on prayer were banned by the Spanish Inquisition.[84] The Lord became her word. The interior light now shines from within and lights all of her life.

Soon she progresses to where she not only can understand her experiences, on her own, but can describe them.[85] She recognizes that the truth comes through her. The word within enlightens others too, because she is not only aware of herself as a whole person but continues to trust her experience and can focus on it, organize it, understand it and describe it to others for their enlightenment. She is no longer only passive, but has gone through a process which enables her to be creative and fructify herself and others.

Now she sees the spiritual master as the one to whom she can articulate experience. Of course Teresa always sees all parts of the Self as graced and therefore object of a direct intervention of her Lord. She will never refer to the insights as coming from a part of herself separate from the recognition of God's grace, Jesus working in her. [86]

Here, after having developed the Jungian maturation process, we can see that the basic parallel in this paper consists in Jung's finding the animus crucial for the development of the psyche while Teresa found grace to be crucial for the development of the soul. Thus, the parallel can be put simply this way: the animus is to the psyche as grace is to the human soul.

We will continue into the next section of this article with an intuition based on phenomenological analysis. Though we are dealing with works from two empirical sciences, we will proceed by intuiting an interpretation of their words, examples and experiences and then arrive at parallels in their experiences.

FOUR WATERS

Teresa's experience of maturity is always put within a religious context and so it should not surprise us that her account of significant growth is situated within the imagery of growth in prayer.

She gives an account of her growth in prayer through the image of different ways of watering a garden.[87]

The ego is seen as a gardener beginning with barren soil filled with weeds. Up to this point the ego did not recognize the seeds of evil (shadow) within the psyche (ground) but now it is visible, the crisis has taken place. The ego is now aware that these aspects of the person need to be dealt with. Before the good seed can flourish, one has to take responsibility for the weeds. The weeds could also be a good representation of negative animus opinions and projections which up to this point have been denied or ignored and have finally forced their way up to consciousness. The focal awareness is not constructive but damaging at this point and can destroy the good seed, or prevent it (the ability to focus in a healthy manner) from growing to maturity.

The first part of the growth of the person must be the preparation, awareness of the shadow, its recognition, and dealing with it.

The plants that Teresa sees eventually, when the garden is prepared and watered, are the virtues. In this term she recognizes the proper and balanced functioning of all aspects of the interior person for fruitfulness and the service of others.

Jung also recognized that the application of the Christian virtues was necessary in the process of individuation:

> To live in perpetual flight from ourselves is a bitter thing and to live with ourselves demands a number of Christian virtues which we then have to apply to our own case, such as patience, love, faith, hope, and humility. It is all very fine to make our neighbor happy by applying them to him, but the demon of self-admiration so easily clasps us on the back and says, "well done!" And because this is a great psychological truth, it must be stood on its head for an equal number of people so as to give the devil something to carp at. But does it make *us* happy when we have to apply these virtues to ourselves? When I am the recipient of my own gifts, the least among my brothers whom I must take in-

to my own bosom? When I must admit that I need all my patience, my love, my faith, and even my humility, and that I
myself am my own devil, the antagonist who always wants the
opposite in everything? Can we ever really endure ourselves?
"Do unto others . . ." — this is as true of evil as of good.[88]

Just as Jung chose to stress the humility needed to overcome
the "demon of self-admiration," Teresa also found in her experience that humility often summed up the whole import of self-
knowledge. Humility for her is not only realizing one's dark side
but also one's giftedness.

We will see this application of the Christian virtues to the self
(that Jung stresses) in the *Life* of Teresa. In fact she will often
and repeatedly refer at each stage in her development of prayer
to the need of applying these virtues to the Self. But the ultimate
result is that they are used in the service of others and faithful-
ness to God.

Just as in the process of individuation one must continually be
involved in all the stages of development, even though one has
achieved integration, so too Teresa recognizes that all four
waters are used in the soul throughout life.[89]

For Jungians the imagery of water represents the unconscious. In Teresa's four waters, the waters spoken of are progressively more visible and available. These waters seem to represent the focal awareness of her animus which is necessary for
the cultivation, recognition, experiencing and sharing with
others of the virtues brought forth from the Self.

The unconscious is hidden deep within the person and will
become for a woman focal awareness. This unconscious material or function needs to be poured forth on the psyche (represented by the garden) to bring forth the Self as the fully integrated, cared for and growing garden. Just as it is a lot of work
to prepare and maintain the garden at first, so too preparing
and maintaining the Self is work which gets progressively easier
as time goes on.

First Water

Beginners care for the interior life by drawing water from a well at this stage. Here we can recognize an attempt on the part of a person to begin the process of drawing out the water (animus) from the depths (repressed, ignored or unrecognized unconscious) so that it can be poured on the ground (constructive use of the animus). The ground (psyche) needs to be watered (nurtured), the water is necessary for the growth of the seed in the garden, and the first attempts are to run between the garden and the well (the animus must be drawn with much labor from the depths of the unconscious to be applied to the conscious life).

The gardener (ego) is having to use energy to search out the water (animus) that can be poured upon the ground so as to raise up the plants. The outpouring of the animus' focal awareness on the psyche brings about wholeness and transforms the psyche into the Self, resulting in the development and growth of the virtues in the person.

She stresses thinking about one's past life. In this way a person gains self-knowledge which will result in the virtues, especially genuine humility (the knowledge of good and bad within). One needs to recognize the source of one's gifts and recognize their goodness while not allowing oneself to become subject to the "demon of self-admiration,"[90] by balancing one's view with the realization of the shadow, the negative animus in oneself (weeds).[91]

Even when the well runs dry (we are exhausted) one receives encouragement by means of another source ("tears" or interior feelings). In this we understand also that the process of individuation once begun can become tiring but the Self has ways of giving insights from the unconscious so that we do not lose heart and turn from the task (God finds ways of getting us to grow through this stage of dryness).

There is a need to persist in trying to draw water from the well, even when it is dry, so as to be there and drawing when the water begins to flow again. (We must continue our mental prayer and keep God, the end, in mind.) So in individuation one wants to give up because it is hard to keep struggling with negative projections and irrelevant opinions, to face how much work is needed before results will show, or to see the demise of one's strength. Nonetheless, one has to push on in sincerity by relating to the animus, keeping the goal (wholeness) in mind. Without keeping the end in mind the way will seem too hard.

The main idea is to remain faithful despite outward appearances of no fruit. One must be selfless in dedication to the goal. It helps if the person recalls that others have gone through the same dryness.

This part of the process (the first water) took Teresa many years.[92] In all she recognized her dependency on God to move her through this period and how much he taught her about herself. She had to learn this dependency on God and her inability to grow on her own. The image of Christ bearing his cross and her helping him by growing in prayer supports her in this process. In individuation, the woman in order to grow must learn to trust and depend on her animus' focal awareness. Only by integrating both the diffused awareness of her ego and the focal awareness of her animus can she come to wholeness. There must be cooperation and balance between the two.

Teresa's trust in the process and its source is continuous throughout these stages.[93] Each person has his own way and "time-line" in this process. Ultimately it is the development of the virtues and their fruits that matters, not the specific path one takes or how swiftly one proceeds. In individuation one then has to have trust in the process and the way in which the Self is leading toward wholeness.

Teresa warns that we must learn to trust our experience and use discernment with regard to trials, weaknesses and setbacks. She believes and teaches an exchange of care between the body and the soul.[94] Furthermore, one can overtire and weaken the body and ego in the process of individuation by too intense a pursuit of the animus. Patience and balance is needed. A guide, an analyst, is helpful in balancing one's zeal and discouragements just as Teresa saw the importance of spiritual masters for temperance and perseverance in prayer.

We are not to be impatient but to take each stage as it comes. To force oneself to go to another stage as if finished with the previous is to make a grave mistake. One stage builds upon another.[95]

"Since this edifice is built entirely on humility, the closer one comes to God the more progress there must be in this virtue; and if there is no progress in humility, everything is going to be ruined."[96] True knowledge of Self is the foundation of individuation. In this one will not assume a speed of progress ahead of Self and yet not tarry unnecessarily.

"5. What I say about not ascending to God unless he raises one up is language of the spirit."[97] One waits for the proper time for the animus to focus one's thinking, one does not try to force it without first going through the necessary preparations. To tell feelings and facts of the situation is necessary to a woman so the animus can speak relevantly.

Articulation of what the animus relates also comes in proper time and not right away. God gave Teresa the experience first, and then the ability to express it in words.[98] The animus will begin to act as word when the groundwork has been done and is appropriate.

> ... It is good to walk in fear of self so as to avoid trusting oneself either little or much when entering into an occasion where God is usually offended. This fear is most necessary until we are whole in virtue ...[99]

The self she speaks of here may be the ego, in which case she recognizes the necessity of its maintainance and strength, yet fears it. It can try to eliminate or suppress the animus, because it hates to lose its central position and is tempted to keep that position at the expense of the rest of the person. At the same time it can be a great tool for integrating the animus in the process. Wholeness makes this concern unnecessary.

"His Majesty wants this determination, and he is a friend of courageous souls, if they walk in humility and without trusting in self."[100] Here the word "determination" denotes the sincerity necessary to seek out the animus and relate to it. She seems to be saying that one must look outside the ego to the Self (His Majesty) for wholeness. The "self" she is speaking of here is most likely the ego.

"For though the soul is not yet strong enough it nonetheless takes flight and goes very high although like a little fledgling it soon tires and stops."[101] There are limits to what can be accomplished at this stage, and even though one may get a glimpse of what the animus can do or what wholeness is, one cannot yet achieve it on a permanent basis.

Second Water

The second water is drawn by a water wheel and so is less work for the gardener but still must be carried and distributed throughout the garden. Teresa calls this form of prayer the prayer of quiet. She points out that not only is there less work but more water is available in this prayer.[102]

> 2. Here the soul begins to be recollected and comes upon something supernatural because in no way can it acquire this prayer through any efforts it may make. True, at one time it seemingly got tired turning the crank, and working with the intellect, and filling the aqueducts. But here the water is higher, and so the labor is much less than that required in pulling it up from the well. I mean that the water is closer because grace is more closely manifest to the soul.[103]

A woman's ego at this stage comes upon and accepts the animus as positive and other than itself (supernatural). What comes forth from that animus is ready made, complete. There is still a struggle to bring the animus forth and give the necessary information for its focus to be on target but it is easier than in the first stage. One is a little more proficient.

> 4. All this that takes place here brings with it the greatest consolation and with so little labor that prayer does not tire one, even though it lasts for a long while. The intellect's work here is very slow paced, and it obtains a lot more water than it pulled

out of the well. The tears God gives are now accompanied by joy; however, although they are experienced, there is no striving after them.[104]

One is capable of working on the animus for longer periods of time and recognizes it easily. Tears accompany this recognition signifying the woman's identifying it with the deepest inner truth. She feels this truth wholly.[105]

> 5. This water of great blessings and favors that the Lord gives here makes the virtues grow incomparably better than in the previous degree of prayer, for the soul is now ascending above its misery and receiving a little knowledge of the delights of glory. This water I believe makes the virtues grow better and also brings the soul much closer to the true Virtue, which is God, from whence come all the virtues. His Majesty is beginning to communicate himself to this soul, and he wants it to experience how he is doing so.[106]

The virtues are strengthened in the process as applied by the Self to the psyche and are recognized in their source as from deep within (God). Because the animus is recognized for what it is, it is heard more clearly.

"In earthly things it would seem to me a marvel were we ever to understand just where we can find this satisfaction, for there is never lacking in these earthly things both the 'yes' and the 'no' . . ."[107]

One no longer needs to project the animus because it is recognized in itself. Polarization is recognized and she sees that though her emphasis is on the masculine animus the ego is eventually to be brought together with the animus so that they work together, the masculine-feminine principles, the 'yes'/'no,' will come together in a creative tension.

> . . . I begged him to increase the fragrance of the little flowers of virtue that were beginning to bloom, so it seemed, and that they might give him glory and that he might sustain them since I desired nothing for myself—and that he might cut the ones he wanted, for I already knew that better ones would flower, I say

"cut" because there are times when the soul has no thought of this garden. Everything seems to be dry, and it seems there is not going to be any water to sustain it — nor does it appear that there has ever been in the soul anything of virtue. It undergoes much tribulation because the Lord desires that it seem to the poor gardener that everything acquired in watering and keeping the garden up is being lost. This dryness amounts to an authentic weeding and pulling up of the remaining bad growth by its roots, no matter how small it may be. By knowing that there is no diligence that suffices it God takes away the water of grace and by placing little value on the nothing that we are, and even less than nothing, the soul gains much humility. The flowers begin to grow again.[108]

Teresa sees that in this stage "little flowers of virtue" are beginning to make their presence known by blossoms and fragrance. In this she seems to point out that the recognition (in the first water) and the acceptance (in the second water) of the animus have already brought about some positive results. This fact helps the Self in allowing the ego to recognize positive results. The cutting represents the non-attachment to these results that is necessary so that one is willing to go on to the next stage of maturity rather than be satisfied with present results as if they were the ultimate goal of the whole process.

At times the ego gives up the work, exhausted. When this happens the ego counts all progress as lost. The results gained (little flowers) disappear. This is the experience, at times, of the selfish ego that pulls back from the task at hand or is too exhausted to continue and allows the results of the first two stages to die. This substantiates the Self as the source of the process as instigator and sustainer, rather than the ego. Alone the ego is incapable of individuation. Just to realize this (as one of the results of this stage) leads to a rebirth of the process and to new results.

Teresa goes on to talk about the "little spark" which is enkindled in the soul which "will begin to enkindle the large fire." Here it seems that she considers the light of the animus as a little help, but as the beginning of what will be a great source of enlightenment in the future as a result of the process.[109]

... We should fix our eyes on the true and lasting kingdom we are trying to gain. It is very important to keep this kingdom always in mind, especially in the beginning ...[110]

She reminds us to keep the goal in mind. One must never lose sight of wholeness as the goal. This wholeness is often represented in psychology with a mandala (Kingdom) that is balanced in all its parts having a center and its outer dimensions as a circle.

One must be aware of and willing to accept the suffering that comes in the process.[111]

15. In sum, so as not to tire myself, this prayer of quiet is the beginning of all blessings. The flowers are already at the point in which hardly anything is lacking for them to bud; and the soul sees this very clearly. In no way is it able to believe at that time that God is not within it. When it sees again the cracks and imperfections in itself, it then fears everything ...[112]

The focal awareness of the animus has become more visible and capable of being evidenced to others. There is still a fear of the negative animus, the failure of the ego to relate the diffused awareness in conjunction with the focal awareness of the animus. But that fear is overridden by the realization that the Self is a reality within that works despite the presence of the shadow.

Third Water

1. Let us come now to speak of the third water by which this garden is irrigated, that is, the water flowing from a river or spring. By this means the garden is irrigated with much less labor, although some labor is required to direct the flow of the water. The Lord so desires to help the gardener here that he himself becomes practically the gardener and the one who does everything.[113]

Here the animus is well directed and used by the ego (recognized, accepted), and put to use. The flow of its particular awareness (focal) is being brought to bear on the psyche (gar-

den) without much busyness except learning the necessary tools
to bring it to bear appropriately (irrigation trough or ditches).
The woman's energy is spent in directing or using her focal
awareness, not in discovering it or in an effort to bring it forth
from the depths of the unconscious. The Self (Lord) seems to
have taken over most of the work and delivers the ego (gardener)
from exhausting activity. The ego can now rest and function as
a partner of the animus though still having to work presenting
diffused awareness adequately so as to direct the focal awareness in the proper directions.[114]

The Self is taking over more and more as the central reality of
the person, thus freeing the ego from a false and exhausting
role. Now it is learning to act as a partner of the animus within
the Self.[115] The light of the animus is in hand. Its light is shining
and is possessed within the Self.[116] So it is that the ego has died to
control and power, and now acquiesces to the greater position
of the Self. It is indeed a true wisdom.[117]

". . . For the truth of the matter is that the faculties are almost totally united with God but not so absorbed as not to function . . ."[118]

The ego still functions separately though within the Self and
perfect balance between it and the animus is not total.

". . . Now the flowers are blossoming; they are beginning to
spread their fragrance . . ."[119]

The virtues (flowers) are developed though not perfected.
The fruits (fragrance) of the individuation process are visible
and affecting others.

> 7. I should like the five of us who at present love each other in
> Christ to make a kind of pact that since others in these times
> gather together in secret against His Majesty to prepare wicked
> deeds and heresies, we might seek to gather together some time
> to free each other from illusion and to speak about how we
> might mend our ways and please God more since no one knows
> himself as well as others who observe him if they do so with love
> and concern for his progress . . .[120]

Teresa still sees the need to relate to others and be able to articulate her experience so as not to suffer from illusion. One always runs the risk of fooling oneself and allowing the ego to control what is happening and thwart the place of the Self. Everyone needs others to whom to articulate the process and one's own progress within it so as to have an objective measure of that progress. Here again is Teresa's continuing stress on spiritual masters and on sharing with others what is experienced and Jung's concern for an analyst to act as guide through the process of individuation:

> . . . I only think it is amazed at seeing how good a gardener the Lord is and how he doesn't desire it to do any of the work other than delight in the fragrance the flowers are beginning to give. For in one of these visits, however brief, the water is given without measure because the gardener is who he is — in truth, the creator of the water. And what the poor soul could not achieve in about twenty years with its labors to bring repose to the intellect, this heavenly gardener accomplishes in a moment. And the fruit grows and matures in such a way that the soul can be sustained from its garden if the Lord so desires. But he doesn't give it permission to distribute fruit until it is very strong from what it has eaten; otherwise it will be giving it to others to taste without their receiving any profit or gain, maintaining them and giving them to eat at its own cost; and perhaps it will itself be left dead from hunger . . . [121]

The Self leads the person to a realization of the process of coming to wholeness so that results are obvious. The animus focuses well when properly approached and seems limitless in its enlightening (discerning) powers. Great accomplishments are achieved in this stage of individuation.

The process is not far enough along for the person to be competent to help others in their process but must be satisfied to gain from this experience and wait until it is mature enough to share its fruits with others. It must know itself and how to integrate the parts of the psyche in the wholeness of Self before sharing its awareness with others.

3. In the sum, the virtues are stronger than in the previous prayer of quiet. The soul can't ignore them, because it sees that it is different and doesn't know how this happened. It begins to perform great deeds by means of the fragrance the flowers give, for the Lord desires that they bloom so that it may see that it possesses virtue although it is very clearly aware that is couldn't have acquired them — nor was it able to — in many years, and also that in that moment the heavenly gardener gave them. Here the humility that remains in the soul is much greater and more profound than in the past . . . It seems to me this kind of prayer is a very apparent union of the whole soul with God . . .[122]

Teresa stresses the greater strength of the virtues, particularly humility.

Apparent wholeness is being achieved in individuation:

Although this prayer seems entirely the same as the prayer of quiet I mentioned, it is different — partly because in the prayer of quiet the soul didn't desire to move or stir, rejoicing in that holy idleness of Mary; and in this prayer it can also be Martha in such a way that it is as though engaged in both the active and contemplative life together . . .[123]

Here Teresa touches upon the specific difference between the second and third waters. The third water is similar to the second except in the role of Martha (active Masculine focal awareness, animus) and Mary (passive feminine diffused awareness, ego) are to work together. There are still elements that need to be integrated but cooperation has begun.

She goes on to delineate the aspects of the role of Martha (the animus) as she sees it:

. . . For it is one grace to receive the Lord's favor; another, to understand which favor and grace it is, and a third, to know how to describe and explain it. And although no more than the first grace seems necessary, it is a great advantage and a gift for the soul that it also understands the favor so as not to go about confused and afraid and so that it may become more courageous in following the path of the Lord, trampling under its feet all worldly things.[124]

The given is the animus and that animus is the focal awareness that allows the woman to know that she knows (is in touch with her unconscious material), has the ability to understand how the animus works, its purpose and how to use it properly together with her diffused awareness (understanding) and the ability to articulate this to others (describe and explain it). With these abilities woman can reject society's demand that she deny her masculine inner animus (trampling under its feet all worldly things) and affirm this part of her Self.

Fourth Water

This water is represented by rain. It is least work, the most visible, although still retaining its hiddenness (cloud), and abundance of all the waters.

> 2. How this prayer they call union comes about and what it is I don't know how to explain . . . The way this happens is comparable to what happens when a fire is burning and flaming, and it sometimes becomes a forceful blaze. The flame then shoots very high above the fire, but the flame is not by that reason something different from the fire but the same flame that is in the fire . . . [125]

> . . . A small fire is just as much a fire as is a large one . . . [126]

Teresa finds that she can only explain the experience of union through images. In individuation this is also true. We use images to explain what we experience in the union of polarities. The flame may represent the animus breaking forth, appearing in the life of the woman to others and at the same time remaining a part of her inner Self.

> . . . What union is we already know since it means that two separate things become one . . . [127]

The unity of all parts of the psyche and the balance of all polarities make up one whole Self.

> Well now, let us speak of this heavenly water that in its abundance soaks and saturates this entire garden; if the Lord were always to give it when there is need, the gardener would evidently have it easy . . . But this is impossible while we are living on this earth . . ."[128]

Total individuation in the sense of perfect achievement of wholeness is impossible. The woman must struggle always to be growing, maturing and discovering new aspects of her Self. To achieve balance at one point is to achieve only part of an ongoing task.

> 14. Now let us come to what the soul experiences here interiorly. Let him who knows how to speak of it since it cannot be understood — much less put into words![129]

Human words cannot convey the totality of the experience of wholeness.

> 1. This prayer and union leaves the greatest tenderness in the soul in such a way that it would want to be consumed not from pain but from joyous tears. It finds itself bathed in them without having felt them or knowing when or how it shed them. But it receives great delight in seeing that the driving force of that fire is quenched by a water that came forth so forcefully and quickly and that seemingly poured from that heavenly cloud.[130]

Now the animus is visible, as a cloud is visible in the sky, and drenches the Self with its awareness. The fear of the diffused awareness being drowned by the focal is no longer because diffused awareness is seen as necessary for the focal to be used.

Tears are woman's symbol of being in touch with her deepest truth.

> . . . The intellect doesn't have to go hunting for this knowledge because it beholds there, all cooked and prepared, what it must eat and understand.[131]

So the animus gives to the psyche the complete worked out truth. Thought comes forth already formed, developed, and formulated.

> . . . It can now, with clear understanding that the fruits are not its own, begin to distribute them since it has no need of them. It starts to show signs of a soul that guards heavenly treasures and has the desire to share them with others and it beseeches God that it may not be the only rich one. It begins to be of benefit to its neighbors almost without knowing it or doing anything of itself. They recognize it because now the fragrance of the flowers has reached the point in which it attracts others. The soul understands that it has virtues, and its neighbors see the desirable fruit. They would like to help it eat this fruit. If the soul is well cultivated by trials, persecutions, criticisms, and ill-nesses — for few there must be who reach this stage without them — and if it is softened by living in great detachment from self-interest, the water soaks it to the extent that it is almost never dry. But if the soil is still hardened in the earth and has a lot of briers, as I did in the beginning, and is still not so removed from occasions and if it doesn't have the gratitude a favor as great as this deserves, the ground will dry up again. And if the gardener becomes careless and the Lord solely out of his good-ness does not desire to let the rains come again, the garden can be considered as lost. So it happened to me sometimes . . . For tears gain all things: one water draws down the other.[132]

Now the woman has not only enjoyed the fruits of the Self but finds that she is concerned to share those fruits with others. Others have been attracted already by the virtues they have witnessed in her as a result of her wholeness process. It is an ef-fortless task to share the results of the process.

One must be open to the fact that even those negative things which happen to us (trials, persecutions, criticisms and ill-nesses) are a necessary part of the growth process. The Self em-braces all or the balance and wholeness will be lost. It is a con-stant working to individuate and integrate everything within the person. This Teresa learned from her own experience, ("So it happened to me sometimes.")

Tears (which are the sign of a woman's being in touch with the inner truth) now also become signs of getting in touch with the process of the working of the animus as well as its having delivered an insight:

> 15. This self-reliance was what destroyed me. For this reason and for every reason there is need of a master and for discussions with spiritual persons . . . [133]

She again stresses the need for a guide and sharing with others who are experienced in these things. ". . . It is his soul, it is he who has taken it into his charge, and thus he illumines it . . ."[134] The Self is whole, in control and thus the animus and ego act as integrated parts of it. They work from within the Self freely.

> When my soul reached this stage where God granted it such a great favor, the evil in me disappeared, and the Lord gave me strength to break away from it. It didn't bother me to be amid the occasions of falling and with people who formerly distracted me any more than if there were no occasions at all; what used to do me harm was helping me. All things were a means for my knowing and loving God more, for seeing what I owed him, and for regretting what I had been.[135]

The Self now incorporates the shadow in such a way that it is no longer seen as a disintegrating force. By "breaking away from it" Teresa has an understanding of a deliverance from a negative force which can no longer affect her. What was formerly an occasion of evil now is an integrated part of the Self. Now all leads to wholeness, nothing is foreign to the Self. "12. Here in this ecstasy are received the true revelations and the great favors and visions — and all serves to humiliate and strengthen the soul, to lessen its esteem for the things of this life, and to make it know more clearly the grandeurs of the reward the Lord has prepared for those who serve him."[136] Now all serves to bring one to true humility and the realization of strength. One knows the Self is on the road to ongoing wholeness. What seemed so important on the outside is now unimportant. The inner journey is what matters and that which results from it in love. All becomes love.

CONCLUSION

So we see that Teresa has the religious dimension in her maturation process of an ongoing trust in God and his constant personal involvement in her process. Everything good comes from him because he, through his grace, is the source of every movement to maturation. God is her all, he is the image of perfection. He is that perfection for which she strives, the ultimate symbol of her wholeness.

When wholeness is a reality the union of all opposites is complete in an ongoing process. The masculine and feminine are united as Teresa and Jesus, and all polarities are dynamically balanced in this symbol.

The point of this whole study is that Teresa found maturity through the process of contemplation. "By their works you shall know them," the Lord said, and so we look to the generativity of Teresa and see that she achieved renown for her accurate assessment of the inner journey and the ability to establish a model for men and women by which this process could be lived for their own maturity and that of others. In fact, her spirit lives on today in thousands of people who use her as a model in their striving to wholeness. Her writings are still used as a blueprint of the process through contemplation.

She came to the integration of her diffused and focal awareness by self-knowledge and came to wholeness, to dynamically balance the polarities within her psyche, to become a generative woman of her times and universally recognized as a model of Christian Wholeness. Is it any wonder that the Church has officially recognized her as a Doctor of the Church?

I chose the *Life* of Teresa for this comparison for three reasons. First she wrote it when she was in her mature years. Secondly, after she wrote it she continually carried a copy of it wherever she went because she felt it was the best expression of who she was as a result of this process. Thirdly, after its completion she felt so profoundly moved by the change she saw in herself, the process of her own growth, that she began to sign her name as Teresa of Jesus instead of Teresa de Ahumada.

This work seems to be the summation of the maturation process as Teresa experienced it in her life. She recognized that though her confessors had commanded her to write it that she had been driven for some time to write it and had been resisting. This drive was from within, her animus was pushing for her to reflect on her life's process to attain the awareness of self and process to be whole.

She changed the way she signed her name to represent the hidden reality, the principle of life, Jesus, the Light, the Symbol of her focal awareness, the animus, united with her conscious person, her ego, her diffused awareness. She recognized herself as whole after writing this book and symbolized it in her signature which then contained the symbol of the ego (Teresa) and the animus (Jesus), Teresa of Jesus.

NOTES

1. C.G. Jung, *Aion: Researches into the Phenomenology of Self*, trans. R.F.C. Hull (Princeton: Princeton Univ. Press, 1959), 3 and 6.
2. Irene Claremont de Castillejo, *Knowing Woman: A Feminine Psychology* (New York: Harper and Row, 1973), 169.
3. Ibid., 78.
4. Richard Gelwick, *The Way of Discovery: An Introduction to the Thought of Michael Polanyi* (New York: Oxford Univ. Press, 1977), 62.
5. Ibid., 57.
6. C.G. Jung, *The Undiscovered Self*, trans. R.F.C. Hull (New York: New American Library, 1958), 111 and 112. Italics in the original.
7. Gelwick, *The Way of Discovery*, 63 and 64.
8. Ibid., p. 67.
9. Ibid.
10. Ibid., 89.
11. C.G. Jung, *The Archetypes and the Collective Unconscious*, Trans. R.F.C. Hull (Princeton: Princeton Univ. Press, 1960), 79f.
12. C.G. Jung, *The Psychology of the Transference*, trans. R.F.C. Hull (Princeton: Princeton Univ. Press, 1966), 134.
13. Ibid., 142.
14. Ibid.,141.
15. C.G. Jung, *Two Essays on Analytical Psychology*, trans. R.F.C. Hull (Princeton, Princeton Univ. Press, 1966), 205.

16. Ibid., 207.

17. Ibid., 208.

18. Claremont de Castillejo, *Knowing Woman*, 86.

19. Jung, *Two Essays*, 209.

20. June Singer, *Androgeny: Toward A New Theory of Sexuality* (New York: Doubleday — Anchor Press, 1976), 197.

21. C.G. Jung, *Memories, Dreams, Reflections*, Aniela Jaffé ed., trans. Richard and Clara Winston (New York: Random House, 1963), 392.

22. Claremont de Castillejo, *Knowing Woman*, the whole chap. on Animus.

23. Ibid., 77.

24. Ibid., 84.

25. Ibid., 170. "The animus is portrayed as woman's representative of the Eternal Logos. He is the word, the power to formulate, to analyse, to discriminate between the opposites."

26. Jung. *Aion*, 62 and 63.

27. C.G. Jung, *The Structure and Dynamics of the Psyche*, trans. R.F.C. Hull (Princeton: Princeton Univ. Press, 1960), 133f:

> . . . qualities that are not individually acquired but are inherited, e.g., instincts as impulses to carry out actions from necessity, without conscious motivation. In this "deeper" stratum we also find the . . . *archetypes* . . . the instincts and archetypes together form the "collective unconscious." I call it "collective" because, unlike the personal unconscious, it is not made up of individual and more or less unique contents but those which are universal and of regular occurrence.

28. Jung, *Aion*, 5.

29. Jung, *The Psychology of the Transference*, 35.

30. Ibid., 71.

31. Ibid., 103.

32. Jung, *Two Essays*, 26; and idem, *Aion*, 229.

33. Jung, *Aion*, 163.

34. Jung, *Structure and Dynamics*, 226.

35. June Singer, *Boundaries of the Soul: The Practice of Jung's Psychology* (New York: Doubleday — Anchor Press, 1971), 272.

36. Clement of Alexandria, *Christ the Educator*, vol. 23: The Fathers of the Church, trans. Simon P. Wood (New York: Fathers of the Church, Inc., 1654), bk. 3, chap. 1, sent. 1-2.

37. L, 13, 15.

38. Jung, *Archetypes and Collective Unconscious*, 275; Singer, *Boundaries of the Soul*, 158.

39. Singer, *Boundaries of the Soul*, 280.

40. Ibid.

41. Ibid., 410.

42. Ann Belford Ulanov, *The Feminine in Jungian Psychology and in Christian Theology* (Evanston: Northwestern Univ. Press, 1971), 67.

43. Ibid.

44. Claremont de Castillejo, *Knowing Woman*, 84.

45. L, 7, 11.

46. Claremont de Castillejo, *Knowing Woman*, 78:

> . . . At the slightest beckon of her finger he appears, throws his light in answer to her question on what seems to be the formula she seeks, and out she comes with a slogan, correct enough probably as a general truth, or in its rightful context, but just as irrelevant to the matter at hand, or the particular case. When he is wide of the mark he is not dangerous because his bad aim is apparent. Often however, he is only a hair's breadth away from the truth and then sounds so plausible that, unperceived, in a few minutes the woman, and not infrequently her hearers, have been subtly led far astray from the matter at hand.

47. Ibid., 80: "*Irrelevance* is, I believe, the unmistakable hallmark of a negative animus statement."

48. Singer, *Boundaries of the Soul*, 252:

> It is a necessary part of man's development to meet the anima first in her projected form, that is out in the world, and deal with her there. Concomitantly, the same thing needs to happen to the woman in connection with her animus. Otherwise, anima and animus remain locked in the unconscious and are not released to create the struggles that bring with them the potential for a widening of consciousness. Anima and animus cannot be experienced until they have first been projected onto the opposite sex.

49. Claremont de Castillejo, *Knowing Woman*, 89: "For one thing, when a woman ceases to project her own aspect of the negative animus onto her man, he becomes free to function unhampered by this incubus."

50. Ibid., 80:

> It is the woman who is not using the animus creatively who is at his mercy for he *must* throw his light somewhere. So he attracts her attention by throwing his light on one formula or slogan after another quite regardless of their exact relevance. She falls into the trap and accepts what he shows her as gospel truth.

51. Ibid., 81: "So also, in an inner dialogue, what the animus tells her will be

a valueless generalization unless she gives him all the facts; above all, the facts of her feelings, their intensity, their object."

52. Ibid., 79.

53. Josef Goldbrunner, *Individuation: A Study of the Depth Psychology of Carl Gustav Jung,* trans. Stanley Godman (New York: Pantheon Books, 1956), 119.

54. Singer, *Boundaries of the Soul,* 273.

55. Emma Jung, *Animus and Anima: Two Essays* (Dallas: Spring Publications, 1957), 3 and 4.

56. Ulanov, *The Feminine,* 269:

> The phase of confrontation for the woman, therefore, is not urged by the animus, as it is by the anima in the man, but by the self. The dominance of the self archtype urges her to individuation in order to come to herself and to develop her own uniqueness and wholeness. The self for the woman is, of course, feminine — and here is a salient point. This highest phase of confrontation and individuation in both sexes is initiated by the feminine: for the man, through the anima, which leads to the self; for the woman, through the feminine self, not through any contrasexual elements . . . The masculine initiates the emergence of consciousness from primary unconsciousness, the feminine initiates the completion of consciousness by re-establishing contact with the unconscious.

57. Jung, *Two Essays,* 173.

58. Jaffé ed., *Memories, Dreams, Reflections,* 196.

59. Ulanov, *The Feminine,* 245 and 246.

60. L, 1, 6.

61. Ulanov, *The Feminine,* 246.

62. Ibid., 247.

63. L, 2, 1-2.

64. L, 2, 7.

65. L, 3, 7:

> Reading the *Letters of Saint Jerome* so encouraged me that I decided to tell my father about my decision to take the habit, for I was so persistent in points of honor that I don't think I would have turned back for anything once I told him. So great was his love for me that in no way was I able to obtain his permission or achieve anything through persons I asked to intercede for me. The most we could get from him was that after his death I could do whatever I wanted.

66. L, 4, 1:

> In those days while I was making these decisions, I persuaded one of my brothers to become a friar, telling him about the vanity of the world. We both agreed to go one morning very early to the convent where that friend of mine was, which was the convent I liked very much. For in this final decision I was determined to go where I thought I could serve God more, or where my father desired. For I was already thinking more of a remedy for my soul than of any easy way of life for myself.

67. Ibid.:

> I remember, clearly and truly, that when I left my father's house I felt that separation so keenly that the feeling will never be greater, I think, when I die. For it seemed that every bone in my body was being sundered. Since there was no love of God to take away my love for my father and relatives, everything so constrained me that if the Lord hadn't helped me, my reflections would not have been enough for me to continue on. In this situation He gave me such courage against myself that I carried out the task.

68. L, 7, 14:

> I believe I served him somewhat for the trials he suffered during mine . . . Since in losing him I was losing every good and joy, and he was everything to me, I had great determination not to show him my grief until he would die to act as though I were well. When I saw him coming to the end of his life, it seemed my soul was being wrenched from me, for I love him dearly.

69. Ulanov, *The Feminine*, 255 and 256.

70. Ibid., 258:

> This patriarchal type of dependence of a woman upon man and man upon woman establishes a symbiosis where each gives up his or her own natural psychological contrasexuality. The man identifies with all that is consciously masculine, with consciousness and the ego structure; the woman identifies with the unconscious. Masculine and feminine are polarized.
>
> A man's unconscious femininity, in form of the anima, is projected onto woman, and a woman's unconscious masculinity, in the form of the animus, is projected onto man.

71. L, 7, 10-13.

72. L, 13, 3: "These first acts of determination are very important, although

in this initial stage it is necessary to hold back a little and be bound by discretion and the opinion of a spiritual master."

73. L, 13, 12: "I want to explain myself further because these matters concerning prayer are all difficult and if one doesn't find a master for himself, they are very hard to understand."

74. L, 13, 13 and 16; 13,21; 19, 15; 23, 10 and 11.

75. L, 23, 8.

76. L, 23, 10:

> It was then that I arranged that the holy gentleman come sometime to see me. Here I saw his great humility, that he wished to talk to someone as wretched as myself. He began to visit me, encourage me, and tell me that I shouldn't think I could give up everything in one day, that little by little God would do the work, that he himself had been for some years unable to make a break with some very trivial things. O humility, what great blessings you bestow where you are present on those who approach the one who possesses you!

77. Ibid.:

> Because I hope in God that your Reverence will be able to help many souls, I mention it here; this gentleman was my complete salvation in knowing how to cure me and in having the humility and the charity to stay with me — and patience while seeing that I wasn't making amends in everything. He proceeded with discretion little by little showing me ways to conquer the devil. I began to have such a great love for him that there was no greater recreation for me than on the days I saw him, although they were few. When he was late, I became very worried because it then seemed to me that since I was so wretched he wasn't going to see me.

78. L, 23, 11:

> Since he was getting to know my very great imperfections, and they would even be sins — although after I spoke with him I made greater amends — and since I mentioned to him the favors granted me by God so that he could give me light, he told me that my imperfections were incompatible with the favors and that these gifts were bestowed on persons who were already very far advanced and mortified, that he couldn't help but fear a great deal because in some things it seemed to him there was a bad spirit, although he didn't come to a definite conclusion. But he thought well of all that he understood about my prayer, and he said so. The difficulty was that I didn't know how to say

either little or much about my prayer; for only recently did God give me this favor of understanding what it is and knowing how to speak about it.

79. Ibid.

80. L, 23,12:

> Looking through books in order to see if I could learn how to explain the prayer I was experiencing, I found in one they called *Ascent of the Mount*, where it touches on the union of the soul with God, all the signs I experienced in that not thinking of anything. This was what I was most often saying: that when I experienced that prayer I wasn't able to think of anything. I marked the pertinent passages and gave him the book so that he and the other priest I mentioned, the saintly one and servant of God, might look it over and tell me what I should do, and that if they thought I should, I would give up prayer completely—for why should I place myself in these dangers.

81. L, 25, 3.

82. L, 24, 5: "I heard these words: 'No longer do I want you to converse with men but with angels.' This experience terrified me because the movement of the soul was powerful and these words were spoken to me deep within the spirit; so it frightened me—although on the other hand I felt great consolation when the fear that, I think, was caused by the novelty of the experience left me."

83. L, 25, 14.

84. L, 26, 5:

> When they forbade the reading of many books in the vernacular, I felt that prohibition very much because reading some of them was an enjoyment for me and I could no longer do so since only the Latin editions were allowed. The Lord said to me: 'Don't be sad, for I shall give you a living book' . . . Afterward, within only a few days I understood very clearly because I received so much to think about and such recollection in the presence of what I saw, and the Lord showed so much love for me by teaching me in many ways, that I had very little or almost no need for books. His Majesty had become the true book in which I saw the truths. Blessed be such a book that leaves what must be read and done so impressed that you cannot forget!

85. L, 30, 4:

> For at that time I didn't understand myself or how to describe my experiences as I do now (for afterward God enabled me to understand and describe the favors that His Majesty granted me), and it was

necessary that the one who understood me and explained these experiences to me should himself have experienced them. Friar Peter greatly enlightened me; I couldn't understand that such an experience was possible at least as regards the visions that were not imaginative. It seemed to me that I didn't understand either how those I saw with the eyes of my soul were possible. As I said, only those that were seen with the bodily eyes seemed to me to merit attention; and I didn't experience them.

86. L, 40, 9: "Once while in prayer I was shown quickly, without my seeing any form — but it was a totally clear representation — how all things are seen in God and how He holds them all in Himself."

87. L, 11, 6:

The beginner must realize that in order to give delight to the Lord he is starting to cultivate a garden on very barren soil, full of abominable weeds. His Majesty pulls up the weeds and plants good seed. Now let us keep in mind that all of this already done by the time a soul is determined to practice prayer and has begun to make use of it. And with the help of God we must strive like good gardeners to get these plants to grow and take pains to water them so that they don't wither but come to bud and flower and give forth a most pleasant fragrance to provide refreshment for this Lord of ours. Then he will often come to take delight in this garden and find his joy among these virtues.

88. Jung. *The Psychology of the Transference*, 142-43.

89. L, 11, 8: "This person has prepared himself better, and so without any labor of his own the flower garden is watered with all these four waters, although the last is still not given except in drops."

90. Jung, *The Psychology of the Transference*, 142.

91. L, 11, 9.

92. Ibid.

93. L, 11, 12:

My Lord, what do you do but that which is for the greater good of the soul you understand now to be yours and which places itself in your power so as to follow you wherever you go, even to death on the cross, and is determined to help you bear it and not leave you alone with it?

Whoever sees in himself this determination has no reason, no reason whatever, to fear. Spiritual persons, you have no reason to be afflicted. Once you are placed in so high a degree as to desire to commune in solitude with God and abandon the pastimes of the world, the most has been done. Praise His Majesty for that and trust in his goodness who never fails his friends. Conceal from your eyes the thought about why he gives devotion to one after such a few days and not to me after so many years. Let us believe that all is for our own greater good. Let His Majesty lead the way along the path he desires. We belong no longer to ourselves but to him. He grants us a great favor in wanting us to desire to dig in his garden and be in the presence of its Lord who certainly is present with us.

94. L, 11, 16:

> There are other exterior things like works of charity and spiritual reading, although at times it will not even be fit for these. Let it then serve the body out of love of God — because many other times the body serves the soul — and engage in some spiritual pastimes such as holy conversations, provided they are truly so, or going to the country, as the confessor might counsel. Experience is a great help in all, for it teaches what is suitable for us; and God can be served in everything. His yoke is easy, and it is very helpful not to drag the soul along, as they say, but to lead it gently for the sake of its greater advantage.

95. L, 12, 1: "It is very good for a soul that hasn't gone beyond this point to refrain from striving to ascend further. This should be kept in mind, for otherwise the soul wouldn't make progress but would suffer harm."
96. L, 12, 4.
97. L, 12, 5.
98. L, 12, 6:

> Many years passed by in which I read a lot of things and didn't understand anything of what I read. For a long time, even though God favored me, I didn't know what words to use to explain his favors; and this was no small trial. In a way amazing to me, His Majesty when he desires teaches me everything in a moment.
>
> One thing I can truthfully say: although I spoke with many spiritual persons who wanted to explain what the Lord was giving me so that I would be able to speak about it, my dullness was truly so great that their explanations benefited me neither little nor much. Or maybe, since His Majesty has always been my Master, it was the Lord's desire that I have no one else to thank. May he be blessed forever because it is very disconcerting for me to speak in all truth about his favors. Without my desiring or asking (for in this matter of understanding these favors I have by no means been curious — it would have been a virtue to have been so — as I have been in regard to vanities), God gave me in a moment completely clear understanding so that I knew how to explain his favor in a way that amazed me more than it did my confessors; for I understood better than they my own dullness. This clear

understanding was given me a little while ago, and so what the Lord has not taught me I do not strive to know unless it be something touching upon matters of conscience.

99. L, 13, 1.
100. L, 13,2.
101. Ibid.
102. L, 14, 1: "Let us speak now of the second manner, ordained by the Lord of the garden, for getting water; that is, by turning the crank of a water wheel and by aqueducts, the gardener obtains more water with less labor; and he can rest without having to work constantly. Well, this method applied to what they call the prayer of quiet is what I now want to discuss."
103. L, 14, 2.
104. L, 14, 4.
105. Claremont de Castillejo, *Knowing Woman,* 86: "But if we are stirred, if we weep, there is no doubt that what the animus is telling us truly belongs, for a woman's tears accompany her deepest truth. An emotional response is usually a woman's surest guide to what belongs to her."
106. L, 14, 5: "This water of great blessings and favors that the Lord gives here makes the virtues grow incomparably better than in the previous degree of prayer, for the soul is now ascending above its misery and receiving a little knowledge of the delights of glory."
107. Ibid.
108. L, 14, 9.
109. L, 15, 4:

> This prayer, then, is a little spark of the Lord's true love which he begins to enkindle in the soul; and he desires that the soul grow in the understanding of what this love accompanied by delight is. For anyone who has experience, it is impossible not to understand soon that this little spark cannot be acquired. Yet, this nature of ours is so eager for delights that it tries everything; but it is quickly left cold because however much it may desire to light the fire and obtain this delight, it doesn't seem to be doing anything else than throwing water on it and killing it. If this quietude and recollection and little spark is from God's spirit and not a delight given by the devil or procured by ourselves, it will be noticed no matter how small it is. And if a person doesn't extinguish it through his own fault, it is what will begin to enkindle the large fire that (as I shall mention in its place) throws forth flames of the greatest love of God which His Majesty gives to perfect souls.

110. L, 15, 11.

111. L, 15, 13: "Well, returning to what I was saying, a solid foundation for the protection of oneself from the tricks and consolations coming from the devil is to begin with the determination to follow the way of the cross and not desire consolations, since the Lord himself pointed out this way of perfection saying: 'take up your cross and follow me.'"
112. L, 15, 15.
113. L, 16, 1.
114. Ibid.: "This prayer is a sleep of the faculties: the faculties neither fail entirely to function nor understand how they function."
115. Ibid.: "This experience doesn't seem to me to be anything else than an almost complete death to all earthly things and an enjoyment of God."
116. Ibid.: "It is like a person who already has the candle in his hand and for whom little time is left before dying the death he desires: he is rejoicing in that agony with the greatest delight describable."
117. Ibid.: "This prayer is a glorious foolishness, a heavenly madness where the true wisdom is learned; and it is for the soul a most delightful way of enjoying."
118. L, 16, 2.
119. L, 16, 3.
120. L, 16, 7.
121. L, 17, 2.
122. L, 17, 3.
123. L, 17, 4.
124. L, 17, 5.
125. L, 18, 2.
126. L, 18, 7.
127. L, 18, 3.
128. L, 18, 9.
129. L, 18, 14.
130. L, 19, 1.
131. L, 19, 3.
132. Ibid.
133. L, 19, 15.
134. L, 21, 10.
135. Ibid.
136. L, 21, 12.

THE DOCTORATE OF EXPERIENCE

Otger Steggink

Otger Steggink is a Carmelite of the Ancient Observance and professor of spiritual theology at the Nimijen University in the Netherlands. He is especially well known for his collaborative efforts with the Discalced Carmelite Efrén Montalva which produced Tiempo y Vida de Santa Teresa, *the almost encyclopedic and indispensible handbook of everyone interested in studying in depth about St Teresa. This text comes from his book of essays* Experiencia y Realismo en Santa Teresa y San Juan de la Cruz (*Madrid, 1974*).

The proclamation of Teresa of Avila as Doctor of the Church has given an opening to some who would extol this event without precedent as allied to the emancipation of women; as if she were part of the feminist movement of social equality with men. To support this contention of an exalted feminism, which really derives from our times, there is a recurrent theme in the popular press — based on quotes, anecdotes and examples of situations from her life — which appears to make Teresa of Avila a protagonist in the so-called "war of the sexes."

Clearly, this interpretation of the doctorate of Teresa runs the risk of disfiguring the personality of the saint by presenting her only as a manly woman. She would be a woman who might have been, in her time, an example of the "virile protest," in the

275

terms of A. Adler, which is characteristic of a woman unhappy with her proper calling and a woman aspiring to take the place of men in all sectors of public and social life. Such an orientation not only alters the historical figure of Mother Teresa of Jesus, inspired as it is by theories and concepts totally foreign to her spirit, but it also takes away from her doctorate as a woman its true and proper meaning. "Saint Teresa is not a feminist, nor an anti-feminist. This is not the issue—and how far from her is this claim!—in the emancipation and promotion of women."[1]

Of course, the proclamation of a woman as a Doctor of the Church is very modern. Teresa of Jesus exercised in her own time the spiritual teaching for which she deserves this title. That historical-doctrinal reality spares us any attempt to place her on the level of men, because her spiritual teaching (and consequently, also, her doctorate) was and continues to be, typically feminine.

One can illustrate the feminine nature of her teaching with many aspects of her rich personality: her activity as reformer and founder; her task as lawmaker for religious women; her spiritual pedagogy and the doctrine of her writings; her varied social relationships; and her imcomparable sense of adaptation. Nevertheless, her contacts and constant relationships with the "letrados" or theologians of the time, are a touchstone—from our point of view—that is very illustrative as much of her spiritual teaching as of her exquisitely feminine personality; while we see it appear more especially in the positions that she took in the struggle between the so-called "intellectuals" and "mystics," or to use Teresa's own words, between the "letrados" and the "espirituales" or "experienced" ones.[2]

MYSTICS AND INTELLECTUALS

From the end of the fourteenth century, according to some, or from the beginning of the fifteenth century onward, according to others, there was a break a "divorce," between mysticism as faith-experience and "theology" as the science of faith.

Under the influence of an exaggerated application of dialectic theology, there grew up an alienation between theology and lived religiosity, between theology and mysticism.[3] Decadent scholastic theology turned aside reflection on Holy Writ for elaborations of conceptualist nominalism. They turned toward questions, sub-questions, disputations, and other scholastic forms of a purely intellectual character. Just how far this alienation went, and how it became a "divorce," may be illustrated by the anti-scientific and anti-scholastic flavor we find in the spiritual writings of the fourteenth and fifteenth centuries. The author of the *Imitation of Christ*, for example, felt obliged to warn his readers against the dangers of the theological science of his time.[4] The alienation between decadent theology and spirituality appeared clearly in the practical moralizing and voluntarism that characterized the ascetic orientation of "Devotio Moderna." The rupture between the science of theology and a life of Christian piety must be considered as the "great schism of the fifteenth century."[5]

That which, in the fifteenth century, was a rupture and a divorce, evolved in the following century into antagonism. In reaction to the tragic situation of a Christianity divided by the Protestant Reformation—that division caused partially by the fifteenth century split between religious experience and theology—a theology in Catholic countries sprang up that was little more than a defense of orthodoxy against the subjective experience of the Protestants and the spirituals. Thus, we have by the middle of the sixteenth century in Spain, a conflict between mystics and intellectuals. This antagonism between men and women of religious experience on the one hand, and the academic theologians on the other, created a profound gap in the theological-spiritual environment of the Spanish Golden Age: a fatal separation between theory and practice of religious living, between experience and mystical teaching—"I believe that it is called mystical theology," writes Teresa[6]—and the official theology of the schools, that of the tenured professors at the universities (who in their function as officials of the Supreme Tribunal of the Inquisition, distrusted the mystical life of the "spirituals" and denounced and censured their practices and writings).

The tension between the hierarchy and the charism, between the institutional and the freedom of the Spirit and the Gospel (part and parcel of the Church's earthly status) was converted into a fanatic, and apparently irreconcilable, opposition. Almost all of the great spiritual authors of the period in Spain, St John of Avila, Louis of Granada, Francis of Osuna, St Peter of Alcántara and St Francis Borja, were distrusted by the Inquisition and censured because "the accusation of being an 'alumbrado' became a commonplace and was thrust at all of the reformers of Carmel."[7]

"TURBULENT TIMES"

Teresa of Jesus lived the confusion of her times very concretely, as they took the form of inquisitorial trials and censures. Well known are the sad cases of false mysticism, like that of the Abbess of Córdoba, Magdalena of the Cross, "who put fear into all of Spain."[8] Certainly, "strong preachers of authority" were not lacking who, on certain occasions, "said many bad things of her [Teresa], comparing her to Magdalena of the Cross."[9] The fact that Spain had "women visionaries," victims of illusions or the "deceit of the devil," did not escape Teresa. She confesses openly: "I began to be afraid, as there have been cases recently in which women have been subjected by the devil to serious illusions and deceptions."[10] Teresa feared, from the beginning, those who would ridicule her, and those who would consider her visions and raptures as the "foolish things" of women — something she had always disliked hearing.[11]

Suggestive of this atmosphere of suspicion toward contemplative women were the words of warning that, without doubt, she frequently heard from confessors and fearful friends, and which made the rounds of devout people. It was said:

> "there are dangers"; "so-and-so went astray by such means"; "this other one was deceived"; "another who prayed a great deal fell away"; "it's harmful to virtue"; "it's not for women, for they will be susceptible to illusions"; "it's better they stick to their

sewing"; "they don't need these delicacies"; "the Our Father and the Hail Mary are sufficient."[12]

A Spanish Jesuit, contemporary of Mother Teresa of Jesus, describes the situation: "We are in a time when one preaches that women take up their hand work and their rosary, and not worry about more devotions."[13] And the celebrated theologian of Salamanca, Melchior Cano, advocated in his *Censure of the Catechism of Bartholomew Carranza* that the reading of Sacred Scripture should be forbidden to women, "Because the more that women seek with insatiable appetite, to eat this fruit (the reading of Sacred Scripture), the more it is necessary to forbid it, and to put out the fire, so that the nation is not burned by it."[14] The "alumbrados" (enlightened) had already sowed terror, even among the "letrados" (learned). In a letter of 17 February 1555, written by Rev Antonio de Córdoba to St Ignatius of Loyola, the famous Dominican theologian Dominic de Soto is described this way: "if he did not have the gospel before him, he would not know how to think of God who is invisible; that he would not know what people would do who spent two hours on their knees before the altar, and certainly he would not be able to do it."[15] Not long before that preachers censured publicly women who desired to know how to read. Because of the fear that their daughters would be influenced by the "alumbrados," some fathers like Cristopher de Balmaseda, a relative of Teresa de Ahumada, forbad his daughters learning how to read and write.[16] In reality, women were considered inept for the practice of mental prayer; and many women, victims of their own illusions, made sure that they were talked about, thus augmenting the suspicions and the prohibitions.

"The times were turbulent," recalls the saint, and in this context of alarm it would not be strange for someone to express the fearful suspicion that "something would be alleged against me, and they would report me to the Inquisitors."[17] It was only natural that such insinuations should come to the ears of the confessors of Mother Teresa of Jesus, and cause a most cautious attitude in them. "I know that they told him (her confessor)," Teresa points out, "to be careful of me, that he should not let the devil deceive him by anything I told him, and they brought up examples to him of other persons."[18] At the time Fr Baltha-sar Alvarez, a young Jesuit, was the confessor for the saint, and he had to direct himself to a small group of well-intentioned men of the city of Avila who sought to unmask the devil in the mystical experiences of the Carmelite nun. Her own words reveal the conflict in her soul: "I had so much to fear that I obeyed him in everything . . ." He "had to calm me and heal the fear I had by putting greater stress on the fear of offending God."[19] Finally, such was the desolation that "I feared that there would be no one to hear my confession, but that all would run from me. I did nothing but weep."[20] "It was enough to make me lose my judgment," she concludes, "the opposition of good men to a weak and sinful little woman like myself, and fearful too."[21]

Reflecting on this panorama of the immediate past, in order to describe it in her autobiography, she was not able to contain her aggressiveness. She was constantly having to defend the practice of mental prayer and mystical experiences, without respect for the misgivings:

> I don't understand these fears. "The Devil! the Devil!, when we can say "My God, my God" and make the devil tremble, Yes, for we really know that the devil can do nothing if the Lord does not permit him to do it. What is this? Without doubt, I fear those who have this great fear of the devil more than I do the devil himself, for he cannot touch me. On the other hand, other people, especially if they are confessors, cause severe disturbance . . .[22]

Given such a situation of distrust against these women dedicated to the life of prayer, it is understandable that Mother Teresa of Jesus felt obliged to put all of her nuns on guard against any semblance of "the holy woman syndrome" or signs of sensational mysticism. "Once again I warn you," she writes in her autobiography, "that it is very important for the spirit not to ascend unless the Lord raise it up."[23] In the *Way of Perfection* she suggests:

> As to the other devotions (raptures and visions) do not be upset if you have not experienced them; they are uncertain anyway. It

could happen that in others they are experiences of the Lord and in your case, His Majesty might allow you to be deluded by the devil, and that you would be deceived by him, as others have been. In women, these illusions are something dangerous.[24]

"WALK IN THE TRUTH"

Teresa de Ahumada possessed an education level much higher than the average woman of her day. Thanks to the teaching of her mother she was able to read by the time she was six years old. She really enjoyed reading and conversations with intelligent men, with the educated and the learned (*letrados*).[25] Dominique Deneuville suggests that it was with some insistence, "not free from some flirtatiousness,"[26] that Teresa repeatedly decried her ignorance of theology to the "learned." Even though she confesses herself always "fond of learning,"[27] she suffered from a real complex about being a non-educated person, a non-theologian. Phrases are always jumping off of her pages like: ". . . since we women have no learning, nor are we subtle geniuses, all of this is necessary that we may understand . . ."[28]; ". . . those of us who have no learning or knowledge of what one can speak about without sinning"[29]; and "Since I have no learning, in my dullness I am able to explain nothing."[30] On the other hand, she was acutely aware of the fact that she was "spiritual" or "experienced." At times, she went so far as to believe that she was a "visionary woman" exposed to the censures of the theologians and the inquisitors."[31]

What she desired with all her soul was to live and *walk in the truth*.[32] This is why she admired learning and felt a true passion for the learned, the theologians. The texts leave no room for doubt: "It is a great thing, understanding, and education for all situations"[33]; "Education is a great thing for shedding light on all"[34]; and "Education is a great thing because those who have it can teach those who understand little and give us light, and by attaining to the truths of Sacred Scripture we can do what we ought. Deliver us from foolish devotions, O God!"[35]

When she discusses spiritual direction Teresa becomes very decisive on the matter. "My opinion has been, and will be, that

any Christian should try to speak with a well-educated person —
and the more educated the better — and those who travel the
way of mental prayer have more need of an educated guide."[36]
"It's my feeling that the people who pray, and discuss the matter
with the educated, if they wish not to be deceived, will not then
be deceived by the devil."[37] It follows that Teresa sought for her
sisters confessors and spiritual directors from among the educated: "You ought to be informed always, my daughters, about
who is well educated, for in those persons you will find the way
of perfection with discretion and truth."[38] On the other side of
the coin, Teresa distrusted "half-educated, the fearful ones
[who] have cost me dearly."[39] She speaks from her own experience:

> I have seen by my experience that it is better if the confessor be
> virtuous and of holy manner — that they have little learning. For
> if they do not understand a matter, they will ask someone who
> understands it, nor do I really trust them. On the other hand, a
> really educated man has never misguided me.[40]

In the end, Teresa preferred the educated as confessors and
spiritual directors, even to the point of giving more credit to
these than to the holy ones, the "spirituals." The norm of conduct in this matter was clear:

> In spite of all this, she was not without fears at times, and it
> seemed to her that spiritual people could be deceived as well as
> she. Therefore, she wanted to speak with very learned men,
> even though they might not be given to prayer, for what she was
> trying to find out was whether or not her experiences were in
> conformity with Sacred Scripture.[41]

Teresa does not claim to be educated, but goes to the theologians to have them discern the character of her spiritual experiences and activities. For this reason, she seeks guidance and
opens herself without reserve to the good theologians, even
knowing that they were on the alert against the "spirituals," and
particularly against the "women visionaries" and those who
practiced mental prayer. Without wavering, she approaches

those very people who censured the "visionary" or the "worthless woman" Teresa of Jesus.

When Fr Bartholomew of Medina, who was tenured professor of Scripture at the University of Salamanca, got to know Teresa, one of the students recounts that "he had publicly, in his class, said that there were worthless women, who went from place to place, and who would be better off if they stayed at home praying and sewing." Teresa asked Fr Peter Fernandez for the opportunity to speak with the professor from the University of Salamanca. She was able to go to confession to him; she gave him her books, and opened her conscience to him. The saint herself says that after this encounter "he assured her more than the others did, and remained her friend afterwards."[42] The same kind of thing happened with the Provincial of the Dominicans, Fr John Salinas,[43] and with the Jesuit Rodrigo Alvarez.[44] Teresa kept the same attitude with regard to her writings and always submitted them sincerely to good theologians for judgment.

EXPERIENCE AND THEOLOGY

Clearly, Teresa sought a confrontation between religious experience and theology, a dialogue between the *spirituals* and the *intellectuals* (the official theologians). Her anxiety about the truth and the authenticity of her experience was not inhibited by an environment of open friction with the theologians, even when the antagonism took on forms that were bitter on the part of the *intellectuals*, with drastic measures taken against the *spirituals*. Here we refer to the prohibition of spiritual books in the vernacular, decreed by the Inquisitor General, Fernando de Valdés, in 1559.[45] On this list of forbidden books were the works of St John of Avila, Fr Louis of Granada, St Francis Borja.[46] This harsh measure was inspired by the conviction that every exposition of spirituality based on the interior life was contaminated with heresy; in other words, through this decree the official theology attempted at all costs to cut off the expression of religious experience.

Without a doubt, this was a hard blow to the *spirituals*. It affected Teresa of Jesus profoundly. She confesses that "When they eliminated many of the books that I read in the vernacular, I was deeply troubled because I enjoyed reading some of them and I was unable to read the Latin editions . . ."[47] Precisely in that year, 1559, on the feast of St Peter, she "felt" for the first time an intellectual vision.[48] At that fearful juncture, when the Archbishop of Toledo (Don Bartholomew Carranza) was shipwrecked, Teresa could only be fearful. She had to revert to trial and error and sought out "spiritual persons diligently, so she could talk with them."[49] Certainly, the circle of her counselors in Avila offered such great problems that she did not know where to turn. It was the "spirituals" Francis Borja and Peter of Alcántara who were able to relieve her doubts momentarily, because of their understanding and spiritual affinity. However, the persons who finally ended the doubts were the educated ones.

The opposite of what one would expect occurred in the life of Teresa, as she sought with more anxiousness educated people, aware that in a confrontation of religious experience with doctrine the truth would win out in the end. It was exactly in this period of 1559-1562, with its difficulties in ecclesiastical Spain, that Teresa underwent the most complex period in her own spiritual development. It was for Spain and for Teresa a time of visions and censures, made all the more confusing by the beginning of her work as a founder and reformer. During this time she dealt more frequently with the theologians, and thereby—in a Teresian, or maybe feminine, paradox—her friendship with the theologians turned into her teaching them.

TEACHER OF THEOLOGIANS

Teresa of Avila understood that mystical experience was predominantly the privilege of women. She writes:

There are many more women than men to whom the Lord grants these favors. This I heard from the saintly friar Peter of

Alcántara — and I have seen it myself . . . He also gave excellent reasons for this, all in the favor of women . . .[50]

When she was giving the reasons for writing the *Book of Her Life* she expressed herself in a way that is unmistakable: ". . . one of the things that gave me courage, knowing my weakness, to obey in writing this account of my wretched life and the favors the Lord has worked in my life, without my serving him but rather offending him, is just this: I would like in this matter to have great authority so that it might be believed."[51] Here she is demanding the right to be heard because, in this matter, her feminine contribution deserves it. In fact, the mental prayer of woman — over the whole spectrum of its stages and depths — is more passive, more receptive, of a type that might be called more affective and concrete than that of men which ends up being more discursive and speculative, more rational. The ontology of the sexes has its repercussions on the level of lived religious experience.[52]

If we are looking at the case of Teresa of Jesus, we need only remember her very feminine definition of prayer: ". . . an intimate sharing between friends . . . with him who we know loves us."[53] With a woman's intuition she realized she brought a decidedly feminine (through the knowledge of love) contribution to men's theology and she never tired of helping others share her experience on the way of prayer, by consulting them to assure herself that the experiences were authentic. From seeking guidance she passes on to teaching — a typical feminine method of imparting teaching; and by opening herself to the learned theologians, she exposed them to her spirituality — the strategy of an intelligent woman.

Very well educated and learned men experienced this process, Dominic Báñez, Peter Ibañez and García de Toledo, the three Dominican confessors of the saint. The process of approaching the theologians is seen most clearly in the autobiography, the work which reflects best the spheres of antagonism between theology and religious experience in the years 1550-1562. Through its pages runs the constant desire of Teresa to see her directors share her experiences. She reveals her anxiety to communicate her interior experiences for the benefit of her directors: "And I shall speak of what it taking place in me so that when it is conformed to the faith, it may be of some profit to your Reverence . . ."[54] When Teresa is writing about the prayer of quiet from her own experience, her *eros pedagogicus* before her theologian-directors has her accent the part of this prayer that is loving acts and she reduces the part of this stage of prayer focused on the understanding: "In fact, a little straw put there with humility . . . will serve the purpose and help to enkindle fire more than a lot of wood, which comes with much learned reasonings . . ."; resolutely she goes on: "This is good advice for the learned men who ordered me to write."[55]

She addresses Fr García de Toledo on a maternal tone: "Oh my son! — the one to whom this is addressed and who ordered me to write is so humble that he wants to be addressed this way"; and at the same time she confesses that he is her director: "My father, as he is my confessor, but he is also my son and I have entrusted my soul to him. Free me with the truth!"[56] Certainly, Teresa did not rest until she had placed him in his proper spiritual orbit, directing to him a "few words" which pierced him to the soul. "These words really seemed to be from God because of the change that they brought about in him," she comments. "He resolved to devote himself to prayer, even though he did not do so right away. The Lord, as he desired this man for himself, used me to say a few truths which were so much on the mark, without my knowing it, that they scared him . . ."[57] "He was so changed by the Lord that he hardly knew himself. The Lord gave him bodily strength for penance, and courage for every good thing . . . it looked like a very particular call from the Lord."[58] It would seem that Teresa could answer with some satisfaction that the theologian García de Toledo was able to integrate in his own personality that lesson of experience which Teresa wished for him:

> This father I'm speaking about was given many things from the Lord, and he has tried to study all these things — for he is well educated — and what he doesn't understand through experience

he finds out from one who has it. In this way, the Lord helps him by giving him deep faith, and so this father has benefited much and has helped other souls, one of which is mine.[59]

Teresa maintained a similar friendly relationship with another Dominican, Fr Peter Ibáñez — an intimate friend of the same García de Toledo. Teresa calls him the "best educated man we had in that place (Avila), and there were few better in his Order"[60]; and "very spiritual and a theologian."[61] Teresa turns to him in the face of the violent reactions that were awakened among the people of Avila by her project of founding the first convent of the Discalced Carmelite nuns; she opened her conscience to him: "I told him everything . . . the visions, the way of praying, the great favors that the Lord had done for me, all with the greatest clarity that I could muster, and I asked him to look at it very carefully and tell me if he saw anything against the Sacred Scriptures, and what he felt about it all."[62] There is no doubt that Fr Peter Ibáñez also benefitted from the experience of the person he directed. In his famous *Pronouncement* in favor of her good spiritual life he confesses: ". . . and I am certain that she has been a great help to many people, and I am one of them."[63] Teresa, for her part, writes: "He greatly reassured me, and I believe I helped him; for even though he was very good, from that time onward he was much more given to mental prayer and he went aside to a monastery of his Order where there was much solitude, so he would be able to pray more . . ."[64] And she described his spiritual progress: ". . . he who before reassured me with his learning, now was able to do it also with his spiritual experience which was very deep in supernatural things . . ."[65]

The great theologian Fr Dominic Báñez, "esteemed in his Order and then lector of theology in the friary of St Thomas at Avila,"[66] also was a member of the group of educated Dominicans Teresa relied upon. He was aware that when Teresa was communicating her interior experiences she wished to see her confessors understand and teach her, but also (she desired to) "attract to virtue those who read the mercies God granted her."[67] Likewise, the Dominican theologian stated that he was convinced that Mother Teresa continued for more than twenty years to consult him "because she saw him so well rooted in the law and in the arguments of reason, so as to be a man created to read and debate all of his life."[68] Even though we have no data showing a decisive influence on the part of Teresa in the spiritual life of this Dominican theologian, the confidential tone of her letters addressed to him, and his statements, confirm for us a perfect interfacing between the experience of the Carmelite nun and the teaching of the master in theology and professor of the University of Salamanca. Certainly, this was an exceptional case for those confused times when, in Spain, antagonism between mysticism and theology prevailed.

FEMININE TEACHING OF EXPERIENCE

In this Teresian paradox is realized the union between experience and doctrine; between a typically feminine contribution, and one of men, to spiritual theology; between orthopraxis and orthodoxy. The timeliness of the doctorate of Teresa of Avila is supported by the feminine teaching of experience, of that science of love which seeks to be recognized and appraised by theory for which it aspires to be the *locus theologicus* or the fountainhead and, at the same time, the authentic expression. Couldn't we suggest that mystical experience constitutes a theological locus or, perhaps better, that the mystic not only poses problems for theology but also feeds into theological reflection?

Mystical experience can also be critical of theology, since it has its place within the faith and not outside of it. Experience is the level proper to faith. Teresa of Jesus, it would seem, understood this very well. That is why she had recourse to theologians and went so far as to criticize them (as happened, for example, in her defense of mental prayer) in such a way that Fr García de Toledo even noted in the margin of the autograph copy of Teresa's *Life*: "It seems that she is blaming the inquisitors for forbidding books on mental prayer."[69] At the same time, one must say that religious experience and mysticism without theology will be nothing more than a vulgar sentimentalism or gnosticism. Thanks to theology, mysticism does not collapse into an apocryphal Christianity or an irrational fanaticism. Mysticism and theology need each other for their proper authenticity. This means that those who teach mysticism are concerned with theology, because they communicate something to the Church to the extent they build up those who believe in Christ. Therefore, it seems to us that the feminine magisterium of the first woman Doctor of the Church is based on her having understood this theological value of her mystical experience. She demonstrated that her teaching — directed to the Church as such — is not the privilege of men. We must recognize that Teresa — teacher of the theologians and promoter of the union of and a dialogue between both theology and mysticism — was right when she wrote with a certain amount of cunning "that even though women are not good as counselors, sometimes, however, we are right."[70] (Trans. D. Graviss)

NOTES

1. Cf. Pierre Blanchard in his prologue to the book of Dominique Deneuville, *Santa Teresa de Jesús y la mujer* (Barcelona: Editorial Herder, 1966), 10.

2. See L, 12, 4; 13, 4; C, 2, 1, 10. Cf., also, E. Colunga, "Intelectualistas y místicos en la teología española del siglo XVI," *Ciencia Thomista* 9 (1914): 209-21; 377-94; 15 (1914-15): 223-42.

3. The classic presentation of this problem is: François Vandenbroucke, "Le divorce entre théologie et mystique," *Nouvelle Revue Théologique* 72 (1950): 372-89.

4. *Imitation of Christ*, bk. 1. chap. 3.

5. Stephanus Axters, *Geschiedenis van de vroomheid in de Nederlanden* vol. 3 *De Moderne Devotie, 1380-1550* (Antwerp: Uitgeverij De Sikkel N.V., 1956), 11.

6. L, 10, 1.

7. Marcelino Menedez y Pelayo, *Historia de los Heterodoxos españoles*, vol. 2, bk. 5, chap. 1: "Sectas Místicas," Biblioteca de Autores Cristianos (Madrid: Editorial Catolica, 1956), 187-88.

8. Francis de Ribera, *Vida de la Madre Teresa de Jesús* (Salamanca, 1590), bk. 1, chap. 9, 75; cf. L, 23, 2.

9. Dominic Báñez in the *Proceso de Salamanca de 1592*, in *Procesos de Beatificación y Canonización de Santa Teresa de Jesús*, ed. and annotated by Silverio de Santa Teresa, Biblioteca Mistica Carmelitana 18, vol. 1 (Burgos: Ed. Monte Carmelo, 1935), 11.
10. L, 23, 2.
11. *Spiritual Testimony*, 58, 5.
12. W (Escorial), 21, 2.
13. *Monumenta Historica Societatis Iesu*, tom. 8: *Litterae quadrimestres*, tom. 3 (Madrid, 1896), 308.
14. See A. Caballero, *Conquenses ilustres* 2 (Madrid, 1871), 597.
15. *Monumenta Historica Societatis Iesu*, tom. 8, *Litterae*, tom. 3, 308.
16. Cf. *Firgures choisies de Carmélites* (Mangalore, 1913), 106 and *Les parents de Sainte Thérèse* (Thichinopoly, 1914), 75.
17. L, 33, 5.
18. L, 28, 14.
19. L, 28, 16.
20. L, 28, 14.
21. L, 28, 18.
22. L, 25, 22.
23. L, 12, 7.
24. W (Valladolid), 18, 9.
25. Cf. Efrén de la Madre de Dios and Otger Steggink, *Tiempo y Vida de Santa Teresa*, Biblioteca de Autores Cristianos, vol, 283, 2d ed. (Madrid: Editorial Catolica, 1977), 34. In her autobiography she answers that "for many years I dealt with the well educated." (L, 28, 6).
26. Dominique Deneuville, *Santa Teresa de Jesús y la mujer* (Barcelona: Editorial Herder, 1966), 45.
27. "I was always a friend of the well educated": L, 5, 3.
28. W (Escorial), 48, 2; (Valladolid, 28, 10).
29. W (Valladolid), 41, 6.
30. C, 6, 4, 9.
31. L, 33, 5.
32. This very teresian expression is used by her in her autobiography to indicate the ideal, to live an unmasked and transparent life. "Unmask me with the truth," she writes to Fr García de Toledo. See L, 16, 6; 25, 21; and 26, 1.
33. C, 4, 1, 5.
34. W (Valladolid), 5, 2.
35. L, 13, 16.
36. L, 13, 17.
37. L, 13, 18.

38. F, 19, 1.
39. C, 5, 1, 8.
40. L, 5, 3.
41. *Spiritual Testimony*, 58,7.
42. Francisco Mena, *Proceso de Avila*, 1610,17°, Biblioteca Mística Carmelitana 19 (Burgos: Ed. Monte Carmelo, 1935), 349; and *Spiritual Testimony*, 58,8.
43. The account of Fr Dominic Báñez in his declaration in the Proceso de Salamanca, 1592, 4°, Biblioteca Mística Carmelitana 18 (Burgos: Ed. Monte Carmelo, 1934), 9.
44. See Jeronimo Gracián , "Scholias y adiciones al libro de la vida de Madre Teresa de Jesús," *El Monte Carmelo* 68 (1960): 156.
45. *Cathaologus librorum qui prohibentur mandato Illustrissimi et Reverend. D.D. Fernandi de Valdes Hispalensis Archiepiscopi Inquisitionis Generalis Hispaniae, Necnon et Supremi Sanctae Inquisitionis Senatus* (Pinciae, 1559). This book exists in a photo facsimile edition, published by the Real Academia Española as *Tres índices expurgatorios de la Inquisición española en el siglo XVI* (Madrid, 1952).
46. Ibid., 37-51.
47. L, 26, 5.
48. L, 27, 2.
49. L, 23, 3.
50. L, 40, 8.
51. L, 19, 4.
52. Adriana Zarri began to demonstrate this thesis in an excellent article published in an international journal of theology—see her "Woman's Prayer and Man's Liturgy," *Concilium* no. 52 (February 1970): 73-86.
53. L, 8, 5.
54. L, 10, 8.
55. L, 15, 7.
56. L, 16, 6.
57. L, 34, 10-11.
58. L, 34, 13.
59. Ibid.
60. L, 32, 16; cf. *Spiritual Testimony*, 58, 8.
61. *Spiritual Testimony*, 3, 13.
62. L, 33, 5.
63. The complete text is quoted in *Tiempo y Vida de Santa Teresa*, 2d ed., 190-91.

64. Fr Peter Ibáñez retired to the monastery of Trianos (León) of the contemplative Dominicans—see L, 33, 5.

65. L, 33, 6.

66. *Procesos de Salamanca*, 1592,2°, Biblioteca Mística Carmelitana 18, 6.

67. Ibid., 7.

68. Ibid.

69. This can be seen in the margin of the seventy-second page of the autograph copy of the *Way of Perfection* (Escorial—see *Reproducción Fotolitographica* (Valladolid: pub. by Doctor don Francisco Herrero Bayona, 1883), 145.

70. Letter to Juan Bautista Rubeo (Seville), end of January, 1576, 7.

BEATIFICATION
OF
EDITH STEIN

POPE'S REMARKS ABOUT
EDITH STEIN

John Paul II

This is not the first time the writings of "Papa Wojtyla" have graced the pages of CARMELITE STUDIES. "The Question of Faith in St John of the Cross" was a resume of his doctoral dissertation in theology which appeared in Vol. 2 of this series.

The following texts are excerpts from the words of Pope John Paul II directed to various groups during his recent second visit to the Federal Republic of (West) Germany. The translation comes from the English language edition of the *Osservatore Romano*, and we thank the *Osservatore*'s editor, Fr Lambert Greenan, OP, for authorization to reproduce the texts. While we present isolated quotations which in places will tend to whet the reader's appetite for longer portions of the papal discourse(s), we feel it better to center the excerpt primarily on Bl. Teresa Benedicta/Edith Stein. Chronology rules the order in which the excerpts appear. The numbers indicate paragraphs given in the *Osservatore Romano*.

ADDRESS AT COLOGNE-BONN AIRPORT

On Thursday, 30 April, Pope John Paul II began his second pastoral visit to the Federal Republic of Germany. On arrival at

Wahn International Airport (Cologne-Bonn), he was greeted by leaders of Church and State. In response to the address of welcome by Federal President Richard von Weizsäcker, the Holy Father spoke as follows:

> 2. "And you will bear witness for me." The momentous events we will be celebrating together in spiritual fellowship in the various dioceses in the days to come will pay special homage to the phenomenon of witness. During the two beatification ceremonies in Cologne and Munich we will be honoring two Christians who fearlessly and heroically bore witness to their faith, in spite of severe trials and extreme peril. Edith Stein, as a Jew and a Catholic nun, demonstrated her solidarity with the Jewish people by sharing their suffering and martyrdom. (. . .)

ADDRESS TO THE BISHOPS AT COLOGNE

Shortly after his arrival in Cologne in the evening of Thursday, 30 April, the Holy Father gave an address to the members of the German Bishops' conference.

> 1. . . . This second visit of mine is given its particular character by two solemn beatifications, the first beatifications a pope has ever had the privilege of performing in this country. The heroic testimony of faith given by Sister Edith Stein and Father Rupert Mayer take us back to a time of great tribulation for the Church and for the whole of your people. (. . .)

> 2. . . . Shining out against this dark historical background are the figures of the three witnesses whose memory we are honoring during these days: the two who will soon bear the title Blessed, Edith Stein and Rupert Mayer, as well as the confessor Cardinal Clemens August von Galen. (. . .)
> . . . Through the solemn beatifications of the coming days, the Church places before us the life and work of Christians who heroically followed Jesus Christ by bearing witness for God and mankind. They are models for our own calling as Christians. For us today, their example challenges and encourages us to bear consistent witness to God and his saving truth in our society

and in all areas of human life. Every Christian is called upon along with the Church to bear this witness as a follower of Christ: "You are to be my witnessess." (Acts 1:8) We today must courageously assume the disciples' mission as witnesses and must pursue it with determination in our times. Our Church's communion of saints and beatified persons, to whom Edith Stein and Father Ruper Mayer will soon belong, invite us to follow in their footsteps.

4. . . . Edith Stein is a shining example to us in this pursuit of spiritualization. She said, "Unbounded loving devotion to God and God's gift in return, full and lasting union, that is the supreme edification our hearts can attain, the ultimate level of prayer. Those souls which have achieved that are truly the heart of the Church." She herself admirably demonstrated this devotion. That is why an eyewitness from Westerbork concentration camp, where Edith Stein was initially taken after her arrest, was able to report, "Sister Benedicta was glad to be able to help with consoling words and prayers. Her deep faith created an aura of heavenly life around her." She herself wrote from the same place of misery and humiliation that she had so far been "able to do some marvellous praying." May she, who will soon be beatified, reveal to us anew the immeasurable spiritual riches of prayer and our profound communion with Christ.

6. My meeting with the Central Council of Jews in Germany and with representatives of other Christian Churches during my second pastoral visit are of great importance, as were the encounters in Mainz in 1980. Edith Stein, who entered the Carmelite convent in Cologne in 1933, was a daughter of the Jewish people: in solidarity with them and in Christian hope she shared their sufferings on the way to the *Shoah*. "After all, salvation is from the Jews," said Jesus during his talk with the Samaritan woman at Jacob's well (Jn 4:22). We Christians must never forget these roots of ours. The apostle of the nations reminds us that "You do not support the root: the root supports you." (Rom 11:18)

ADDRESS TO THE CENTRAL COMMITTEE
OF GERMAN CATHOLICS

In the evening of Thursday, 30 April, at Cologne, the Pope met the Central Committee of German Catholics and spoke to them.

As you are aware, my second pastoral visit to your country is connected with the beatifications of Sister Edith Stein and Father Rupert Mayer. We honor the courageous testimony for Christ and for selfless love of their fellow men manifested in the lives of these two saints. Edith Stein saw her being transported to Auschwitz as an expression of solidarity with the Jewish people, of which she was a member and with which she felt connected right up to the moment of her agonizing death. She said to her sister, "Come, we will go for our people." Testimony for Christ and helping our fellow men are part and parcel of Christain life and closely connected with the Church's doctrine of salvation and all the elements of the Church.

HOMILY AT THE BEATIFICATION
OF EDITH STEIN (Friday May 1, 1987, 10 AM)

"These are the ones who have survived the time of great distress; they have washed their robes and made them white in the blood of the Lamb" (Rv. 7:14).

1. Today we greet in profound honor and holy joy a daughter of the Jewish people, rich in wisdom and courage, among these blessed men and women. Having grown up in the strict traditions of Israel, and having lived a life of virtue and self-denial in a religious order, she demonstrated her heroic character on the way to the extermination camp. Unified with our crucified Lord, she gave her life "for genuine peace" and "for the people" (see *Edith Stein, Judin, Philosophin, Ordensfrau, Martyrin*).

Cardinal, dear brothers and sisters:

Today's beatification marks the realization of a long-outstanding wish on the part of the Archdiocese of Cologne as well as on the part of many individuals and groups within the Church. Seven years ago the members of the German bishops conference sent a unanimous request for this beatification to the Holy See. Numerous bishops from other countries joined them in making this request. As such, we are all greatly gratified that I am able to fulfill this wish today and can present Sister Teresa Benedicta of the Cross to the faithful on behalf of the Church as blessed in the glory of God. From this moment on we can honor her as a martyr and ask for her intercession at the throne of God. In this I would like to express congratulations to all, most of all to her fellow sisters in the order of Our Lady of Mount Carmel here in Cologne and in Echt as well as in the entire order. The fact that Jewish brothers and sisters, relatives of Edith Stein's in particular, are present at this liturgical ceremony today fill us with great joy and gratitude.

A Call for Help

2. "O Lord, manifest yourself in the time of our distress and give us courage" (Est. 4:17).

The words of this call for help from the first reading of today's liturgy were spoken by Esther, a daughter of Israel, at the time of the Babylonian captivity. Her prayer, which she directs to the Lord God at a time when her people were exposed to a deadly threat, are profoundly moving.

"My Lord, our king, you alone are God. Help me, who am alone and have no help but you, for I am taking my life in my hand . . . You, O Lord, chose Israel from among all peoples . . . and our fathers from among all their ancestors as a lasting heritage . . . be mindful of us, O Lord . . . Save us by your power" (Est. 4:17).

Esther's deathly fear arose when, under the influence of the mighty Haman, an archenemy of the Jews, the order for their destruction was given out in all of the Persian empire. With God's help and by sacrificing her own life Esther rendered a key contribution toward saving her people.

3. Today's liturgy places this more than 2,000-year-old prayer for help in the mouth of Edith Stein, a servant of God and a daughter of Israel in our century. This prayer became relevant again when here, in the heart of Europe, a new plan for the destruction of the Jews was laid out. An insane ideology

decided on this plan in the name of a wretched form of racism and carried it out mercilessly.

Extermination camps and crematoriums were rapidly built, parallel to the dramatic events of World War II. Several million sons and daughters of Israel were killed at these places of horror—from children to the elderly. The enormously powerful machinery of the totalitarian state spared no one and undertook extremely cruel measures against those who had the courage to defend the Jews.

4. Edith Stein died at the Auschwitz extermination camp, the daughter of a martyred people. Despite the fact that she moved from Cologne to the Dutch Carmelite community in Echt, her protection against the growing persecution of the Jews was only temporary. The Nazi policy of exterminating the Jews was rapidly implemented in Holland, too, after the country had been occupied. Jews who had converted to Christianity were initially left alone. However, when the Catholic bishops in the Netherlands issued a pastoral letter in which they sharply protested against the deportation of the Jews, the Nazi rulers reacted by ordering the extermination of Catholic Jews as well. This was the cause of the martyrdom suffered by Sister Teresa Benedicta a Cruce together with her sister Rosa, who had also sought refuge with the Carmelites in Echt.

On leaving their convent Edith took her sister by the hand and said: "Come, we will go for our people." On the strength of Christ's willingness to sacrifice himself for others she saw in her seeming impotence a way to render a final service to her people. A few years previously she had compared herself with Queen Esther in exile at the Persian court. In one of her letters we read: "I am confident that the Lord has taken my life for all (Jews). I always have to think of Queen Esther, who was taken away from her people for the express purpose of standing before the king for her people. I am the very poor, weak and small Esther, but the king who selected me is infinitely great and merciful."

Incessant Search for Truth

5. Dear brothers and sisters, the second reading in this special Mass is from St Paul's letter to the Galatians. He wrote there: "May I never boast of anything but the cross of our Lord, Jesus

Christ. Through it, the world has been crucified to me and I to the world" (Gal. 6:14).

During her lifetime, Edith Stein too encountered the secret of the cross that St. Paul announces to the Christians in this letter.

Edith encountered Christ and this encounter led her step by step into the Carmelite community. In the extermination camp she died as a daughter of Israel "for the glory of the Most Holy Name" and, at the same time, as Sister Teresa Benedicta of the Cross, literally, "blessed by the cross."

Edith Stein's entire life is characterized by an incessant search for truth and is illuminated by the blessing of the cross of Christ. She encountered the cross for the first time in the strongly religious widow of a university friend. Instead of despairing, this woman took strength and hope from the cross of Christ. Later she wrote about this: "It was my first encounter with the cross and the divine strength it gives those who bear it . . . It was the moment in which my atheism collapsed . . . and Christ shone brightly: Christ in the mystery of the cross."

Her own life and the cross she had to bear were intimately connected with the destiny of the Jewish people. In a prayer she confessed to the Savior that she knew that it was his cross that was now being laid on the Jewish people and that those who realized this would have to accept it willingly on behalf of all the others. "I wanted to do it — all he has to do is show me how." At the same time she attains the inner certainty that God has heard her prayer. The more often swastikas were seen on the streets, the higher the cross of Jesus Christ rose up in her life. When she entered the Carmelite order of nuns in Cologne as Sister Teresa Benedicta a Cruce in order to experience the cross of Christ even more profoundly, she knew that she was "married to the Lord in the sign of the cross." On the day of her first vows she felt, in her own words, "like the bride of the lamb." She was convinced that her heavenly groom would introduce her to the profound mysteries of the cross.

Ethical Idealism

6. Teresa Blessed by the Cross was the name given in a religious order to a woman who began her spiritual life with the conviction that God does not exist. At that time, in her school

girl years and when she was at university, her life was not yet filled with the redeeming cross of Christ. However, it was already the object of constant searching on the part of her sharp intellect. As a 15-year-old schoolgirl in her hometown of Breslau, Edith, who had been raised in a Jewish household, suddenly decided, as she herself put it, "not to pray anymore." Despite the fact that she was deeply impressed by the strict devotion of her mother, during her school and university years Edith slips into the intellectual world of atheism. She considers the existence of a personal God to be unworthy of belief.

In the years when she studied psychology, philosophy, history and German at the universities of Breslau, Gottingen and Freiburg, God didn't play an important role, at least initially. Her thinking was based on a demanding ethical idealism. In keeping with her intellectual abilities, she did not want to accept anything without careful examination, not even the faith of her fathers. She wanted to get to the bottom of things herself. As such, she was engaged in a constant search for the truth. Looking back on this period of intellecutal unrest in her life she saw in it an important phase in a process of spiritual maturation. She said: "My search for the truth was a constant prayer." This is a comforting bit of testimony for those who have a hard time believing in God. The search for truth is itself in a very profound sense a search for God.

Under the influence of Edmund Husserl and his phenomenological school of thought the student Edith Stein became increasingly dedicated to the study of philosophy. She gradually learned to "view things free of prejudice and to throw off 'blinkers.'" She came into contact for the first time with Catholic ideas through a meeting with Max Scheler in Göttingen. She described her reaction to this meeting as follows: "The barriers of rationalistic prejudice, something I grew up with without being aware of it, fell and suddenly I was confronted with the world of faith. People I dealt with on a daily basis, people I looked up to in admiration, lived in that world."

Her long struggle for a personal decision to believe in Jesus Christ was not to come to an end until 1921 when she began to read the autobiographical *Life of St Teresa of Avila*. She was immediately taken with the book and could not put it down until she had finished it. Edith Stein commented: "When I closed the book I said to myself: 'That is the truth!'" She had read through the night until sunrise. In that night she found truth—not the truth of philosophy, but rather the truth in person, the loving person of God. Edith Stein had sought the truth and found God. She was baptized soon after that and entered the Catholic Church.

Continuing Heritage

7. For Edith Stein baptism as a Christian was by no means a break with her Jewish heritage. Quite the contrary, she said: "I had given up my practice of the Jewish religion as a girl of 14. My return to God made me feel Jewish again." She was always mindful of the fact that she was related to Christ "not only in a spiritual sense, but also in blood terms." She suffered profoundly from the pain she caused her mother through her conversion to Catholicism. She continued to accompany her to services in the synagogue and to pray the psalms with her. In reaction to her mother's observation that it was possible for her to be pious in a Jewish sense as well, she answered: "Of course, seeing as it is something I grew up with."

Although becoming a member of the Carmelite order was Edith Stein's objective from the time of her encounter with the writings of St Teresa of Avila, she had to wait more than a decade before Christ showed her the way. In her activity as a teacher and lecturer at schools and in adult education, mostly in Speyer, but also in Münster, she made a continuous effort to combine science and religion and to convey them together. In this she only wanted to be a "tool of the Lord." "Those who come to me I would like to lead to him," she said. During this period of her life she already lived like a nun. She took the vows privately and became a great and gifted woman of prayer. From her intensive study of the writings of St Thomas Aquinas she learned that it is possible "to approach science from a religious standpoint." She said that it was only thus that she was able to decide to return seriously (after her conversion) to academic work. Despite her respect for scholarship, Edith Stein became increasingly aware that the essence of being a Christian is not scholarship, but rather love.

When Edith Stein finally entered the Carmelite order in Cologne in 1933, this step did not represent an escape from the world or from responsibility for her, but rather a resolved commitment to the heritage of Christ on the cross. She said in her first conversation with the prioress there: "It is not human activity that helps us — it is the suffering of Christ. To share in this is my desire." On being registered in the order she expressed the wish to be named "Blessed by the Cross." She had the words of St John of the Cross printed on the devotional picture presented to her on taking her final vows: "My only vocation is that of loving more."

8. Dear brothers and sisters. We bow today with the entire Church before this great woman whom we from now on may call upon as one of the blessed in God's glory, before this great daughter of Israel who found the fulfillment of her faith and her vocation for the people of God in Christ the savior. In her conviction, those who enter the Carmelite order are not lost to their own — on the contrary they are won for them. It is our vocation to stand before God for everyone. After she began seeing the destiny of Israel from the standpoint of the cross, our newly beatified sister let Christ lead her more and more deeply into the mystery of his salvation to be able to bear the multiple pains of humankind in spiritual union with him and to help atone for the outrageous injustices in the world. As Benedicta a Cruce — blessed by the cross — she wanted to bear the cross with Christ for the salvation of her people, her church and the world as a whole. She offered herself to God as a "sacrifice for genuine peace" and above all for her threatened and humiliated Jewish people. After she recognized that God had once again laid a heavy hand on his people, she was convinced "that the destiny of this people was also my destiny."

His Suffering

When Sister Teresa Benedicta a Cruce began her last theological work, *The Science of the Cross,* at the Carmelite convent in Echt (the work remained incomplete since it was interrupted by her own encounter with the cross) she noted: "When we speak of the science of the cross this is not . . . mere theory . . . but rather vibrant, genuine and effective truth." When the deadly threat to the Jewish people gathered like a dark cloud over her as well she was willing to realize with her own life what she had recognized earlier: "There is a vocation for suffering

with Christ and by that means for involvement in his salvation
. . . Christ continues to live and to suffer in his members. The
suffering gone through in union with the Lord is his suffering,
and is a fruitful part of the great plan of salvation."

With her people and "for" her people Sister Teresa Benedicta
a Cruce traveled the road to death with her sister Rosa. She did
not accept suffering and death passively, but instead combined
these consciously with the atoning sacrifice of our savior Jesus
Christ. A few years earlier she had written in her will: "I will
gladly accept the death God chooses for me, in full submission
to his holy will. I ask the Lord to accept my suffering and death
for his honor and glory, and for all interests . . . of the holy
Church." The Lord heard her prayer.

An Example

The church now presents Sister Teresa Benedicta a Cruce to
us as a blessed martyr, as an example of a heroic follower of
Christ, for us to honor and to emulate. Let us open ourselves up
for her message to us as a woman of the spirit and of the mind,
who saw in the science of the cross the acme of all wisdom, as a
great daughter of the Jewish people and as a believing Christian
in the midst of millions of innocent fellow men made martyrs.
She saw the inexorable approach of the cross. She did not flee in
fear. Instead, she embraced it in Christian hope with final love
and sacrifice and in the mystery of Easter even welcomed it with
the salutation *ave crux, spes unica.* As Cardinal Höffner said in
his recent pastoral letter, "Edith Stein is a gift, an invocation
and a promise for our time. May she be an intercessor with God
for us and for our people and for all people."

9. Dear brothers and sisters, today the Church of the 20th century is experiencing a great day. We bow in profound respect
before the testimony of the life and death of Edith Stein, an outstanding daughter of Israel and, at the same time, a daughter of
Carmel, Sister Teresa Benedicta a Cruce, a person who embodied
a dramatic synthesis of our century in her rich life. Hers was a synthesis of a history full of deep wounds, wounds that still hurt, and
for the healing of which responsible men and women have continued to work up to the present day. At the same time, it was a synthesis of the full truth on humankind, in a heart that remained
restless and unsatisfied "until it finally found peace in God."

Spirit and Truth

When we pay a spiritual visit to the place where this great Jewish woman and Christian experienced martyrdom, the place of horrible events today referred to as *Shoah*, we hear the voice of Christ the Messiah and Son of Man, our Lord and Savior.

As the bearer of the message of God's unfathomable mystery of salvation he said to the woman from Samaria at Jacob's well:

"After all, salvation is from the Jews. Yet an hour is coming, and is already here, when authentic worshipers will worship the Father in spirit and truth. Indeed, it is just such worshipers the Father seeks. God is Spirit, and those who worship him must worship in spirit and truth" (Jn. 4:22-24).

Blessed be Edith Stein, Sister Teresa Benedicta a Cruce, a true worshiper of God — in spirit and in truth.

She is among the blessed. Amen.

ADDRESS TO JEWISH CENTRAL COUNCIL

In the afternoon of Friday, 1 May, the Pope met the members of the Jewish Central Council at the residence of the Archbishop of Cologne. He mentioned among other things:

3. Today the Church is honoring a daughter of Israel who remained faithful, as a Jew, to the Jewish people, and, as a Catholic, to our crucified Lord Jesus Christ. Together with millions of fellow believers she endured humiliation and suffering culminating in the final brutal drama of extermination, the *Shoah.* In an act of heroic faith Edith Stein placed her life in the hands of a holy and just God, whose mysteries she had sought to understand better and to love throughout her entire life.

May the day of her beatification be a day for all of us to join together in praising God, who has done marvelous works through his saints and exalted himself through the People of Israel. Let us pause in reverent silence to reflect on the terrible consequences which can arise from a denial of God and from collective racial hatred. (. . .)

4. By virtue of the life she lived, the blessed Edith Stein reminds us all, Jews and Christians alike, of the call of the Holy Scriptures: "You shall be holy because I am holy." (Lev 11:45) (. . .)

ADDRESS TO THE PEOPLE OF MÜNSTER

In the afternoon of Friday, 1 May, the Holy Father went from Cologne to Münster, where he delivered an address.

2. . . . And I recall Sister Edith Stein, whom I beatified in Cologne this morning on behalf of the Church. It was here in Münster that she received her calling. From here her path led to Mount Carmel and then to a violent martyrdom and thus into God's eternal salvation.

HOMILY AT MASS IN GELSENKIRCHEN

In the evening of Saturday, 2 May, the Holy Father celebrated Mass at Gelsenkirchen and delivered a homily.

4. On this visit I am able to venerate on behalf of the Church witnesses from your country who show you how to be real disciples of Christ in our time. Yesterday, Edith Stein, the Carmelite nun, in Cologne; tomorrow, Rupert Mayer, the Jesuit priest in Munich.

HOMILY AT THE BEATIFICATION OF RUPERT MAYER

On the morning of Sunday 3 May, in the Olympic Stadium at Munich, the Holy Father celebrated Mass during which he beatified Father Rupert Mayer, SJ. In his homily the Pope said:

1. . . . The day before yesterday I beatified in Cologne the Carmelite Sister, Teresa Benedicta a Cruce, the woman "blessed by the Cross." Both of these Blessed belong together, for Father Rupert Mayer was also blessed by the Cross. (. . .)

HOMILY DURING MASS IN AUGSBURG

In the evening of Sunday 3 May the Holy Father celebrated Mass in Augsburg for the people of the diocese. In his homily he preached:

> 5. . . . Wasn't it necessary for men and women like Saint Maximilian Kolbe, Blessed Edith Stein, Max Josef Metzger or Dietrich Bonhoeffer to give thier lives so that through their sacrifice new Christian life might arise in this country and reconciliation might be made possible once again between neighboring peoples?

HOMILY DURING MASS IN SPEYER

In the afternoon of Monday 4 May the Holy Father arrived in Speyer. He visited the cathedral, the largest church in Germany, and prayed at the tombs of the emperors. Afterward in the square in front of the cathedral he celebrated Mass and preached a homily.

> 10. God has also sent holy people to us in our time to help us to distinguish between what is essential and inessential, to assess fully man's possibilities in the light of his Creator and Redeeemer and to find the way to our Father's eternal home even through the darkness. As representatives of them all I mention Father Rupert Mayer of the Society of Jesus and the Carmelite nun Edith Stein who belonged to the Jewish people, both of whom I have beatified on this visit. They very definitely possessed the gift of discernment of spirits because they took God as their yardstick. They saw through the mass hysteria and misleading propaganda of their time.
>
> Blessed Edith Stein, Sister Teresa Benedicta of the Cross, spent important periods of her life and of her slow rise to the status of Christian philosopher and mystic here in Speyer. Be faithful guardians of her message and of her life testimony! With her life and work, Edith Stein is the successor of the outstanding holy women, confessors, mystics and worshippers of ancient Europe, of whom I will only mention St Hildegard of

Bingen. The women of this age in particular should be able to see in those who have been newly beatified a genuine model for a life of real self-fulfillment and self-reliance deriving from the true and unerring source of solidarity with God.

FAREWELL ADDRESS AT SPEYER

In the evening of Monday 4 May the Holy Father left Speyer by helicopter for Stuttgart-Echterdingen Airport. At the heliport in Speyer Federal Chancellor Helmut Kohl bade farewell to the Pope, who replied:

1. ... In this moment of farewell I recall with pleasure and gratitude, together with you, the solemn beatification of Sister Teresa Benedicta of the Cross in Cologne and of Father Rupert Mayer in Munich, as well as the other Eucharistic celebrations, gatherings in prayer, and the many meetings with various groups. On those occasions we have honored God in prayer and praise, God who is glorified in his saints. At the same time we have together considered what the example of the two newly beatified persons and of Cardinal von Galen and other courageous preachers of the faith from your country's recent past means for our calling as disciples of Jesus Christ. Just as they, "convenient or inconvenient" (cf. 2 Tim 4:2), were fearless witnesses to Christ and his liberating word and sacrificed their lives for this purpose, we too should, together with Christ, bear witness in the world of today to truth and justice in the community, to solidarity and fraternity at work, to the unity of all Christians as established in baptism, to our common responsibility for a Christian Europe and for extending God's kingdom throughout the world. The Church presents the blessed and the saints for our veneration, but above all for our imitation.

EDITH STEIN, JEWISH CATHOLIC MARTYR

Ambrose Eszer

Ambrose Eszer is a German Dominican friar who works as a Relator of the Congregation for the Causes of Saints at the Vatican. Just recently he became a Corresponding Fellow of the Pontifical Theological Academy in Rome. He completed this study about the martyr status of Bl Teresa Benedicta/Edith Stein late in March 1987 for distribution by the Vatican Press Office at the time of her beatification. Intimately connected with the process of beatification, his words offer a quite fascinating eyewitness account of the deliberations which paved the way for the ceremonies held in Cologne this past May. (We maintain here the numbering found in the Italian version of his text from which our translation comes.)

When World War II ended Sr Teresa Benedicta of the Cross/Edith Stein, OCD was mostly forgotten or simply unknown. The persons who had lived with her for a while had been dispersed, and the Carmel of Cologne (in which she had found her spiritual refuge) ended up totally destroyed. No one knew what end Sr Teresa Benedicta had met. Early information about it, however, began to be published rather soon, e.g., in the book of the Franciscan Dr Stokman[1] in which rather direct mention is made of the events which led to the violent death of the Carmelite nun. In the meanwhile her sisters of Cologne Carmel (who had moved into the former Carmelite monastery of

Our Lady Queen of Peace) also began to gather all kinds of documentation regarding Stein, including her correspondence. The fruit of these efforts was the biography written by Sr Teresa Renata of the Holy Spirit, OCD who had been Mistress of Novices during the novitiate of Sr Teresa Benedicta.[2] In spite of the fact that a veritable spate of other biographies or specialized studies followed this book, still today it can be considered fundamental. Its greatest worth consists in its clearly Carmelite character, also in the deep spirituality of its author.

In 1958 the Archbishop of Cologne, Cardinal Joseph Frings, asked Sr Teresa Renata to draft an official study on Sr Teresa Benedicta Stein. Thus began the gathering together and publication of this Carmelite nun's philosophical and theological writings, conducted by the Edith Stein Archive of Louvain and its directress [sic], Dr Lucy Gelber. All this brought about, little by little, conditions (suitable) for the opening of a Cause of Beatification and Canonization of Sr Teresa Benedicta.[3]

2.1 Consequently, in 1962, twenty years after her violent death, Cardinal Frings proceded to the opening of the Ordinary Process. During this process and the subsequent Petitionary Processes from New York, Regensburg, Westminster, Southwark, Speyer, Bamberg, Trier, Roermond, Liège, Aachen, Namur, Malines, Basel, Augsburg, Limburg, Salzburg and Freiburg-im-Breisgau, 103 texts were drafted by numerous leaders of the scholarly and intellectual world, and by several Jews, including Dr Erna Biberstein (née Stein), the sister of Sr Teresa Benedicta.

2.2 Furthermore, the Brief for the Introduction of the Cause is rich in documentation: texts from distinguished persons like Fr Erich Przywara, SJ and Rev Prof Schulemann; a considerable collection of letters of petition; as well as the Judgments (*Vota*) of two theological censors, one of which is—in my opinion—a real masterpiece.

2.3 In 1972 the successor of Cardinal Frings, Cardinal Joseph Höffner, was in a position to send to Rome the entire file of (beatification) process materials. On September 19, 1972 the Congregation for the Doctrine of the Faith gave its "Nihil obstat" and, so, preparations could proceed on the Brief for the Introduction of the Cause, which was ready only in 1983. Even though, according to the former rules, the *Brief for the Introduction* had as (its) primary aim proof of the fame of sanctity of the Servant of God while alive, at death and after death, our *Brief* succeeded in offering shining proof of the heroic degree of Sr Teresa Benedicta's virtues, a proof normally supposed to be supplied in the Apostolic Process investigating the Virtues! The Judgment of the Rev Promoter of the Faith turned out to be very positive on the whole. As a result it did not seem to be a difficult undertaking to reply to the few objections.

2.4 Up to that time the Cause had advanced, but really not so quickly. The work had been exhausting. In 1980 the Vice-Postulator of the Cause, Msgr Jakob Schlafke (a Canon of Cologne Cathedral), published a small work[4] containing documents found in the Rijksinstitut voor Oorlogs Dokumentatie (Royal Institute for War Documentation) in Amsterdam, documents which possibly were already known to the above mentioned Fr Stokman, OFM. By his study of these documents Canon Schlafke offered the thesis of Martyrdom suffered for the Catholic faith, a thesis which had already been taken into consideration spontaneously in some of the texts of the Petitionary Processes but never studied in depth by Rome, given the fact that from its inception the Cause had been oriented toward proving the heroic virtues of Sr Teresa Benedicta. Consequently, this small work of the learned Vice Postulator produced no reaction. But, on March 3, 1983, Cardinal Höffner as President of the German Episcopal Conference wrote another Letter of Petition to the Holy Father which Cardinal Jozef Glemp (Primate of Poland) seconded in the name of the Polish Episcopal Conference. In this letter, both of these prelates stress the fact that the Dutch "Christian Jews" were spared from the general deportation of all Dutch Jews at an early stage and that, only as a result of the *public* protest of the *Catholic* Bishops of the Netherlands, the Jews who had become Catholic—and among them Sr Teresa Benedicta—were deported and exterminated as well. Nevertheless, even the Letter of Petition of the two Episcopal Conferences almost ended up forgotten, for the fact that a year and a half later it was rather difficult to find. Therefore it would be not only risky, but also false and calumnious to declare that either the Bishops or the Congregation for the Cause of Saints moved hastily in order to "get around" the obstacle of a missing acknowledged miracle. The lack of a miracle is understandable, among other things, for want of a real tomb of Sr Teresa Benedicta in spite of the undeniable and solid presence of a reputation for possible miracles due to numerous favors granted to the requests for help from the Carmelite nun.

3.1 The early months of 1983 saw the arrival of new regulations for the causes of the Saints and for the Congregation to which they are entrusted. At that time the *Apostolic Process*, which till then had followed on the *Ordinary Process*, plus the *Introduction of the Cause* also necessary for the opening of the *Apostolic Process*, were abolished. In place of these two procedures there is now a *Single Process*; but for the causes begun under the former stipulations it was necessary to seek carry-over solutions.

3.2 On May 11, 1984 the cause of Sr Teresa Benedicta was entrusted to one of the "examining judges," just established by the Congregation, that is, to one of its Relators. During a brief vacation-time stay in Cologne he lost no time in familiarizing himself with the work of Msgr Schlafke. He felt it his duty to take into consideration *also* the possibilities it contained, namely, a possible declaration of the martyrdom of Sr Teresa Benedicta by the Congregation and the Magisterium of the Church. Very quickly he took encouragement also from the Letter of Petition of the German and Polish Episcopal Conferences. In the meantime he ordered some new textual depositions and did some personal research to help reply to objections of the Rev Promotor of the Faith.

3.3 Once back in Rome the Relator wrote out his Report for the Meeting of the Congregation while Msgr Luigi Porsi, Advocate of the Cause, began preparing a *Supplementary Brief*. The validity of the Process was declared on November 15, 1985 and on January 10, 1986 the Rev Fr Postulator General of the Discalced Carmelite Order — interpreting the desire of the German and Polish Episcopal Conferences — wrote a letter of petition to the Holy Father to ask him to allow that the new brief of the cause of Sr Teresa Benedicta would be entitled, presented and discussed, no longer and merely restricted to "investigating heroic virtues," but specifically "investigating martyrdom." The Congregation at its meeting of January 17, 1986, consented to this request and the martyrdom was included with the heroic virtues in the *Supplementary Brief* that appeared in March 1986. On October 28th of the same year the Theological Consultors met to consider the heroic virtues and the martyrdom of Sr Teresa Benedicta. This meeting was followed, on January 13, 1987 by the Plenary convocation of the Cardinal and Archbishop/Bishop Members of the Congregation. On January 25, 1987, in the presence of the Holy Father, the Decree confirming the *heroic degree of the virtues*, as well as the *martyrdom* of Sr Teresa Benedicta, was read — an event without precedent in the centuries-old history of the Congregation. What, then, is the evidence for the martyrdom of Sr Teresa Benedicta?

4.1 In 1942 the Nazi leaders in the Netherlands had decided to wipe out Dutch Judaism, except that one must emphasize there was deportation into forced labor for German industry of not only Jews but also Dutch "Aryans" on the one hand, while exceptions were made (from the beginning) of baptized Jews whether Catholics or Protestants on the other. Still, the religious leaders were especially worried about their fate, even though it was not clear whether or not any of them had been taken captive. At any rate, all the Christian churches showed their indignation over the deportation underway by a telegram sent on July 11, 1942 to Reichscommissar Dr Arthur Seyss-Inquart, to General Commissars Schmidt and Rauter, and also to General Christiansen the Commander in Chief of the German Armed Forces in Holland.[5] As was normal, this telegram (which at first received no reply) showed the ecclesiastical authorities pointing out their preoccupation for the fate of the "Christian Jews" to the extent that these had not found places of worhip in the area. This offered the Nazis the chance, as in fact it turned out, to present an image of almost idyllic "normalcy" in the deportation itself. The Secretary General of the Ministry of the Interior, a Dutchman, stated that the deportation of the Jews was a European problem whose solution could not be altered. This meant that all the Dutch state functionnaries would have tacitly approved of the deportation. Among the Jews people thought that those able to work would be transported to the East to prepare living quarters for subsequent deportees.[6] The Nazi authorities, while not replying directly to the churches' telegram, then immediately prohibited public reading of the telegram from the pulpit when they heard the churches planned to do this. At the same time they told the churches that they could intervene in favor of their faithful of Jewish blood who would be exempted from the deportation if the pulpit announcement (of the telegram) did not take place.[7] With this, the Nazi authorities showed they accepted officially the reason of "inadequate places of worship," precisely to render more credible their "idyllic" version of the exile of the Dutch Jews. The Protestant churches, at least a majority of them, "were not closed to such reasoning," as was stated in an internal report to the Nazi high command in Holland which defined the capture of 4000 "Christian Jews" as a "consequence" of the behavior of the churches.[8] But the Protestant Jews were either not incarcerated or "were quickly released."[9] At first the Nazis had believed that the Protestant churches had also disobeyed the order of the Reichscommissar; only, the Protestant churches had been able to offer the excuse that, because of poor telephone connections,[10] they were unable to revoke the decision to have the telegram read. At any rate, according to the information which reached the Nazi authorities, an unspecified "synod" of the Protestant churches had, on July 24th, decided not to publish the protest telegram. Nonetheless, "according to the declarations that have to this point reached us from outlying offices, *this synodal decision was obviously not followed everywhere. Investigations are now going on.* The measures against the Church [author's note: the word should read "against the churches"] now are still being weighed. The small group of the "Evangelical-Lutheran Ecclesial Community" had refused to participate in the pulpit announcement and reading of the telegram from the very beginning."[11] It seems that the number of "disobedient" Protestant churches was larger than expected, and this would explain — at least partially — the fact that, in Autumn of 1942, the Nazis began to deport Protestant Jews too. The Catholic Archbishop of Utrecht, Bishop de Jong, claimed that the Protestant churches had not kept quiet.[12] Another reason for the behavior of the Nazis toward the "Protestant Jews" could have been some attempt by the Dutch populace to save Jews by regarding them, for the time being, "baptized Jews." Such subterfuges in favor of the Jews were probably known to the Nazis from what was going on in Italy and in the countries occupied by the Italian army. As an extra punishment or as an alternative to the deportation of the "Catholic Jews," the Nazi authorities considered secularizing some large charitable institutions of the Catholic Church in Holland, viz., the "large Catholic hospitals of Groningen."

All these institutions had nothing to do with the Jews; still, taking them over was being considered as a direct punishment on the Catholic Church for having defended them.[13] If the plan was not realized, the reason probably was that, to carry it out, the Nazi authorities would have had to concern themselves also with the sick people admitted to these institutions (with an easily predictable outcome). Still, *the simple existence of the above-mentioned plan establishes proof that the motive for the capture of the Catholic Jews was not some generic racial hatred but hatred against the Catholic Church. With its protest message the latter had not only disobeyed the order of the Reichscommissar but also blown away that "idyllic" image of the deportation of the Jews which the Nazis wanted to justify* in the eyes of the Dutch populace. The proclamation of the Dutch Catholic Bishops contained, besides the text of the protest telegram, a long prayer for the persecuted Jews that cited the words of Jesus in Lk 19:43-44 in a free translation which inevitably applied to the Third Reich.[14] This truly very beautiful text brought on the implacable hatred of the Nazi leaders against the Dutch Catholic Church.

4.2 Just the same, some theologians could question where it

is possible to find in Sr Teresa Benedicta's case *the profession of faith* traditionally required of the victim called a "valid provocation" directed at the "Tyrant." There is no doubt that Sr Teresa Benedicta was ready to make this profession: "When first challenged (in the concentration camp) about who she was, Edith Stein said 'I am Catholic.' The SS said 'You damned Jew, stand there.' Sr Rosa, 'I am a Jew.'"[15] It should be noted that "Sr Rosa" was the sister of Sr Teresa Benedicta: like her sister she was converted to the Catholic religion and had joined her at the Carmel of Echt where she worked later on as a third order sister. But as far as "Tyrants" are concerned, we have to take note that those of our century are substantially different from the "Tyrant" of ancient and medieval times. The latter did not present himself so much as anti-religious as anti-Christian. Even the French Revolution established a "Religion of Reason!" Totalitarian "Tyrants" of our times come, instead, from the Christian religion (Stalin had been even a seminarian) and they want to destroy every religion from within, in order to replace them with their own totalitarian ideology (this expression was coined by Giovanni Gentile who can be identified as the most lucid theoretician of totalitarianism), that is, with a pseudo-religion. At the same time, the modern "Tyrants" use every means available to maintain the sham of *not persecuting any religion,* even unto criminalizing the true confessors of any religion. Even though he was the founder of a new, radically anti-Christian weltanschauung, Hitler never wanted to leave officially the Catholic Church and paid public taxes for the Church until his death. He and others saw in the Church, especially in the Catholic Church, *a burdensome relic from the past which little by little would be transformed.* This rendered the criminalization of a real believer all the more easy for him. In our case, the *provocation* of the "Tyrant" was made by the action of the Dutch Bishops, to which Sr Teresa Benedicta definitely adhered, given the fact she had always criticized in a radical fashion any behavior which could be considered too condescending toward Nationalsocialism. Regarding her own spiritual preparation for martyrdom, as well as her perseverance, we see it in her act of offering herself as a victim for peace and the unbelief of the Jewsish people in her 1939 will.[16] Only, the Nazi "Tyrant" did not want to ask the fatal question, establishing the deportation of the Dutch Catholic Jews as a measure to punish the Dutch Catholic Church—not as a religious community but as a social group, because Nationalsocialism did not persecute any church or religion officially. In other cases, too, the Nazis punished not individual persons, but entire families (*Sippenhaft*).

To return to religious persecutions, we must say that National-socialism, in the case at hand, *not only intended to avoid causing but felt most obliged to suppress any eventual confession of faith* which, in its own way, would have been able to "provoke it." Thus, the Nazis sought to reduce those persecuted to an infantile state in which they'd be unable to give expression to their faith and, furthermore, suffer the humiliation of their human dignity. The "Catholic Jews" of Holland knew very well, instead, why they had to suffer. Thus, the third order Dominican, Dr Lisamarie (Mary Magdalen) Meirowsky, wrote from Westerbork Camp: "I consider it a grace and a privilege to have to suffer in such circumstances and so give witness to the word of our Fathers and Shepherds in Christ. Even if our sufferings have been worsened a little, grace is doubled, and a magnificent crown awaits us in heaven. Rejoice with me."[17]

4.3.1 It remains to be clarified, as much as possible, the difference between the hate of the Nazis for the Jewish people and the "hatred for the faith" (*odium fidei*) which led to the persecution and annihilation of the Catholic Jews of the Netherlands. Some will find this complicated and abstruse beyond words. Nevertheless, it behooves us to emphasize that the complications are derived, not from any procedures of ecclesiastical courts, nor from norms of Canon Law, nor from theological concepts, etc., but rather from the Nazis' immorality and from the deep moral and social disorder created by them. Furthermore, the Nazis were not that horde of dumb and brutal creatures who came in from the darkness of history in some unexplainable fashion, but (a group) that constituted instead an example of the consequences of a massive collapse of Christian ethics over vast segments of the population of entire nations, in particular the Austro-Germanic population. Only, to comprehend this fact we have to recognize also the value of Christian morality and not disqualify it, as an old "Liberalism" has done and modern progressives still do, by considering it as a collection of absurd "taboos."

We should not forget that to a great extent the responsibility of the slaughter of the Jews in Europe falls on those "Liberal" forces which, during the second half of the 19th and the first decade of the 20th centuries did all they could to bring down that Christian-humanistic social order which, for example in the Austro-Hungarian dominions, protected the crowds of Jews expelled systematically by the pogroms of the Western-minded jurisdictions of the Russian Empire.

4.3.2 Doubtlessly, both the Antichristian and Antisemitic hate of the Nazis have had a common root: in the *Diaries* of Cosima Wagner you read that he whom Hitler considered his one worthy predecessor defined Catholics and Jews mutually "the plague of this world." The interpretation of *Parsifal* is equally rather well-known, this opera innocently admired by many a Catholic, in which the magician Klingsor is really "the" Jesuit who directs the harlot Kundry, that is, the Catholic Church, to besmirch the innocence (not moral, but racial) of that "pure fool" Parsifal.

At the same time, materialism makes a showing in another way, given the fact that in *Parsifal* — as Msgr Scheffczyk, the eminent professor of systematic theology at the Ludwig-Maximilian University in Munich, has explained — it's not the bread and wine which are transformed into the Body and Blood of Christ, but the Body and Blood of Christ are transformed into bread and wine! In fact, Nationalsocialism, not so much for "moral" or "religious" reasons as for its grim and materialistic social Darwinism, saw in Judaism the material substratum of the Catholic Church.[18] According to Josef Goebbels, head of the Propaganda Ministry of the Third Reich (*Reichsprogagandaministerium*), Hitler saw in Christianity "a symptom of decadence and a branch of the Jewish race."[19] But, even though both of them were aware of their connection with Judaism, Hitler forbade Goebbels to leave the Catholic Church.[20] Due to over-riding concerns of the war, the Führer felt the "final solution" (*endlösung*) of the Catholic problem was to be held off until it was over. Hence, Hitler and his colleagues had to put the brakes on their own anticatholic hate because, even though they felt they were apostles of a new religion founded on race, they had not yet determined its liturgy, however well-disposed they were to the "liturgical-cultic lunacies" of Rosenberg, the author of the "Myth of the Twentieth Century," as well as those of Himmler and Darré.[21] On the other hand, with the Catholic Church des-tined to be destroyed after the victory, it would have been easier to put together a pseudo-Catholic liturgy from the model of the "festival stage play" *Parsifal*, whose composer and librettist was precisely Richard Wagner, the one Hitler venerated so much.[21a]

4.3.3 Today no one questions how *racial* antisemitism was a structural element of the nascent neo-primitive religion of Na-tionalsocialism. Even though it presupposed the existence of a popular-racist antisemitism, on the scene before WWI broke out especially in the Austro-hungarian Empire and afterwards predominantly in Germany itself, Nazi antisemitism underwent a series of strange modifications. Even with the elimination of the Jewish race always considered the ultimate goal, there was always a system of dispensations from persecution in place from the beginning. Such dispensations would not have stopped the extermination of the Jewish race and the definitive ascent of the "blond, blue-eyed" Aryan race. Richard Wagner—that simply hysterical antisemite—had already introduced this system of dispensations by opening Villa Wahnfried also to Jews, on con-dition, however, that they accept his verdict of extinction against their people. Two such cases were poor Maestro Her-mann Levi, taken advantage of more than any other "Hausis-raelit" (as a kind of "*Hofjude*") and the pianist Joseph Rubens-tein in whom "a firm faith was formed regarding the possibility of being redeemed through the German spirit."[22] Given the fact that the most worthy predecessor (Wagner—in between one or another discourse on the best method for eliminating the Jews) had acted this way, his "disciple" Hitler also could feel he was authorized to make use of a "dispensation" or "absolution" of the evil of Jewish blood. And he also had to do it, because in the veins of many Nazi hierarchs flowed generous doses of Jewish blood, and it was for this reason that the only woman leader of the party at Munich, Elsa Schmidt-Falk, had to provide cleansed family trees so as to offer her services to the party.[23] The system of "dispensation" from elimination would make possible the appointment of the Jew Erhard Milch as Field Marshal and Vicecommander of the Third Reich's Airforce; and Reichsmarschall Herman Göring used to say cynically: "I determine whoever's Jewish." Other examples include Mrs Ingeborg Malek Kohler, half-Jewish, who obtained from Hitler himself his signed permission to marry Dr Herbert Engeling, an Aryan and director of the movie company "Tobis,"[24] and the very popular actor-singer Hans Albers who lived with a Jewish woman, simply refusing to obey repeated and severe invitations to send her away.[25] Examples could be multiplied, but it should be said that often enough the Nazis made Jews emigrate, particularly well-known people. A large part of the family of Sr Teresa Benedicta emigrated; and it would have been completely within the rules followed by the Nazi authorities if they had dispensed her from arrest and deportation, seeing how the Swiss consulate and other foreign dignitaries had shown an interest in her. Still, even a "dispensation" of brief duration regarding all the Dutch Catholic Jews would have been sufficient to save Sr Teresa Benedicta, since the immigration papers to Switzerland for her and her sister Rosa were almost ready and it is well known that the Federal President of Switzerland was actively committed in her favor.

4.3.4 After having become a structural element of the Nazis' neoprimitive religion, *antisemitic hate was institutionalized and became the State's antisemitism (but, for as much as it sounds absurd, without a real measure of hatred).* The extermination of the Jews seemed to the very Nazis an integral part of a universal plan of Divine Providence (the word "Providence" was one of Hitler's favorite terms). But here too it should be emphasized that the heads of the new "religion," due to their being mostly ex-Catholics, could logically dispense from carrying out the horrendous plan so long as the absolute domination of the blond, blue-eyed Aryan race was not in danger. Whoever would claim that such affirmations are preposterous should read the following sentences of the American historian, Gerald Reitlinger:

> The direction of the extermination of the Jews had been entrusted to Himmler and Heydrich certainly as far back as March 1941. But there is no evidence that at that time Himmler was an embittered anti-Semite or indeed that he ever became one. It is a peculiar thing that Himmler's surviving speeches are largely free from the savagely anti-Jewish utterances which were fashionable even among the more moderate of Hitler's Ministers. Himmler's one and only public allusion to the extermination of Jewry, which he made at Posen on 4 October 1943, incredibly though it reads, is worded in a whining, apologetic style.[26]

We could cite numerous quotations, either from Reitlinger's work or from others, which confirm such realities. And it is also very well known that Himmler himself continually admonished his troops to "remain clean," that is, *to repress every push toward personal hatred and toward sadism.* In this context the historian Karl-Dietrich Erdmann writes:

> Genocide applied to the Jews did not succeed in being a terrorist measure. Terror, as it was exercised, for example, in the French Revolution or in the Bolshevik Revolution . . . is directed against political adversaries. It is carried out in public life as a means of intimidation. What happened with the Jews was not supposed to be known by anyone, not even by the German people itself. The people who were murdered — without taking into consideration the problem whether they represented or not a political factor — were judged to be of poor quality. Hence, the Nazi extermination activity cannot be compared to crude break-outs of hate for the Jews as have been witnessed time and again throughout European history, whether for political or economic reasons. The SS proceded with a systematic bureaucracy . . . Mass extermination was the Nazi theory of biological materialism, carried out with horrific consistency . . . Murderers seek out their victim in another human being with which they confront themselves, be this an individual or a group. But the extermination of the Jews

appears characterized by a touch of total anonymity. The expression used by the Nazis to define the elimination of non-desirable life was "extermination." Extermination could have been directed against any kind of life which had been judged "not worthy of life."[27]

4.3.5 The way the Nazi authorities in Holland proceeded against the "Catholic Jews" reveals some very differing psychological motivations: *this was an act of revenge against the Catholic Church decided, moreover, cum ira (with anger) and premeditation with which the preceding decree of exemption from deportation was abolished.* Even though the deportation and killing of the Catholic and non-Catholic Dutch Jews was an action materially one and the same—after the abolition of the exemption, first off tacit and then later explicit, of the Catholic Jews from deportation—in it still appear two different motives and two formally different actions. The goal of the extermination of the Dutch Catholic Jews was the punishment of the Catholic Church in Holland by means of the killing off of its Jewish children, while the goal of the general massacre of the Jewish people was exactly the wiping out of this people and the exaltation of the Aryan race. Whoever does not accept Catholic rules for judging human acts might think this looks like some kind of sleight-of-hand, but it should be said right away that it is impossible to judge the acts of a religious community unless you understand and recognize its own internal logic.[28] The linch pin of Catholic logic is Jesus Christ, the Messiah and Savior, and every Christian and Catholic person is judged by the Catholic Church along the lines of his or her relationship with Christ which is the only thing that counts. Regarding this fact nothing has changed since apostolic times and nothing can change. One must, nevertheless, emphasize once again that every objective observer will notice clearly *the substantial difference between antisemitic hatred of an institutionalized and industrialized type, and that spontaneous (and till that moment suppressed) hatred against the Catholic Church of Holland.*

4.4 There is one question left to answer: how could one of Hitler's henchmen, after promising and offering him a deadline to annihilate the Jewish people in his district, then "dispense" a part of the intended victims from deportation and massacre?

Dr Seyss-Inquart (1892–1946), Commissar of the Reich in the Netherlands, came from a middle-class background and, in his homeland of Austria, showed himself more of a nationalist than a Nationalsocialist. In 1936, while the Austrian Nazi party was still clandestine, he entered the fifth cabinet of the Federal Chancellor Kurt von Schuschnigg (11 Feb. 1938) but only to become, within a couple of weeks, the last Chancellor before the *Anschluss.*[29] Even though he was a self-proclaimed fanatical Nazi, Seyss-Inquart was more of an opportunist who sought to cash in on the changing political situations, just as they presented themselves. If it is true that he wrote Hitler that the Dutch Jews would be eliminated by a certain date, that did not exclude absolutely the possibility he would exempt from extermination a particular number of Jews, a minority less than 10%, especially if this could help keep the Dutch populace calm. In fact, Seyss-Inquart sought support from the Dutch at that time by a combination of maneuvres to say the least strange. As an honorary SS lieutenant-general (*Gruppenführer*), he worked against the SS in the Netherlands (*Nederländische SS*) which were under the Hauptamt (or General Command) of the SS in Berlin by entering into an alliance with the nationalsocialist movement of Adriaan Musserts whom Himmler despised as "corrupt." Already on January 5, 1941 SS Lieutenant-General Gottlob Berger had reported on these politics of Seyss-Inquart in a letter to Rudolf Brandt, Himmler's secretary: this state of things lasted until the collapse of the Nazi domination of the Netherlands.[30] From this it becomes rather clear that the Commissar of the Reich not only could not have been "shot down" by the SS but he was, in his own "kingdom," even more powerful than they were. If he were to exempt the Catholic Jews from the planned extermination they, as it were, would become non-Jews. A colleague of Seyss-Inquart, Wilhelm Kube, who was Reichscommissar for White Russia, changed from a fanatical antisemite into an equally decided protector of the Jews: for more than two years he sabotaged systematically and with all the means at his command the actions of the infamous *Einsatzkommandos* (quick intervention shock troops) of the SS until, on September 22, 1943, he was killed by a bomb that his partisan housekeeper placed under his bed. Not even Himmler himself was able to get rid of him even though he had told Hitler all that was happening in White Russia.[31] Hitler's henchmen actually possessed a wide range of discretionary powers. This fits with the situation of general chaos that reigned supreme between the different "satrapies" and big fiefs of the Third Reich, something Hitler slyly kept alive according to the old adage of "Divide and conquer!" There's no doubting, then, the Seyss-Inquart was in a position to turn the Dutch Catholic Jews into non-Jews and vice versa. As it was, he became furious and took it personally when the Dutch Bishops' public protest, marked by such harshness and therefore so surprising, seriously disturbed his well laid out plans designed to increase the popular prestige of Nationalsocialism and of the Dutch Nazi party which he supported. (Trans. J. Sullivan)

NOTES

1. Het verset van de Nederlandsche Bischoppen tegen National Socialismus en Duitsche tyrannie (Utrecht, 1945).
2. Teresia Renata a Spiritu Sancto, OCD, *Edith Stein/Schwester Teresia Benedicta a Cruce: Ein Lebensbild, gewonnen aus Erinnerungen und Briefen* (Nürnberg, 1954), 238pp.
3. In June 1958 Cardinal Archbishop Josef Frings assigned Mother Teresia Renata of the Holy Spirit the task of writing a profile of the life of Sr Teresa Benedicta which would be of use for an eventual Beatification and Canonization Process. See Jokob Schlafke, *Edith Stein: Dokumente zu ihrem Leben und Sterben* (Köln, 1980), 24. Eng. ed. trans. Susanne M. Batzdorff (New York: Edith Stein Guild, 1984), 20.
4. Ibid., 24-35 (Eng. ed., 20-31).
5. Teresia Renata, *Ein Lebensbild*, 238; Schlafke, *Dokumente*, 29 (Eng. ed., 24-25).
6. Schlafke, *Dokumente*, 32 (Eng. ed., 28).
7. Ibid., 31 (Eng. ed., 27-28).
8. Ibid., 32 (Eng. ed., 28).
9. Positio sup. Intr., Summ., pag. 172.
10. Teresia Renata, *Ein Lebensbild*, 246.

11. Schlafke, *Dokumente*, 35 (Eng. ed., 31). In another document of the Nazi authorities cited in *Dokumente*, 30 (Eng. ed., 25) we read: "In case the majority of Protestant churches also read the telegram addressed to the Reich Commissar, the Protestant Jews will also be deported. For this purpose, lists are to be prepared."

12. Teresia Renata, *Ein Lebensbild*, 246.

13. Schlafke, *Dokumente*, 30 (Eng. ed., 25).

14. Ibid., 35 (Eng. ed., 30-31).

15. Positio sup. Intr., Summ., pag. 409, #1005.

16. Schlafke, *Dokumente*, 9 (Eng. ed., 5).

17. Positio suppl. pag. 126.

18. Hans Gunter Hockerts, "Die Goebbels Tagebucher, 1932-41: Eine neue Hauptquelle zur Erforschung der nationalsozialistische Kirchenpolitik," *Communio*, 13 (1984): 539-56; 544.

19. Ibid., 547.

20. Ibid., 543.

21. Ibid., 544.

21a. As far as Hermann Rauschning is concerned, in a hysterical outburst Hitler lauded Wagner as the greatest poet the German people ever had. See Hermann Rauschning, *Hitler m'a dit: Confidences du Führer sur son plan de conquête du monde*, trans. from German (Paris, 1939), 255: "Hitler refused to admit to predecessors. The only exception was Wagner . . .; and 256: "Wagner received the revelation, he was the harbinger of the tragic destiny of the Germans. He wasn't only a musician and poet. He was especially the greatest prophetic figure that the German people ever had. He, Hitler, had come upon the teachings of Wagner — whether by chance or by predestination — early on. With almost morbid excitement, he stated that everything he read in the works of this great mind corresponded to intuitive ideas which lay dormant, as it were, in the depths of his own consciousness."

See Hartmut Zelinsky, "Hermann Levi und Bayreuth oder Der Tod als Gralsgebiet," Beiheft 6 des Instituts für Deutsche Geschichte (Tel Aviv, no. 103, 1984):350.

22. Cosima Wagner, *Die Tagebücher*, 2nd ed., vol. 3 (München-Zürich, 1982), 521. For the suicide of Rubinstein see Zelinsky, *Levi und Bayreuth*: 319. See also Hartmut Zelinsky, "Richard Wagners 'Kunstwerk der Zukunft' und seine Idee der Vernichtung," *Von kommenden Zeiten: Geschichtspropheten im 19. und 20. Jahrhundert*, eds. Joachim H. Knoll and Julius H. Schoeps (Stuttgart-Bonn, 1984), 84-105.

As for Hitler, he said that no one could understand Nazi Germany without a knowledge of Wagner. See Robert Gutman, *Richard Wagner: Der Mensch, sein Werk, seine Zeit*, 4th ed. (München, 1970), 478.

23. Wilfrid Daim, *Der Mann, der Hitler die Ideen gab: Die Sektiererischen Grundlagen des Nationalsozialismus*, vol. 4 of Böhlaus zeitgeschictliche Bibliothek, 2nd ed. (Wien-Köln-Graz, 1985), 40 and 275 n. 42.

24. *Die Welt*, 23 June 1986, no. 142, p. 8.

25. Deutsche Welle radio broadcast, 11 July 1986.

26. Gerald Reitlinger, *The SS: Alibi of a Nation, 1922–1945*, 1st Am. ed. (Englewood Cliffs NJ: Prentice Hall, 1981), 277–78.

27. Karl-Dietrich Erdmann, *Die Zeit der Weltkriege*, vol. 4 of Bruno Gebhard's Handbuch der deutschen Geschichte, 8th new and rev. ed. by Herbert Grundmann (Stuttgart, 1959), 297.

28. About this topic see Joseph Bochenski, *Logik der Religion* (Köln, 1968), 23–25. Even if some do not want to acknowledge the truth of the Catholic faith they'd have to admit that the Church must follow its own internal logic, otherwise it would destroy itself.

29. Erdmann, *Weltkriege*, 233ff.

30. Heinz Höhne, *Der Orden unter dem Totenkopf: Die Geschichte der SS*, 3rd ed. (München, 1981), 399 and n. 208.

31. Ibid., 340–42.

The Institute of Carmelite Studies promotes research and publication in the field of Carmelite spirituality. Its members are Discalced Carmelites, part of a Roman Catholic community — friars, nuns and laity — who are heirs to the teaching and way of life of Teresa of Jesus and John of the Cross, men and women dedicated to contemplation and to ministry in the Church and the world. Information concerning their way of life is available through local diocesan Vocation Offices, or from the Vocation Director's Office, 514 Warren Street, Brookline, MA 02146.